Official Kai's Power Tools® Studio SECRETS®

D1517897

TED ALSPACH & STEVEN FRANK

OFFICIAL KAI'S POWER TOOLS® STUDIO SECRETS®

IDG BOOKS WORLDWIDE, INC.

AN INTERNATIONAL DATA GROUP COMPANY

Foster City, CA ▲ Chicago, IL ◆ Indianapolis, IN ▼ Southlake, TX

Official Kai's Power Tools® Studio SECRETS®

Published by

IDG Books Worldwide, Inc.

An International Data Group Company

919 E. Hillsdale Blvd., Suite 400

Foster City, CA 94404

Library of Congress Catalog Card No.: 96-76832

ISBN: 0-7645-4002-5

Printed in the United States of America

10 9 8 7 6 5 4 3 2 1

1B/RR/QZ/ZW/FC

Distributed in the United States by IDG Books Worldwide, Inc.

Distributed by Macmillan Canada for Canada; by Contemporanea de Ediciones for Venezuela; by Distribuidora Cuspide for Argentina; by CITEC for Brazil; by Ediciones ZETA S.C.R. Ltda. for Peru; by Editorial Limusa SA for Mexico; by Transworld Publishers Limited in the United Kingdom and Europe; by Academic Bookshop for Egypt; by Levant Distributors S.A.R.L. for Lebanon; by Al Jassim for Saudi Arabia; by Simron Pty. Ltd. for South Africa; by Pustak Mahal for India; by The Computer Bookshop for India; by Toppan Company Ltd. for Japan; by Addison Wesley Publishing Company for Korea; by Longman Singapore Publishers Ltd. for Singapore, Malaysia, Thailand, and Indonesia; by Unalis Corporation for Taiwan; by WS Computer Publishing Company, Inc. for the Philippines; by WoodsLane Pty. Ltd. for Australia; by WoodsLane Enterprises Ltd. for New Zealand. Authorized Sales Agent: Anthony Rudkin Associates for the Middle East and North Africa.

For general information on IDG Books Worldwide's books in the U.S., please call our Consumer Customer Service department at 800-762-2974. For reseller information, including discounts and premium sales, please call our Reseller Customer Service department at 800-434-3422.

For information on where to purchase IDG Books Worldwide's books outside the U.S., please contact our International Sales department at 415-655-3172 or fax 415-655-3295.

For information on foreign language translations, please contact our Foreign & Subsidiary Rights department at 415-655-3021 or fax 415-655-3281.

For sales inquiries and special prices for bulk quantities, please contact our Sales department at 415-655-3200 or write to the address above.

For information on using IDG Books Worldwide's books in the classroom or for ordering examination copies, please contact our Educational Sales department at 800-434-2086 or fax 817-251-8174.

For authorization to photocopy items for corporate, personal, or educational use, please contact Copyright Clearance Center, 222 Rosewood Drive, Danvers, MA 01923, or fax 508-750-4470.

is a trademark under exclusive license to IDG Books Worldwide, Inc., from International Data Group, Inc.

ABOUT IDG BOOKS WORLDWIDE

WINNER
Eighth Annual
Computer Press
Awards 1992

WINNER
Ninth Annual
Computer Press
Awards 1993

IDG BOOKS
WORLDWIDE

Welcome to the world of IDG Books Worldwide.

IDG Books Worldwide, Inc., is a subsidiary of International Data Group, the world's largest publisher of computer-related information and the leading global provider of information services on information technology. IDG was founded more than 25 years ago and now employs more than 8,500 people worldwide. IDG publishes more than 270 computer publications in over 75 countries (see listing below). More than 90 million people read one or more IDG publications each month.

Launched in 1990, IDG Books Worldwide is today the #1 publisher of best-selling computer books in the United States. We are proud to have received eight awards from the Computer Press Association in recognition of editorial excellence and three from *Computer Currents'* First Annual Readers' Choice Awards. Our best-selling *...For Dummies*® series has more than 25 million copies in print with translations in 30 languages. IDG Books Worldwide, through a joint venture with IDG's Hi-Tech Beijing, became the first U.S. publisher to publish a computer book in the People's Republic of China. In record time, IDG Books Worldwide has become the first choice for millions of readers around the world who want to learn how to better manage their businesses.

Our mission is simple: Every one of our books is designed to bring extra value and skill-building instructions to the reader. Our books are written by experts who understand and care about our readers. The knowledge base of our editorial staff comes from years of experience in publishing, education, and journalism — experience which we use to produce books for the '90s. In short, we care about books, so we attract the best people. We devote special attention to details such as audience, interior design, use of icons, and illustrations. And because we use an efficient process of authoring, editing, and desktop publishing our books electronically, we can spend more time ensuring superior content and spend less time on the technicalities of making books.

You can count on our commitment to deliver high-quality books at competitive prices on topics you want to read about. At IDG Books Worldwide, we continue in the IDG tradition of delivering quality for more than 25 years. You'll find no better book on a subject than one from IDG Books Worldwide.

John J. Kilcullen

John Kilcullen
President and CEO
IDG Books Worldwide, Inc.

IDG Books Worldwide, Inc., is a subsidiary of International Data Group, the world's largest publisher of computer-related information and the leading global provider of information services on information technology. International Data Group publishes over 276 computer publications in over 75 countries. Ninety million people read one or more International Data Group publications each month. International Data Group's publications include: **ARGENTINA:** Annuario de Informatica, Computerworld Argentina, PC World Argentina; **AUSTRALIA:** Australian Macworld, Client/Server Journal, Computer Living, Computerworld, Computerworld 100, Digital News, IT Casebook, Network World, On-line World Australia, PC World, Publishing Essentials, Reseller, WebMaster; **AUSTRIA:** Computerwelt Osterreich, Networks Austria, PC Tip; **BELARUS:** PC World Belarus; **BELGIUM:** Data News; **BRAZIL:** Annuário de Informática, Computerworld Brazil, Connections, Super Game Power, Macworld, PC Player, PC World Brazil, Publish Brazil, Reseller News; **BULGARIA:** Computerworld Bulgaria, Networkworld/Bulgaria, PC & MacWorld Bulgaria; **CANADA:** CIO Canada, Client/Server World, ComputerWorld Canada, InfoCanada, Network World Canada; **CHILE:** Computerworld Chile, PC World Chile; **COLOMBIA:** Computerworld Colombia, PC World Colombia; **COSTA RICA:** PC World Centro America; **THE CZECH AND SLOVAK REPUBLICS:** Computerworld Czechoslovakia, Elektronika Czechoslovakia, Macworld Czech Republic, PC World Czechoslovakia; **DENMARK:** Communications World, Computerworld Danmark, Macworld Danmark, PC Privat Danmark, PC World Danmark, PC World Danmark Supplements, TECH World; **DOMINICAN REPUBLIC:** PC World Republica Dominicana; **ECUADOR:** PC World Ecuador; **EGYPT:** Computerworld Middle East, PC World Middle East; **EL SALVADOR:** PC World Centro America; **FINLAND:** MikroPC, Tietoverkko, Tietoviikko; **FRANCE:** Distributique, Golden, Hebdo-Distributique, Info PC, Le Guide du Monde Informatique, Le Monde Informatique, Reseaux & Telecoms; **GERMANY:** Computer Partner, Computerwoche, Computerwoche Extra, Computerwoche Focus, I/M Information Management, Macwelt, PC Welt; **GREECE:** GamePro, Multimedia World; **GUATEMALA:** PC World Centro America; **HONDURAS:** PC World Centro America; **HONG KONG:** Computerworld Hong Kong, PCWorld Hong Kong, Publish in Asia; **HUNGARY:** ABCD CD-ROM, Computerworld Szamitastechnika, PC & Mac World Hungary, PC-X Magazine; **ICELAND:** Tolvuheimur/PC World Island; **INDIA:** Information Systems Computerworld, PC World India, Publish in Asia; **INDONESIA:** InfoKomputer PC World, Komputek Computerworld, Publish in Asia; **IRELAND:** ComputerScope, PC Live!; **ISRAEL:** People & Computers; **ITALY:** Computerworld Italia, Computerworld Italia Special Editions, Macworld Italia, Networking Italia, PC Shopping, PC World Italia, PC World/Walt Disney; **JAPAN:** DTP World, HP Open World Japan, Macworld Japan, Nikkei Personal Computing, Open World Japan, OS/2 World Japan, SunWorld Japan, Windows World Japan; **KENYA:** East African Computer News; **KOREA:** Hi-Tech Information/Computerworld, Macworld Korea, PC World Korea; **MACEDONIA:** PC World Macedonia; **MALAYSIA:** Computerworld Malaysia, PC World Malaysia, Publish in Asia; **MEXICO:** Computerworld Mexico, Macworld, PC World Mexico; **MYANMAR:** PC World Myanmar; **NETHERLANDS:** Computer! Totaal, LAN Magazine, LanWorld Buyers Guide, Macworld, Net Magazine, Totaal! Beurskrant; **NEW ZEALAND:** Absolute Beginner's Guide, Computer Buyer, Computer Industry Directory, Computerworld New Zealand, MTB, Network World, PC World New Zealand; **NICARAGUA:** PC World Centro America; **NIGERIA:** PC World Nigeria; **NORWAY:** Computerworld Norge, Computerworld Privat (Datamagasinet), CW Rapport Norge, IDG's KURSGUIDE, Macworld Norge, Multimediaworld, PC World Ekspress, PC World Nettverk, PC World Norge, PC World's Produktguide, Windows World Spesial; **PAKISTAN:** Computerworld Pakistan, PC World Pakistan; **PANAMA:** PC World Panama; **P. R. OF CHINA:** China Computer Users, China Computerworld, China Infoworld, China Telecom World Weekly, Computer & Communication, Electronic Design China, Electronics Today, Electronics Weekly, Game Camp, Game Soft, Network World China, PC World China, Popular Computer Weekly, Software Weekly, Software World, Telecom World; **PERU:** Computerworld Peru, PC World Profesional Peru, PC World Peru; **PHILIPPINES:** Computerworld Philippines, PC World Philippines, Publish in Asia; **POLAND:** Computerworld Poland, Computerworld Special Report, Macworld, Networld, PC World Komputer; **PORTUGAL:** Cerebro/PC World, Computerworld/Correio Informático, Dealer World Portugal, MacIn/PCIn, Multimedia World Portugal; **PUERTO RICO:** PC World Puerto Rico; **ROMANIA:** Computerworld Romania, PC World Romania, Telecom Romania; **RUSSIA:** Computerworld Russia, Mir PK, Sety; **SINGAPORE:** Computerworld Singapore, PC World Singapore, Publish in Asia; **SLOVENIA:** MONITOR; **SOUTH AFRICA:** Computing S.A., InfoWorld S.A., Network World S.A., Software World; **SPAIN:** Computerworld España, COMUNICACIONES WORLD, Dealer World, Macworld España, PC World España; **SWEDEN:** CAP&Design, Computer Sweden, Corporate Computing, MacWorld, Maxi Data, MikroDatorn, Nätverk & Kommunikation, PC/Aktiv, PC World, Windows World; **SWITZERLAND:** Computerworld Schweiz, Macworld Schweiz, PCtip; **TAIWAN:** Computerworld Taiwan, Macworld Taiwan, PC World Taiwan, Publish Taiwan, Windows World; **THAILAND:** Thai Computerworld, Publish in Asia; **TURKEY:** Computerworld Turkiye, MACWORLD Turkiye, PC WORLD Turkiye; **UKRAINE:** Computerworld Kiev, Computers & Software, Multimedia World Ukraine, PC World Ukraine; **UNITED KINGDOM:** Acorn User, Amiga Computing, Appletalk, Computing, GamePro, Macworld, Network News, Parents and Computers, PC Advisor, PC Home, PSX Pro UK, The WEB; **UNITED STATES:** Cable in the Classroom, CD Review, CIO Magazine, Computerworld, Computerworld Client/Server Journal, Digital Video Magazine, DOS World, Federal Computer Week, GamePro, InfoWorld, I-Way, JavaWorld, Macworld, Multimedia World, Netscape World Online, Network World, PC Entertainment, PC World, Publish, SunWorld Online, SWATPro Magazine, Video Event, WebMaster; **URUGUAY:** PC World Uruguay; **VENEZUELA:** Computerworld Venezuela, PC World Venezuela; and **VIETNAM:** PC World Vietnam.   7/16/96

To the memory of Lucy, who graces several of these pages.

—Ted

To my family, for all of their support and encouragement on this and many other projects.

—Steve

FOREWORD

The fun thing is, the best is yet to come.

JOHN WILCZAK

What a delight to see the hundreds of accumulated hours of technique development and know-how captured in this book. When MetaTools was first approached about a book on its products, the first thing that came to mind was who would be the writers. Fortunately, we got two of the best in Ted Alspach and Steve Frank. This book delivers new dimensions and insights into how to use the incredible tools Kai and our great development team have produced for the creative community over the past several years. The fun thing is, the best is yet to come.

Just a short time ago, in January of 1993, we released our first product, Kai's Power Tools. Thinking back on those early days, I recall the initial response to the product . . . everything from "amazing," "looks like the cockpit of a spaceship," "creative fun," "why didn't you guys make it look like the rest of the Mac?" and on and on and on. There is no doubt of one thing—Kai and I agreed from the very beginning on some fundamental principles regarding software development and our business model:

1. Never forget the basic rule of interface design—make the user happy! Everything Kai designs is intended to make it easier for users to access power they never dreamed they would have at the desktop.

2. Provide real-time capabilities wherever and whenever possible. This approach changes everything by notching up creative freedom and productivity. It may not be that you save time . . . but rather that you get more opportunities to explore creative alternatives.

3. Provide powerful tools at prices everyone can afford. Funny how in the early days a number of other companies in the business urged us to raise our prices, feeling that we were selling our products too inexpensively (code words for "you may force us to lower our prices").

4. Continually work on developing a sense of community in the graphic arts field, whether through our online chats, the posting of Kai's now famous "power tips and tricks," donating time to teach at places such as the American Film Institute, or hosting the bashes MetaTools is known for at major trade events as gathering places for the digerati.

This and a whole lot more has been happening while we provide our team members with an exciting environment to work and play in. Our continuing challenge is to create truly innovative products that enable and enhance creative expression for ever-wider audiences, whether professional or consumer.

Kai's Power Goo, our first consumer creative entertainment tool, and MetaSquares, our first interactive online game, both push the envelope in providing consumers with a new level of creative expression and social game-play fun. Why teach our children and young adults to be insensitive to violence, playing shoot-em-up, rip-em-apart games, when they can have a creative experience or interact with others in strategy games that don't debase society? It makes me feel proud when someone tells me that our products provided them with inspiration or just plain fun. We wanted them to do that!

Over 120 people at MetaTools today are responsible for providing you with the best that we can offer. When we shipped Kai's Power Tools 1.0, we were just eight people! Kai's ability to design groundbreaking software and our basic research and development efforts have paid off in inventing software that performs well beyond what many of you have come to expect from other products. Our employees—from our receptionist to engineering and development, the Web team, product management, creative services, quality assurance, customer service, technical services and support, marketing, sales, accounting, legal, facilities, shipping, and other functions—are all committed to providing you with the products, service, and support that you have come to expect from MetaTools.

If you are in the area, stop by our headquarters in Carpinteria, California. It's up the coast from Los Angeles, just 12 miles south of Santa Barbara. After all, you are part of the family!

John Wilczak
Chairman and CEO,
MetaTools, Inc.

PREFACE

"You know, you can't do that with KPT."

"Uh, actually, you can. First, I'll open a path-based image with Vector Effects ShatterBox, then copy it to Photoshop, where I'll apply Texture Explorer and a custom setting from Convolver. Finally, I'll take the resulting image and apply it as a texture to a Brycean object. Voilà."

"Geek check. Gotcha."

Scarily enough, it's conversations like this that brought this book into your hot little hands. In this case, we were having a hard time determining computer-generated artwork that *couldn't* be done using the KPT line of products. And that was before Kai's Power Goo, which stretches (*sic*) the boundaries of what one can do graphically on a desktop system.

Of course, naming the entire book *KPT Can't Do That* would have been catchy, but we doubted we could fill an entire book with things that fell into that category (we settled for a chapter, eventually). Instead, the thoughts of all the amazing things that *could* be done with KPT products overwhelmed us; in fact we were so overcome with great ideas while cooking up this book that Steve often had fainting spells, while Ted busily brainstormed with the casts of several Rogers and Hammerstein productions.

Eventually, IDG Books and we decided to cover KPT as part of the Studio Secrets series. After some discussion, we determined the book would be more interesting if it included those secrets we knew of, as opposed to secrets no one was willing to tell us. Of course, while we knew all sorts of secrets, we didn't know everything, so we recruited the most talented KPT artists on the planet to assist us. And assist us they did, giving us pages full of pointers and Zip cartridges full of artwork. Of course, now that this book is published, it no longer contains what could be accurately called "secrets," but instead "stuff that was printed in a book that everyone could read," which isn't quite as catchy as the current title.

The end result, of course, is a volume stuffed to the gills (Steve pointed out at this point that books don't have gills, while Ted countered that they must, because they seem to inhale when wet) with the juiciest, most inside stuff you'll find on the entire line of KPT products. We had to bribe officials in very high places for some of this information. We went to the opposite end of the food chain and bribed engineers that had worked on the products. We even bribed unidentifiable species (such as product managers at MetaTools). (Actually, we didn't have to bribe anybody.)

This book isn't meant to be read in one long sitting. Instead, take this book with you on the plane, to the "reading room," and then find a home for it next to your computer. The next time you're waiting for a Microsoft product to load, pick up the book and thumb through it, and you'll find something that strikes your fancy each time. Of course, you'll have to jump out of Word or Excel in order to use the techniques within these pages, at least until MetaTools releases the much-anticipated "Kai's Accounting Tools" or "KPT Spelling Designer."

MUCH MORE THAN A BEAUTIFUL DOORSTOP

We've split the book into two sections: Part 1 is titled "Product Secrets," where we showcase each and every MetaTools product, providing scores of undocumented tips and techniques for using them, and Kai Krause's thoughts on each. Part 1 also includes a history of MetaTools and a revealing look at where its products are going in the future.

Part 2, "Studio Secrets," is filled with the sexy stuff—those tips and techniques for creating artwork (using KPT products both individually and together) that will put you on the top of the graphics heap. It's filled with the work and techniques of the most accomplished KPT artists around, including chapters that cover commercial and artistic design applications of type magic, multidimensional backgrounds and textures, evocative creations of shadows and light, and killer special effects.

CD-ROM OR COASTER: YOU MAKE THE CALL

Oh, and you'll find a circular saw blade—wait—no, we've just been informed otherwise. You'll find a CD-ROM safely tucked into an envelope inside the back cover. This little piece of plastic is packed with valuable KPT stuff—much of which you'll find nowhere else. For example, you'll find a selection of Kai Krause's personal presets, as well as an exclusive QuickTime interview with Kai, a searchable PDF transcript of the entire interview, Bryce elements and animations, Final Effects movies, stunning image galleries, an interactive QuickTime tutorial showcasing some of our KPT secrets, "Goovies" made with the delightfully cool Kai's Power Goo, and demos of the MetaTools product line. And, after you've sucked all the information off of the disc that you can, it makes a very handsome oversized coaster.

FAST FORWARD

We've known all along that this book would be a "hit," and would fly off the shelves faster than the latest O.J. juror tell-all, and that loyal readers such as yourself would want even *more* KPT secrets that we couldn't squeeze into this volume. But we're modest little KPT users. So instead of doing the silly Hall & Oates thing (do you really think we'll ever see a *Rock and Soul Greatest Hits, Part Two*?), we've made no assumption there'll be a glamorous follow-up to this book, but between you and us, there will be. So, if you have some incredible tips or some great artwork that you'd like to see published in a future edition of *Official Kai's Power Tools Studio SECRETS*, send them to us at microquill@aol.com. We can't promise that we'll take you up on your generous offer, but we have been known to respond more favorably to certain artwork, like rectangular, small, green, double-sided, ornate-pattern-encrusted, text-heavy pieces. . . .

Of course, because this is the "official" MetaTools book (and not some flaky "Kai's SuperDuper Tips" rip-off), we've tried to capture the MetaTools spirit throughout. So prepare to be inspired, awed, and possibly, even a little secretive. . . .

ACKNOWLEDGMENTS

Writing *Official Kai's Power Tools Studio SECRETS* has been such a massive undertaking, we're still researching the long-term effects of this book on the U.S. economy (although we're betting that NASDAQ and MetaTools stock in particular—MTLS—goes way, way up upon publication). More people were involved with this book than either of us could count; we couldn't have written this book without them, and we're humbly thankful for their support and contributions.

First off, we'd like to thank the incredible artists for their work in this book. We'd list them all here, but then the Artists Index at the back of the book would be redundant. As you're paging through this book, note the names of the artists, and remember that most of them welcome your comments and the chance to prove themselves again on a freelance basis. All of the artists whose work appears throughout this book have used MetaTools' products in ways that will surely enlighten even the casual reader of these pages. We extend a special thanks to Jackson Ting, Greg Carter, Michael Tompert, Pieter Lessing, and Craig Lawson, who went above and beyond what we asked of them to really propel this book to a higher plane.

Without the constant supervision and guidance supplied by Mike Roney, this book would never have made it into your hands. Mike's foresight and persistence with various "powers that be" led to all the great extras that might not have made it into the book, such as color pages and all the great stuff on the CD-ROM. We also want to extend our thanks to all of the folks at IDG who did great work on a very tight schedule to get this book to you: Michael Welch, our editor "on the inside"; Jayne Jacobson for her copy editing; Jim Tierney, who provided technical editing assistance; Margery Cantor, who designed the book; Phyllis Beaty and the rest of the production team who put it all together; Christine Langin-Faris and Mary C. Oby who proofread the text; and Elizabeth Cunningham for the index.

Of course, this being the official MetaTools book, we couldn't have done it without the incredible help from all the wonderful folks at MetaTools. That goes double for Diana Smedley and Jean Fiegenbaum, whose early support and enthusiasm we especially appreciated. Great big thanks also to Brian, Keith, Guy, and Manuel in Inside Sales—we couldn't have asked for a better cheering section. Scott Krinsky and Birgit Spears were invaluable in helping us pull off the interviews with Kai and John. Thanks of course to John, not only for his help with the book, but also for getting together with Kai to make such a cool company in the first place. Thanks to Jim Mervis and Kari Zeni for handling contracts and all the legal stuff admirably. Lastly, thanks to Rob Sonner and all of the others who shared their technical expertise with us, often via lengthy late-night phone calls.

Special thanks go to Bill Niffenegger, whose excellent *Photoshop Filter Finesse* and other projects paved the way for this book. Bill's artwork appears at the beginning of many chapters in Part 1 (Bill has designed the packaging for most MetaTools products).

Funny how things work, but we would never have been in a position to cowrite this book were it not for Sree Kotay, and a bizarre chain of PostScript-based events. His input into the quality and features of most MetaTools' products can't be overstated; his efforts resulted in countless innovations and hidden stuff (most of it useful) that we've unearthed here (after he showed us the stuff). He also gave Steve his first software credit (to see it, hold down the Option key while you win the "breakout" Easter egg in Vector Effects).

Certain family members and friends had a big part in making sure this book got done. In fact, were it not for Jennifer Alspach's adamant refusal to play any more games of *Marathon II* with us, we doubt we would have ever written anything. In addition to her computer game prowess (and largely because of it), Steve and Ted both agree that she is the perfect woman. Thanks from us both. Mike and Robin Frank provided both hospitality and welcome encouragement (and made sure that Steve was fed and watered daily). We're grateful to Lisa Van Tassell for saving us with her timely and skillful transcribing of the Kai and John interviews. As this is Steve's first book, he would like to especially thank Mom, Dad, Nikkie, Mike, and Lisa for all their years of love, encouragement, and inspiration; thanks to Judy and Ron, Becky and Mike, Craig, Maz, Jimmy, Krish, Scott, Sree, Hessan, Todd, and all my friends for always being there; and thanks especially to Aunt Jo, for being a good friend as well as a great aunt, and also to Uncle Paul who (along with Aunt Jo) helped me get my very first computer all those years ago.

Yote encouraged Steve to concentrate in solitary confinement, while Toulouse made sure everyone knew when lunch-time and dinner-time rolled around. Linus, Pyro, and Lucy helped both of us stay on our toes (if we hadn't, we would've broken our necks tripping over them). Finally, Zeeber tried to help out whenever he could, affecting all sorts of things associated with *Official Kai's Power Tools Studio SECRETS* (including an unsuspecting camera bag).

Speaking of our title, no one deserves more thanks than the "visionary guru" (heh) himself: Kai. His innovations and revolutionary way of creating interfaces and software have forever changed the way people use computers—and the way they design funky cool stuff with them. Besides all that, he's a genuinely nice guy, even though he still claims he was never one of the original Pink Floyd band members.

CONTENTS AT A GLANCE

CONTENTS

CHAPTER 3
BRYCE   37

About the amazing technology and secrets of the latest incarnation of KPT Bryce.

CHAPTER 4
CONVOLVER   63

The least flashy of all the KPT products is incredibly powerful; this chapter shows the depth and breadth of the software, while revealing several little-known secrets.

CHAPTER 5
VECTOR EFFECTS   73

Vectors Rule, Pixels Drool? Secrets from the first plug-in package to take the vector world by storm (aka KPT ShatterBox).

CHAPTER 8
GOO, GAMES, AND MORE 115

Kai's Power Goo isn't a toy, but a brand new way to manipulate artwork. MetaTools' AOL games are fun and challenging, but they also give onliners a more relaxed and enjoyable atmosphere in which to communicate. All this, and a look at what's coming soon from the amazing digital gurus at MetaTools.

PART 2 : STUDIO SECRETS 127

CHAPTER 9
TYPE MAGIC 129

Exploring fantastic type effects and uses with the KPT series of products—the possibilities are nearly endless.

CHAPTER 10

MIXING AND MATCHING MEDIA   139

Creating a killer image—whether for viewing in print, on-screen, or on the Web—often requires the use of several tools. The techniques in this chapter focus on the ways in which artists have combined digital resources for a variety of target media.

CHAPTER 11

PATTERNS, TEXTURES, AND BACKGROUNDS   147

These are the elements of illustrations that give them life, providing depth and realism. This chapter looks at the art of textosity with Bryce, Kai's Power Tools, Vector Effects, and Convolver.

CHAPTER 12
TAKING KPT TO THE NEXT LEVEL 155

Combining KPT products to produce finished illustrations, productions, and more, with plenty of case studies.

CHAPTER 13
KPT CAN'T DO THAT! 105

Oh yes it can! How to accomplish effects you didn't think were possible with KPT products.

CHAPTER 14

SPECIAL EFFECTS SHOWCASE   179

A grouping of wowza images and illustrations that encompass KPT techniques and combinations of techniques not found elsewhere.

PART 1
PRODUCT SECRETS

CHAPTER 1
ONCE UPON A METATIME

While the focus of this book is on MetaTools' extraordinary software products and the secrets behind them, we feel that it is only appropriate to start off with a little background on Kai Krause, John Wilczak, and the company they created. Rather than simply regurgitate a lot of facts, we will focus on the significant events in MetaTools' history, talk about MetaTools' unique approach to bringing a product to market, and delve into Kai's brain to get a deeper understanding of what the company is all about and why. Along the way, we'll sprinkle in some interesting, unusual, and (for the most part) true stories about the people and events that have shaped the company.

HSC WAS ONCE A LITTLE GREEN SLAB OF CLAY: THE EARLY DAYS

1978. Disaster Number One: A flooded basement ruins the components for 3,000 digital waveform generators that Kai and his good friend Martin Schmitt had planned to build and sell as the focus of their recently-formed company, Prototype Systems. Instead of purchasing more components and trying again, Kai and Martin bought a computer (a Compucolor with a whopping 8K of memory!) and began writing fractal generation and manipulation programs.

As the years passed, Kai's and Martin's computers evolved, their programming skills advanced, and their early fractal-manipulation programs turned into

I like the notion of living ten minutes in the future. I've always done that.

KAI KRAUSE

ART OF DREAMING
Bill Ellsworth

CHECKERS VIRUS
Edmond Alexander

KAI AND JOHN
Courtesy of MetaTools, Inc.

3

ELECTRIC POWWOW
Michael Tompert

sophisticated 3D charting software (called DDD.graph and sold to Corvus Concepts for bundling with their computer systems). This same software is still in use today as the core charting engine for many popular software programs such as CorelDraw, Persuasion, and Quattro Pro. In addition to his computer-graphics endeavors, Kai was also breaking new ground in the field of electronic music and sound effects, working with prominent recording artists and movie studios and even earning a Clio award for work he did on a commercial for *Star Trek: The Movie*. By 1982, though, Kai knew that the path to achieving his own creative vision lay in computers; he sold all of his sound equipment and began to concentrate almost exclusively on his graphics software endeavors.

1978. Disaster Number Two: John Wilczak takes a computer programming course during his graduate studies at Columbia University. (Sorry John, we just couldn't resist.) While not actually *disastrous*, John's experience with computer programming was enough to convince him that he would never crunch code for a living. What it did do, though, was to spark a lifelong interest in computers and software development—an interest that would eventually lead him to form a company specifically to develop and market computer software. Between this initial contact with computers and the formation of HSC Software (the predecessor to MetaTools), John held positions with an impressive list of companies including General Electric and Touche Ross.

METAPHILOSOPHY:

INSIDE THE MIND OF KAI KRAUSE

KAI'S OUTLOOK on life is every bit as unique as any interface he's ever designed. In fact, his personal philosophy and his interfaces share many similarities. How Kai interacts with the world, the people in it, and his own ideas and dreams, is shaped by his unique philosophies—philosophies that give him unique tools with which to manipulate his real-world "images."

The following are selections from the interview Kai gave us during the prepration of this book. For your further reading pleasure, we have included Quick- Time

clips and the entire interview transcript (in PDF/Acrobat format) on the accompanying *Official KPT Studio SECRETS* CD-ROM.

When John did get into the computer business, it was in 1987, founding Harvard Systems Corporation, a company providing electronic publishing, imaging and multimedia consulting and systems integration services. In 1989, he made the strategic decision to change the focus of the company to software publishing and then development, when he had found a technology partner.

MR. KRAUSE, I PRESUME: JOHN AND KAI GET TOGETHER

While both John and Kai were very successful in their chosen endeavors individually, it's probably safe to say that at their first meeting neither one of them imagined how astonishingly successful they would be together.

Kai's earlier accomplishments—especially the creation of the core charting technology used in so many commercial applications—had provided him with a substantial income, enough to enable him to work for the joy of pursuing a vision, rather than simply for a paycheck. To this end, Kai had already worked in a situation where he was able to hand designs over to a team of programmers who would then create an actual product or technology.

John's success with early products such as The Graphics Link Plus and Santa Fe Media Manager convinced him that his future was definitely in software publishing; but he needed a cutting-edge product—and a cutting-edge visionary—upon which to exercise his business skills.

INVASION
Greg Carter

Q: You've been labeled by many in the media as a visionary. How do you react to that?

KAI: Contempt. Disregard. Nuisance. (laughter) "Visionary" is better than this "Guru" stuff that they used to slap on me in the old days. I've made a considerable effort to try to get away from that. I've had an idea or two that I had a little earlier than the next guy, and I intend to keep doing that. And I like the notion of living ten minutes in the future. I've always done that.

Q: If you hadn't met John and gotten together and formed MetaTools, what do you think you'd be doing right now?

KAI: Well, I had a company like that before; and I was up on a hill designing stuff; and there was a company in the valley down in L.A.; and I was in Malibu in the mountains. My closest friend back then was Martin Schmidt, and we designed a whole bunch of software; we had a little company because we didn't want employees coming up to the hill; and I had a person running that company for me. Probably, I would have done that same set-up, somehow, because it appealed to me a great deal: to be in the lab, to run through the design, to never show up at the company, and just do it. But somebody does need to do that, so I needed a partnership; and that was the two musketeer situation there. John is very good at keeping the stuff running. I very much want to have a partner who runs the day-to-day company; and when it comes to interfacing with the bankers or the lawyers of this world, I'd pass the hat over gladly; and he, as it happens, gladly took it. It was a nice synergy to do that.

VISAGE
Pieter Lessing

Most of you don't know the name of Uwe Maurer; but if you appreciate the latest copy of KPT or Bryce, it's Uwe that you have to thank for it. A longtime friend of Kai's from Germany, Uwe approached John in 1991 and offered to introduce him to Kai. Uwe felt that John's business savvy and Kai's technological prowess would be a perfect match. He couldn't have been more right. Kai and John worked together on a home video-editing package for Sony (which, unfortunately, never made it to market); and in April 1992, decided that the best way for them to enter the retail software development world would be to create a set of plug-in filters for Adobe Photoshop. The rest, as they say, is history.

GET THEM WAGONS ROLLING: THE MOVE TO SANTA BARBARA

By the end of 1993, HSC had begun to experience some of the growth pains that followed the success of Kai's Power Tools—new employees were swelling the ranks of the Santa Monica, California-based company, doubling and tripling the number of people on the payroll. Computers and equipment were purchased in quantity, workspace had to be found for everyone, and available phone lines were becoming scarce. In addition to these logistic woes, the traffic, smog, crime, and grime of Los Angeles didn't exactly

---

Q: Of all the MetaTools products that are out right now, what's your favorite?

KAI: Hmmmm; the focus is everything (laughter). I don't think—that's like asking me about my children. Each one, when we did them, had their own unique little space; and each one was very enjoyable to bring out. I mean, Vector Effects is an example of the most painless, I mean, it was one weekend of a sketch for me. The next time I saw them, it was hooked up. It was scary. I had Phil Clevenger in there; and, I mean, one design of a button; and he took it and extrapolated the

rest of it. Miraculously. I love that. Bryce 2 was probably the most deep. We went—they stayed at my house, there in the lab, and we just cocooned ourselves for twenty-hour days. We did that for long stretches and really brought something home there. Bryce 2 was really probably the closest to what I really wanted to do in some designs. The subtlety of being able to have new solutions and tiny little changes was good fun.

Q: If there's one piece of software that's already done, that you wish you

had done, and maybe spruced up the interface, what product would that be?

KAI: Hmmmm; I don't think you would know it. I've seen some interesting financial analysis stuff at AT&T, you know, the really big stuff. I keep looking at military. I love to look a little bit ahead on the curve. Take this million dollar piece of software and then give it to the kids for eighty dollars.

Out of the current state of software in our bracket, the two, three, four hundred dollars, I don't know that there's anything there that I would see. I'm not

inspire the creative and artistic expression that was critical for a company like HSC.

John and Kai knew that a major shakeup of the company was in order, but neither one of them knew just how major it would be. As it turned out, the shakeup measured exactly 6.7 on the Richter scale. The Los Angeles earthquake of January 1994 turned out to be the perfect impetus that John and Kai needed to find HSC the room to grow (both physically and creatively).

Inspired by the beauty of the Santa Barbara area (and the cracks in the walls of their Santa Monica offices), John and Kai began looking into moving the company to Santa Barbara. In an amazingly short time, John had made the necessary arrangements to lease space in an ideal location, an office building on a bluff overlooking the Pacific Ocean.

HSC's new home in Carpinteria (about 12 miles south of Santa Barbara and a little more than an hour north of Los Angeles) provided plenty of room to grow as a company, as well as a safe, clean, beautiful place for the company's employees and their families to live and play. As of this writing, MetaTools is once again expanding (in the same location) to make room for its more than 120 employees (85 more than worked for the firm at the time of the move!).

POWER TOOLS
Douglas Chezem

interested to try to invade any of those spaces at all. I'd leave Photoshop alone, leave Painter alone, leave Quark alone. They all do what they do, and I happily send people back to those and say, "If you really need to have Lab modes and CMYK and this and that and the other, there it is. Works perfectly fine. Do it all day long." I like to go into this other— the virgin snow. No footprints. Nobody's there. That's very important to me: to not overlap, to actually create the unexpected. See from KPT 2.1 to 3, you should have seen the feedback we got. It was all

totally linear extrapolation of point one more. And when we then did spheroids and Interform movies and the lens. None of it was what was expected by any of them. And that's what I think are the funnest. It's also the secret into why you can continue to invent yourself like that.

Q: How about a graphics utility like DeBabelizer?
KAI: You know something? DeBabelizer is a good example of very nice functionality with a bit of a problem on the front. But it is the tool for people

who need to solve these problems, and I'm afraid I am going way the other way. You know, that's making five thousand people bleedingly happy because they need it every day. I can do that. But I would much rather make five hundred thousand, or five million people happy. I mean, I look at feature films, I look at these mass games, and if I see one more guy ripping the soul out of it, it just makes me sick, what's going on there. I'd love to get in. Hey, I'd love to get completely out of this whole realm and design physical things, design an

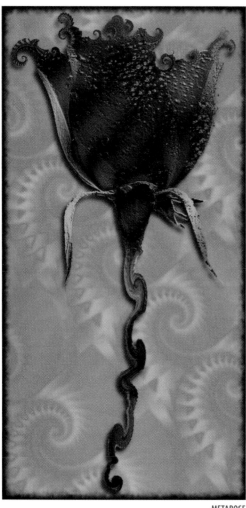

METAROSE
Joseph A. Linaschke

A ROSE, BY ANY OTHER NAME: HSC BECOMES METATOOLS

Back before HSC Software became MetaTools, employees used to have fun making up new meanings for the HSC acronym (1.1). A favorite during the crunch time associated with new product launches was "Have Some more Caffeine." When the IPO (Initial Public Offering of stock) was approaching, the front-runner was "Highly Successful Company." A couple of other choice phrases also made the rounds (which, unfortunately, we can't share with you in a family book).

A frequently asked trade show question was, "What the heck does HSC stand for anyway?" The correct answer is "Harvard Systems Corporation." But knowing what the letters stood for didn't tell anyone anything about the company. It had long been a priority for John and Kai to come up with a more descriptive name for the company; but with the development and release of new software always taking everyone's time and energy, a new name kept getting relegated to the back burner. The approach of the IPO, however, pushed the need for a new name to the forefront. It was imperative that the company go public with a new and descriptive name. The question was, what name?

As the executive staff and creative services department pondered possible names—including "M9 Software" (for Magnitude 9) and "Planet Zontar" (an internal "Name the Company" contest resulted in some highly amusing but not-even-close-to-accept-

HDTV remote. Do a feature film. I got a couple scripts lying around the house. Who knows we'll do this again a couple years from now, and it'll be another SECRETS book.

Q: The biggest thing going on right now in computer graphics is World Wide Web page design. What do you see as MetaTools', or even your position regarding tools that are Web-based or especially for the Web?

KAI: Whew, that's a big one. I mean, I have a philosophical connection to this that's much deeper than the product in ink. I mean, I was literally up there on stages all over the world, "Rah, rah, rah, the Web is coming." Four years ago. People went, "Web? What is he, a spider?" I mean, they had no idea. I'm now getting extremely skeptical. I'm scared gutless on this whole thing, I swear to God. I started with 500 bookmarks. It might as well be 50,000 bookmarks now. I mean, every time you drive by a gas station, it's got a Web page. It's scary. It's diluting itself so much that it becomes meaningless. I think the Web's very impor-

tant. I see the positivity of it. I like to see it in a different way, though. With giving much, much higher bandwidth levels to it, we'll be able to solve the problem again. With the current level at twenty-eight eight, to go through the stuff we now do is a bunch of vanityware; and it won't last very long. It's a necessary phase that we have to plow through to get to the good stuff. It's our Model T that we're playing with right now.

What's important is, you've got mankind. Six billion people on this little blue planet. You link up the common knowl-

able entries from the rest of the employees)—the Greek word "meta," meaning "above" or "beyond," kept going round and round in Kai's head. At one meeting, Kai brought up "meta" again, and John, whose AOL screen name is "Cool Tools," suggested "MetaTools." Because HSC was a company that made tools to take artists above and beyond their current level of productivity, the name worked perfectly (1.2).

YOU LIKE ME, YOU REALLY, REALLY LIKE ME! METATOOLS GOES PUBLIC

One of the big advantages of being a small, privately-held company is that you can develop the products you want, when you want, and the way you want. It was this freedom that brought us Kai's Power Tools and Bryce. The problem, though, is that in a small company, it is virtually impossible to develop more than one product at a time; and you have limited resources for the marketing and distribution of your product(s). To alleviate these problems, John and company approached Paul Allen, cofounder of Microsoft, to discuss MetaTools' (then HSC's) future. Paul was impressed with the company and its potential and became a significant investor. This enabled the company to expand both its personnel and product line, but additional capital would be needed for the company to move to the next level.

On December 12, 1995, MetaTools became a publicly-owned corporation (NASDAQ symbol "MTLS")

with an initial stock offering that netted the company over $46 million in working capital. This capital will ensure that MetaTools has the resources to attract top talent and to bring more and more products to an ever-expanding market.

WHO'S WHO:
KEY PLAYERS AND RISING STARS

MetaTools, perhaps more than any other company, relies heavily on key individuals to make everything work. If you remove any of these talented people from the equation, MetaTools, and the products it produces, would suffer.

1.1

1.2

edge of all of them—cumulative, final knowledge—and you let anybody access anything. That's what it's really about, and there we need new tools to make sense of this. I'd like to go in and let you see a hundred fifty Web sites and be able to bring different variables in and to have it coded in 3D by height, by color, by cross-imposition. That's worthwhile. That will do something. Little tools to make another button: I'm not interested. A lot of people will use our stuff anyway. I mean, I hop around. We've got about two trillion links right now to some guy who wants, maybe, to use the texture explorer to some little button. Hey, you know, why not? It's a visual style; have some fun. But that's not where I see my focus. I don't want to just serve up Kai's Web Tools, and it's another little pretty font with an edge on it. Duh.

1.3 *Kai Krause*

1.4 *John Wilczak*

As the single most indispensable member of the team, Kai Krause (1.3) provides the creative vision and philosophical direction that drives the company. Obviously, without Kai, Kai's Power Tools would never have become a reality.

John Wilczak (1.4), is a perfect yin to Kai's yang. John's business and marketing prowess has enabled MetaTools to take the software development world by storm. Industry insiders are impressed with John's uncanny ability to always have MetaTools in the right place at the right time.

Ben Weiss (1.5) is the original MetaTools wunderkind. Ben's actual title at MetaTools is "Imaging Scientist," which aptly describes his function within the company. It was Ben's algorithms that first breathed life into the original Kai's Power Tools, and his core mathematical handiwork lies at the heart of most of the software developed by MetaTools.

Andrea Pessino (1.6) is another key member of the MetaTools team. Like Ben, Andrea's work focuses not on individual software applications, but on core technology that serves as a foundation for the products that have made MetaTools the company that it is today. A native of Italy, Andrea was introduced to MetaTools through Colleen Chamberlain, John's very able executive assistant. Andrea joined Ben on Kai's "mini xerox PARC" team, developing dynamic core technology for the company.

Sreekant Kotay (1.7) is a relative newcomer to the company. Sree has built his already-formidable reputation on his uncanny ability to cut right to the heart

1.5 *Ben Weiss*

1.6 *Andrea Pessino*

of a programming problem. Sree developed the product that would become Vector Effects on his own before joining the MetaTools team, and has since worked on both Kai's Power Tools 3 and Bryce 2, adding impressive new features and coding efficiency to both products. A little known fact about Sree is that MetaTools doesn't actually pay him money for his work. Instead, a rented truck pulls up to his house once a month and unloads a cargo of Now and Laters, Twizzlers, Spree, M&Ms, Coke, Sprite, and pizza (Sree's special diet—doctor's orders).

Phil Clevenger (1.8) has a wonderful way of quietly taking Kai's wild imaginings and preliminary UI designs and (along with Kai, of course) turning them into actual interfaces. In addition to his interface work, Phil also coordinates the in-house development of UI elements and does a million other things to bring a software program from initial concept to final product. Phil is literally Kai's right hand at MetaTools (and sometimes his nose and left foot, too).

Colleen Heining (1.9) is the heart and soul of customer service. The company has received dozens of letters and e-mail messages declaring her sainthood. It isn't hard to understand why MetaTools customers perceive the company as a friend of the family—Colleen knows how to make them feel loved.

Jon Swift keeps a cool head running the technical services department. This is nothing less than making sure such things as networks, phone systems, tradeshow systems, and everything else is in good shape—no small feat given the company's growth in just three years, and Jon still makes room for parasailing in his spare time.

Brian Dightman has worn almost every important sales hat in the company, and no organization survives without selling its product or service. Brian handles the company's biggest distribution accounts today, loves the technology, and still finds time to write screenplays.

Jim Dudman has provided over five years of important multimedia production, 3D animation, and now video special effects product development management. Enter his office and you immediately find his NT workstation, PowerMac, and SGI systems humming away on renderings, Web e-mail, and software development testing.

Scott Hawthorne has probably done more demos and worked on more multimedia and graphics projects than anyone in the company to date. The company welcomes his sense of humor when we need a bit of levity during crunch time.

In addition to these key players, dozens of others have made invaluable contributions: Todd, Josh, Hessan, and the rest of the engineering crew; Julie and Rob who keep the online stuff up-to-date and actually "online"; Michelle, who makes sure an insane number of tradeshows and events run smoothly; Lars and the production team; the entire product management team; Darin, Donna, and Gregg, whose art graces almost every ad you see; the inside and outbound sales gangs; the wonderful men and women of the accounting department; the customer service team, the extraordinary tech support crew; Greg,

1.7 *Sreekant Kotay*

1.8 *Phil Clevenger*

1.9 *Colleen Heining*

METATOOLS INSIDE INFORMATION

The development of a product's user interface is one of the most critical and time-consuming aspects of product development at MetaTools. Kai develops initial interface ideas and sketches them out for the development team to work on. One of Phil's primary responsibilities is to then take Kai's initial designs and turn them into actual UI prototypes. These prototypes are then taken back to Kai, who tweaks them further (or quite often scraps them altogether and starts over from a new angle). This process of design and tweak continues until a solid prototype is arrived at. This is then given to the engineers, who start hooking different chunks of code into the interface. Sometimes there are chunks of code that don't have an interface element, which requires more design work by Kai and Phil. Sometimes there are interface elements that don't have an equivalent chunk of code, which requires the engineers to think up new features to put into the program.

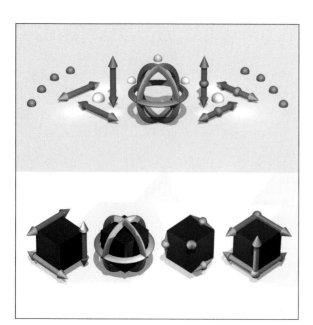

1.10

Susan, and their marketing cohorts; and everyone else in the company.

METAPHYSICS: THE MAKING OF BRYCE 2

During our conversations with Kai, Phil, and other members of the development team, we were fascinated to learn exactly how a MetaTools product evolves from creative spermatozoa to hale and hearty software program. And because we thought it was so interesting, we figured that you might want to hear about the process, too. We have chosen to use Bryce 2 as an example, primarily because it is MetaTools' most recent release (as of this writing) and so is still fresh in everyone's mind.

1. Version 3 of Kai's Power Tools is finally finished and out the door. After a luxurious 3.5 minutes of sleep, it's time for the development team to tackle Bryce 2.

2. Kai, Phil, and the engineering team meet to discuss the preliminary feature set for the new version of Bryce. Ideas are thrown in and tossed out until a rough idea of what the software should do is formed. At this stage, everything is a loose democracy (that is, mob rule). Even features that are not feasible (from an engineering standpoint) are left in because, well, who knows what engineering marvels we might come up with?

3. Eric Wenger, who has been revising core Bryce code by himself since the release of the original Bryce, meets with Kai and Phil to show what he has come up with. Possibilities and impossibilities are discussed. A more realistic feature set is arrived at.

4. Sree is sent to Paris to work with Eric on Bryce. Eric is skeptical about the youngster's abilities (Sree, like Ben, is only 23). Sree shows Eric anti-aliased wireframes with cast shadows that are significantly faster than Bryce 1's aliased, shadowless wireframes. Eric is suitably impressed. Code gets crunched in a big way.

5. While Eric and Sree crunch code, Kai and Phil travel back and forth across the pond to provide input and to flesh out interface ideas and requirements. When Sree isn't in Paris working with Eric, he is at his home in Philadelphia working with Phil on UI possibilities.

6. Feature lock, perhaps the saddest moment in MetaTools' product development, forces its way onto the scene. At this point, no new features can be added to the software. Feature lock is a hard and fast, irrevocable, carved-in-stone rule of the software development industry that must be adhered to without fail. "Feature lock? We don't need no stinkin' feature lock!" This is, of course, never the case at MetaTools, the home of "cool features and lots of 'em," many of which find their way into the software at the last minute because they're just too cool *not* to be included.

7. UI after UI after UI is proposed and discarded (1.10). In many cases (at least three for Bryce 2), entire UIs are scrapped after considerable background and element artwork is painstakingly produced. Finally, a Kai-approved UI is created and UI elements are hooked into existing software capabilities.

8. Sree works his magic on the software, enhancing existing features or UI functionality as needed and carving the code into a lean, mean, rendering machine (1.11).

9. The entire development team works day and night (and any other time that they can find) to pull together the thousand different loose ends that inevitably crop up in a project of this magnitude.

10. At the 11th hour (and sometimes at the 11th hour, 59th minute, and 59th second) bugs are frantically squashed, readme files and installers are created, CDs are burned and fingers are crossed. And the result, once again, is a quantum leap for the software program itself and for the expectations for the next version.

INTO THE FUTURE

Clearly, MetaTools has a winning combination of personalities and ideas. The results are plain to see in its software, through the comments of its millions of happy users, and in the techniques and examples you see in this book. There clearly is much more excitement to come, some of which is described or otherwise hinted-at in Chapter 8, "Goo, Games, and More." For now, sit back and enjoy the views. . . .

METATOOLS INSIDE INFORMATION

Like many software development companies, MetaTools goes through very distinct (and generally quarterly) cycles of cranking up for the release of a new product, followed by a period of relative relaxation before the development of the next product. Because of MetaTools' rapid recent growth, the "cranking up" portions of the cycle have sort of taken over the "relative relaxation" portions. It's not unusual to see pillows and sleeping bags stashed in cubicles, or towering pyramids of soda cans surrounded by protective walls of pizza boxes as engineers and product managers alike go "into the cave" to get a product out on time. To blow off steam, many cubicles have juggling blocks, basketballs, the odd guitar, and Nerf guns stashed somewhere for the occasional covert "hit" (the ping-pong table, unfortunately, had to go to make room for more cubicles). Ben and Andrea, both of whom are accomplished pianists, have a terrific keyboard system set up in their office, and many times the clicking of keyboards and muffled conversations are interrupted at four o'clock in the morning by full, rich (and usually very loud) strains of Beethoven, Mozart, Bach, or any of a dozen other favorite composers.

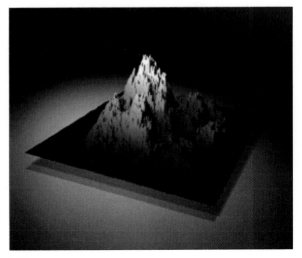

1.11

CHAPTER 2
KAI'S POWER TOOLS

This is it. The product that started the whole KPT "thang." Kai's Power Tools 3 (2.1) is the latest incarnation of the best-selling plug-in collection for Photoshop and Photoshop wannabees. The interface is the stuff of legends (although the glassy green days are over). The effects are nothing sort of legendary. This is the product that jump-started a new software niche—the Plug-In Application.

Kai's Power Tools is primarily a set of special effects tools, though some are quite useful in productivity as well.

The interface is . . . well, actually, there isn't just one interface. There are really three major types of interfaces (2.2) and one subvariation throughout the software.

The images shown on the next page show the three basic interface categories: Really Big Ones, Lens fx, and Credit Cards.

Each one of the products has a little bit of that extra charm for me. They're like little children.

KAI KRAUSE

KAI'S POWER TOOLS EXAMPLES

The following pages show some examples of artwork created and/or modified with various Kai's Power Tools 3 filters. In some cases, more than one—even several—filters were used to generate the final effect. Note, however, that Final Effects (another MetaTools product) is discussed in Chapter 6.

"Rancho Caliente" by Ted Alspach (2.3) showcases several different textures generated with KPT Texture Explorer. The images were then given a three-dimensional look by using channel operations.

2.1

2.2

2.3

This *Business Week* cover art by Pamela Hobbes (2.4) was created primarily in Kai's Power Tools (with a little help from Bryce).

Bill Ellsworth's "Ten Dragons Draggin'" (2.5) was created with a multitude of Kai's Power Tools filters and Bryce, resulting in a surreal portrait of the different Lens fx waiting to be used.

2.4

METAPHILOSOPHY:

**INSIDE THE MIND OF
KAI KRAUSE**

Q: Can you tell me briefly what you think is the knock-out feature of each product? Let's start with Kai's Power Tools.

KAI: Each one of the products has a little bit of that extra charm for me. They're like little children. Where you say KPT, I remember distinctly the process of taking it to the new interfaces and the limitations. Like the spheroids. How I had 38 different interfaces. And it was meant to be on the CD-ROM—you get to pick your own. And it turned out to be just a little bit more complicated to switch the resources because we had extra little floating ele-ments and layers of shadows . . . it wasn't just one resource picture to swap. Other-wise we would have done that.

We had that piece of rock—there is just one way to do it. I had it in shiny alu-minum, and silver reflectors, and a mirror of another world behind you. I had one that was a mirror, and I took a picture of myself behind it. And if you look really closely inside the vault, there's me look-ing at you like that, you know. We have a lot of fun with that sort of thing.

In KPT—you know the annoying part is when the engineers go, "Hey, Kai, we're

"Lisa" by Joseph A. Linaschke (2.6) was created almost entirely with one image which was then modified in various ways through the use of Kai's Power Tools.

"Party Time" by Lester Yocum (2.7) was created with heavy use of the noise filter as well as KPT Spheroid and KPT Gradient Designer.

This *Popular Mechanics* cover by Michael Tcherevkoff (2.8) combines several images, but your eyes focus directly on the lifelike "3D" created by applying a radial metallic gradient within the letters.

This brochure by Sullivan & Brownell, Inc., Art Director, Kent Gardner (2.9) was created using both KPT Texture Explorer and KPT Gradient Designer to achieve the high-tech look of our planet.

2.6

2.5

2.7

72 hours away from shipping. We did a little something as a joke." And they put this entire thing in there, you know, the whole movie-making sphere thing, the Genesis editor, as a surprise to Kai! If only I had known that we could do that. You know, if only they had stopped goofing around with that stuff, we would have finished the lens that's draggable (laughter)! So, there are little stories which aren't always clear to people, "Gee, the Genesis Editor. Why can't you set presets?" Well, guess why: We had two hours before the plane left. It was fun to do.

2.8

2.9

THE REALLY BIG FILTERS

The next few pages provide secrets and tips for the basically monstrous KPT filters. These filters are definitely not in the classic one- or two-option filter category: instead they're mammoth dialog boxes with billions and billions of options and built-in previews. In fact, rather than calling these things "filters," Meta-Tools refers to them as "Application Extensions," which sounds pretty darn impressive.

KPT GRADIENT DESIGNER

Probably the most useful of all the Kai's Power Tools filters, KPT Gradient Designer (2.10) has been part of the Kai's Power Tools filter set since version 1.0 was introduced. It's actually very easy to use despite the six box controls, live adjustable preview, double gradient bracket, and seven color controls at the bottom. No, really!

To select a preset gradient, click and hold on the bottom bar near the little triangle. The gradient *presets* (preconfigured settings) appear. One of the nice things about presets in Kai's Power Tools is that you can view them either graphically (2.11) or in a text-based pop-up menu (2.12). Switch between the two modes by pressing the Spacebar before you click the preset bar. You can also permanently change the appearance through an option in the Preferences dialog box.

2.10

If you'd like to create a gradient that isn't based on any existing gradient, click and hold on the left edge of the gradient bar. The Gradient color picker appears. Drag it to the color you want and release the mouse button. The leftmost color will now be the color you selected (2.13) and will blend to the existing rightmost color. Repeat this color selection for the rightmost color, and you'll have created a basic two-color gradient.

Create gradients with more than two colors by manipulating the black bracket above the gradient bar. This bracket allows you to control the areas of the gradient you're affecting. To affect a smaller area than the entire gradient bar, click and drag the edges of the bracket inward. You can move the bracket around by clicking in the middle of the bracket and dragging it left or right. To reset the bracket so it covers the complete gradient bar again, double-click on the middle of the bracket. Use the shift key to constrain the movement of the bracket to $1/32$ adjustments, allowing for easily made multicolor gradients.

Some of the modes (such as Radial) enable you to manipulate their centers in the preview window. Just click in the preview window to change the center of the current gradient.

The Repeat button controls how many times the gradient is repeated when it is applied, by clicking and dragging on the button (to the right) to increase the repetitions. However, if you click just once on the repeat button after you've repeated the gradient, the number of gradient repetitions is applied to the gradient bar itself.

One of the least known, but most powerful aspects of KPT Gradient Designer is its secret Layer Bin (2.14). Yes, there's a palette within the dialog box. To view it, press Command-Shift-L, and it appears to the left of the dialog box. On a 13-inch monitor (640 × 480 resolution), you will only be able to see the far right edge of the palette; you'll need to click to the far left of the dialog box and drag it onto the dialog box to use it.

The initial gradient you're designing appears at the bottom of the Layer Bin. Clicking the little "+" at the top of the Layer Bin adds another gradient to the bin; modify this gradient as you would any other. To com-

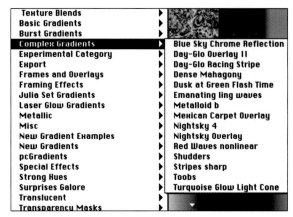

2.12

2.13

2.11

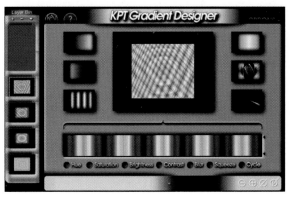

2.14

bine these gradients, you must give them some sort of transparency by using either the alpha masks, the Opacity slider, or one of the Glue settings. Save Layer Bin presets (a collection of all the gradients and how they're stacked) by clicking on the menu triangle at the top of the Layer Bin and pulling down to Add Preset. Delete a gradient in the Layer Bin by selecting it and clicking the "-" that appears at the top of the Layer Bin. You can even rearrange the gradients by moving them up and down within the Layer Bin.

See the Gradient Designer presets pages at the end of this chapter.

METATOOLS INSIDE INFORMATION

Incredible features such as the Layer Bin in KPT Gradient Designer usually inspire questions such as, "Why isn't this outstanding feature documented?" or "What's the smallest number of coins you need to buy something that costs 73¢?" Why don't you ever learn about the feature from MetaTools or any other "official" source (besides this book, of course)? Probably because the feature is usually thrown in by a talented engineer with a few spare hours on his hands; and, because it was never properly tested, it can't be supported well by the technical support people at MetaTools. And by the way: You don't need any coins at all if you have a dollar bill.

KPT TEXTURE EXPLORER

Where KPT Gradient Designer stops, KPT Texture Explorer (2.15) picks up the pace. KPT Texture Explorer is a texture generator that you don't completely control. Instead, you direct it to the texture you end up using. We're pushing MetaTools to change the name of the next revision of KPT Texture Explorer (which will undoubtedly contain more controls for manipulating textures) to "KPT Texture Director" (which would be a little more accurate). Other names we've considered include "KPT Textural Modification Manager" and "KPT Textile Manufacturing Exploration Production Assistant," but we don't think they'll fly. . . .

In previous versions of KPT Texture Explorer, we considered the most severe limitation of the software to be the fact that you couldn't really start anywhere if you had a rough idea of the texture you were looking for. Instead, you had to click repeatedly on the topmost ball on the tree, and wait for your envisioned texture to appear. Once it did, you could work your way down the tree looking for textures that got closer and closer to the one you thought you wanted. Of course, the benefit of all this clicking around was that oftentimes you'd end up with a totally different texture that just happened to catch your eye for some reason or another.

In KPT Texture Explorer 3.0, this is no longer a problem thanks to the wonderful graphical presets included with the filter. KPT Texture Explorer, like

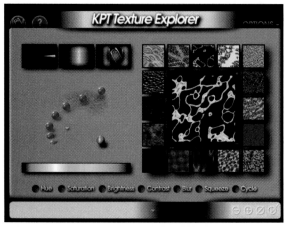

2.15

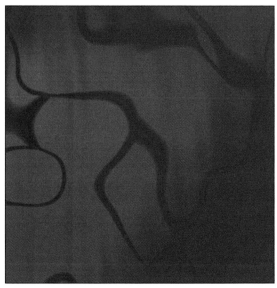

2.16A

KPT Gradient Designer, takes a good idea (presets in general) and turns it into a invaluable component of the software. Instead of randomly guessing around with the tree (which you can still do if you're of a mind to), now you can view thumbnails of all the presets and select the one closest to your idea for the texture.

If you want more than one color in your texture, you can specify the exact colors you'd like using the little gradient bar under the variations tree. By clicking on the bar, you can select a "color set" based on a gradient preset. You might have to make sure you have a gradient preset with the needed colors in it first (you would have to create this in KPT Gradient Designer). This example (2.16) shows a texture with both a simple two-color gradient and a multiple color gradient applied. Note that the pattern stays the same, but the colors are extremely different.

See the Texture Explorer presets pages at the end of this chapter, and try out Kai's personal TE presets included on this book's CD-ROM.

KPT INTERFORM

In a way, KPT Interform is the next step in the KPT Texture Explorer process of generating textures, although you might need a few extra steps. For instance, Interform combines two existing KPT Texture Explorer textures quickly and easily. You have control over how the two textures interact and their position, but you must use preset textures created in KPT Texture Explorer. Existing textures cannot be modified in KPT Interform. In addition to combining textures, Interform also can create original QuickTime movies that are great backgrounds for movies modified with After Effects or Premiere (2.17).

After the textures have been selected, you can "give them a push" by dragging your cursor over them.

DANGER, WILL ROBINSON

With all KPT filters that have presets—but especially with KPT Texture Explorer—be sure to save your preset (click on the "+" and name it) once you've determined it is the one you want to use. Although the last-used texture reappears in the mother box the next time you open the dialog box (the cousin textures will also be there), you're only one minor change and a click of the Cancel button away from losing that texture forever. The last texture/gradient/spheroid created (and cousins) will still be there even if you do hit Cancel.

If you've used a texture and haven't saved it as a preset, there's no way to get back to it once you go to another texture! You're completely out of luck. KPT Texture Explorer can generate billions of different textures (Ted counted), and you'll never be able to return to the exact one you used before.

2.16B

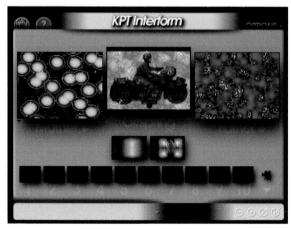

2.17

Each texture moves in the direction and at the approximate speed of the drag. If you'd like to have the textures move nonlinearly, select a movement option from the lists that pop-up from the lower left corner of the textures (Manual Scooting is the option that allows you to manually "push" them). To make the textures stop moving, click without dragging on the textures. To make the textures go away without using your mouse, just close your eyes. To make them come back . . .

KPT Interform can also be used to create QuickTime movies of your moving textures. Click on a frame in the filmstrip along the bottom to insert the current combination in that frame. Interform creates a movie (you can preview this by Option-clicking on the little projector) that moves along all the keyframes, fading to black between each of the frames. You can change the speed of the frames and a few other options in the movies options menu under the projector.

The *Official KPT Studio SECRETS* CD-ROM includes a collection of Kai's own Interform presets.

KPT SPHEROID DESIGNER

Without question, this is the coolest looking interface the gurus at MetaTools have ever cooked up. Originally created with KPT Bryce 1.0, the entire KPT Spheroid Designer interface resembles the interior of a cave, or the floor of a clay basin, or a magnified epidermal surface (ick). No matter what it looks like, KPT Spheroid Designer is both the most fun and the most fascinating of all the Kai's Power Tools filters.

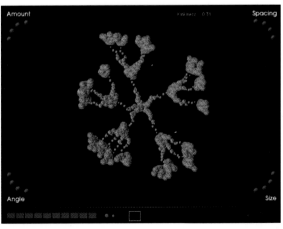

2.18

The best thing about KPT Spheroid Designer is that you have complete control over the eventual look of your spheres. You can custom design the layout for several spheres at a time, the texture, the curvature, and even the lighting.

You're probably thinking to yourself, "What, no QuickTime movies? Boy, those MetaTools people are slackers." And we'd agree entirely were it not for the fact that, yes indeed, you can create QuickTime movies within KPT Spheroid Designer, and they're just this   far apart (imagine two fingers almost touching) from absolutely astonishing.

To get to the QuickTime movie section, pull down the Apply Options pop-up menu (beneath the quantity spheres) and select the Genesis Editor option. Your screen first goes black and then fills with a pattern of spheres (2.18).

There are controls for sizing and selecting the angle, the spacing, and the number of spheres located in the corners of the screen. Click on those words to display controls for each of those attributes. At the bottom of the screen are the tools used for making the movie itself.

Click on a frame to make the current view a keyframe. Click on the large red dot to write a QuickTime movie to disk. Click on the little red dot to preview the movement of the spheres. Click on the box to their right to change the background color.

THE COMPACT FILTERS

A large number of filters consist of a much smaller dialog box and many less options than the filters previously discussed; these are referred to often as the "credit card" filters or Compact UIs (User Interface). We'll call them the compact filters.

All of the compact filters have the standard opacity and glue options, and also a Mode option with options specific to that particular filter. Each of the compact filters has a preview display that shows the effects of the current settings. Because the display is rather small, it updates live on most systems.

KPT 3D STEREO NOISE

This filter creates those wonderful stereoscopic images you can find on posters and full-color books. Initially, they look like static. However, if you stare at the image long enough, it is supposed to pop out at you (2.19).

We have a bit of trouble with this (Steve claims not to see anything, while Ted sees things that aren't supposed to be there), but you or your friends might see these things perfectly. We've provided a few of these images here and scattered several others throughout the rest of the book for your enjoyment (or frustration). After toying with the idea of putting the original images for all of them on the CD, we've decided against it, hoping that our readers will send us nasty e-mail demanding to know what the images are.

To create a stereoscopic image with KPT 3D Stereo Noise, follow these steps:

1 Create a basic image (preferably black and white) composed of basic shapes or text. Photographs do not work.

2 Blur the image a little. We used a Gaussian Blur of 2 for our examples.

3 Choose Filter⇨KPT 3.0⇨3D Stereo Noise.

4 Choose the color mode by clicking on the Mode button.

5 Increase the depth of the effect by dragging across the image to the right. The little white rectangle with the two black boxes that appears shows the depth of the eventual 3D image.

If you can't see your image in the resulting mass of pixels, don't be alarmed.

The technique for doing so is to focus on a point beyond the image (on your computer screen, look for your own reflection within the image). Keep focusing on this point for about a minute, and the texture becomes liquid, seeming to flow around and maybe forwards and backwards. Eventually, the image pops out or in.

Some people (like Steve) may find that stereoscopic images are just not worth their time, while others (like Ted) may discover things that don't exist in this particular universe.

KPT PAGE CURL

This is one of those effects that is so very cool and hip and wonderful that in 1997 and beyond, it will be considered anything but cool and hip and wonderful.

It's the effect that's been around since KPT 1.0. It's the effect you've seen millions of times on book covers, newspaper ads, and posters. It's KPT Page Curl, and it must be stopped.

KPT Page Curl, oddly enough, curls the corner of pages, giving the "back" of the page a shiny look. Using the opacity settings, you can set the curl to be partially transparent, thus allowing yourself to look "through" the curls onto the page beneath.

To change the size of the curl, click on the arrows and drag. Clicking on the little curls around the image lets you change the corner that is being curled.

KPT PLANAR TILING

KPT Planar Tiling automatically tiles your selection off into the distance. The second mode of KPT Planar Tiling is Parquet Tile, which tiles the image and rotates it automatically. Change modes by clicking the Mode button.

While in Planar Tile mode, click on the image and drag around to set the direction and height of the plane. In Parquet Tile mode, click and drag up and down to scale the tiles, or left and right to rotate them around.

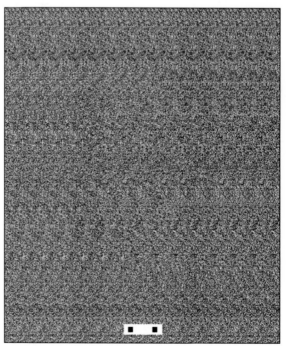

2.19

2.20

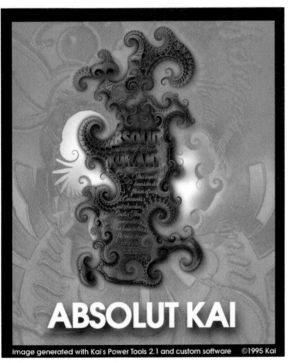

Image generated with Kai's Power Tools 2.1 and custom software   ©1995 Kai

2.21

Because the preview for this filter is quite misleading legions of KPT users avoid it entirely. The preview separates the tiles with a black border. The finished, rendered image does NOT include this border. This knowledge should give new life to this filter for most users.

KPT SEAMLESS WELDER

This is the perfect tile maker: it sets any rectangular shape to automatically have perfectly smooth edges. There are two modes within KPT Seamless Welder: Seamless Welder, which reads from outside the selected area, and Reflective Welder, which reads from the selection only. Increase the intensity of the effect by dragging to the right (2.20).

Follow these steps for a good seamless weld:

1 Create the pattern tile at about 120 percent of the size of the image it will eventually fill, or larger.

2 Use the KPT Planar Tiling filter Parquet mode to create edges around the original image.

3 Select just the central tile and Use KPT Seamless Welder with an intensity of 100 percent.

4 To use the new tile as a pattern fill, use KPT Planar Tiling's Parquet mode.

KPT VIDEO FEEDBACK

This special-effects filter is great for creating images that twist and zoom around. There are two modes: Video Feedback, which uses rectangular shapes, and Telescopic Feedback, which uses elliptical shapes. These shapes are superimposed on each other again and again and rotated (via the Angle control). The number of superimposed objects is controlled by the Feedback Intensity control; while the position of the central, smallest object is controlled by clicking on the preview image.

The best effects seemed to be gained by rotating from an object within your selection, so it appears that the object, not the background, is rotating.

THE LENS FX FILTERS

The Lens fx filters (2.22) are a set of standard effects filters with a unique interface that makes them much more entertaining to use (and often more useful) than those with a standard dialog box.

Using a Lens fx filter is like looking through a printer's loop that has various settings on it. You can switch back and forth between each of the modes (filters) by clicking on the little down arrow right by the Kai logo.

The central image in the center of the lens is a preview of the filter and settings that are currently applied. Oddly enough, this works not just over your selection in Photoshop (or whatever software you're using) but also over the rest of the image, other windows in the background, icons, and even your desktop pattern!

KPT GAUSSIAN FX

The KPT Gaussian fx filter applies a Gaussian blur effect to your images.

The modes pop-up menu provides several different options, including Gaussian Weave, Gaussian Glow, Gaussian Block, and Diamonds. Of all of these modes, Gaussian Diamonds can produce the most stunning effects, as shown in Jennifer Alspach's outstanding illustration (2.23).

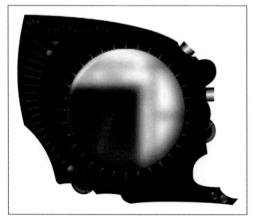

2.22

2.23

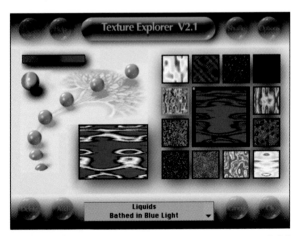

2.24

KPT METATOYS

This is a classic case of "uh-oh." As the Lens fx interface was developed, two of the filters in the set (KPT Glass Lens and KPT Twirl) didn't really work the way they should have. The end result was correct: but because the middle preview was small, and these were distortion filters, the preview didn't match the end result at all. For instance, KPT Glass Lens would create a spheroid effect within the lens of the batcuff, but the rest of the image would appear untouched. However, when the green button was clicked (or Return/Enter was pressed), the entire selection would become spheroided, making the preview mostly useless. This made these two filters less tools than toys, so they were called MetaToys.

KPT GLASS LENS FX

KPT Glass Lens fx works just like the KPT Glass Lens filter (see the KPT Glass Lens filter back in the Compact UIs section), except that now you're using the Lens fx interface. The three modes: Normal, Soft, and Bright, control the highlight size and intensity, while the Options gauge provides a frontlight and backlight option.

Keep in mind that this filter is applied to the entire selected area and will undoubtedly not look like the preview shown in the lens of the interface.

KPT TWIRL FX

KPT Twirl fx twirls the selection. Once again, the preview and the resulting image can vary dramatically. Twirl is the standard twisting effect, while the other mode, Kaleidoscope, slices the image into sections.

CLASSIC KPT

With progress comes all sorts of potential pitfalls. Take, for instance, the wonderful new KPT 3.0 Texture Explorer. While it offers more options, more controls, and more features than previous versions of KPT Texture Explorer, it actually is missing a few features (namely tilable textures). And there was no need to update Fractal Explorer, a staple of previous versions of Kai's Power Tools.

KPT Texture Explorer 2.1 and Fractal Explorer 2.1 are both included with Kai's Power Tools 3.0. The following sections discuss some of the important differences between KPT Texture Explorer 2.1 and 3.0, and KPT Fractal Explorer 2.1.

KPT TEXTURE EXPLORER

The main difference between this version of KPT Texture Explorer 2.1 (2.24) and the newer one is the ability to tile patterns and to create tiles of varying sizes. In addition, presets (they're not graphical) for KPT Texture Explorer 2.1 don't work with KPT Texture Explorer 3.0.

All textures that are created by KPT Texture Explorer 2.1 are either tiled or stretched to fit the current selection. Change the tiling option by clicking on the preview window and selecting an option from the pop-up menu. Options range from Stretch to fit to a small 96 × 96 pixels all the way up to 1024 × 1024.

In addition, entirely different algorithms were used to create the tiled pieces in KPT Texture Explorer 2.1 than are used with KPT Texture Explorer 3.0. The textures themselves look drastically different between the two versions.

See the KPT Texture Explorer presets pages at the end of this chapter.

KPT FRACTAL EXPLORER

Fractals are another form of textures, yet they're much more distinct than any texture has a right to be. Fractals are generated by certain mathematical processes that generate endless patterns within patterns. Fractals can be used as backgrounds, as textures, or as the central point to an illustration.

KPT Fractal Explorer generates complex textures based on mathematical formulae, using colors taken from the gradients created in KPT Gradient Designer. The interface includes the usual preview, zoom and opacity features, as well as a central Fractal Map which allows you to navigate through fractal space in search of new Mandelbrot and Julia fractal forms, as well as untold hybrids of the two. The fractal formulas result in art that repeats itself in its own detail. The closer you look at a fractal image, the more of the original shapes you'll find in the tiniest portions.

See the KPT Fractal Explorer presets pages at the end of this chapter.

KPT SYNERGY

While Kai's Power Tools are an immense set of powerful features stuffed full of capabilities, it's all too easy to lose sight of their usefulness and instead focus on the gee-whiz type of artwork they easily generate. The best uses for all the of the filters are not just a quick application of a texture to a background, or a page curl to a digital piece of paper, but instead the more subtle results of a gentle gradient that follows the contours of a shape, or the Gaussian glow applied carefully to lights within an image.

Many times during our review of artwork for this book, we found ourselves confused as to what Kai's Power Tool filter was used in the image. These images, it turns out, are among the best ones you'll find throughout this book.

> **TIP**
>
> Initially, while exploring in KPT Fractal Explorer (2.25), you might find that all the patterns have an annoying similarity to them. One way to start exploring more of the options that result in much more varied fractals is to change the gradients. The outside gradient is usually the predominant one. In addition, change the spiral that lies between the two gradients from its usually multicolored state to a less varied amount, by increasing the upper left control and decreasing the lower right control.

2.25

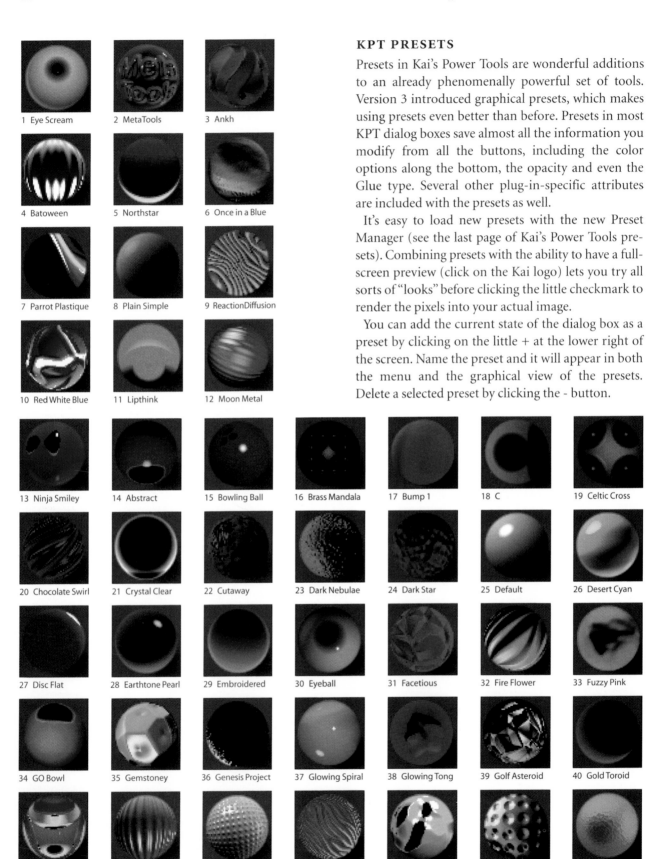

1 Eye Scream 2 MetaTools 3 Ankh
4 Batoween 5 Northstar 6 Once in a Blue
7 Parrot Plastique 8 Plain Simple 9 ReactionDiffusion
10 Red White Blue 11 Lipthink 12 Moon Metal
13 Ninja Smiley 14 Abstract 15 Bowling Ball 16 Brass Mandala 17 Bump 1 18 C 19 Celtic Cross
20 Chocolate Swirl 21 Crystal Clear 22 Cutaway 23 Dark Nebulae 24 Dark Star 25 Default 26 Desert Cyan
27 Disc Flat 28 Earthtone Pearl 29 Embroidered 30 Eyeball 31 Facetious 32 Fire Flower 33 Fuzzy Pink
34 GO Bowl 35 Gemstoney 36 Genesis Project 37 Glowing Spiral 38 Glowing Tong 39 Golf Asteroid 40 Gold Toroid
41 Golden Emeral 42 Golden Gourd 43 Golf Ball 44 Green Purple 45 Green Gargle 46 Green Metal 47 Hammered

KPT PRESETS

Presets in Kai's Power Tools are wonderful additions to an already phenomenally powerful set of tools. Version 3 introduced graphical presets, which makes using presets even better than before. Presets in most KPT dialog boxes save almost all the information you modify from all the buttons, including the color options along the bottom, the opacity and even the Glue type. Several other plug-in-specific attributes are included with the presets as well.

It's easy to load new presets with the new Preset Manager (see the last page of Kai's Power Tools presets). Combining presets with the ability to have a full-screen preview (click on the Kai logo) lets you try all sorts of "looks" before clicking the little checkmark to render the pixels into your actual image.

You can add the current state of the dialog box as a preset by clicking on the little + at the lower right of the screen. Name the preset and it will appear in both the menu and the graphical view of the presets. Delete a selected preset by clicking the - button.

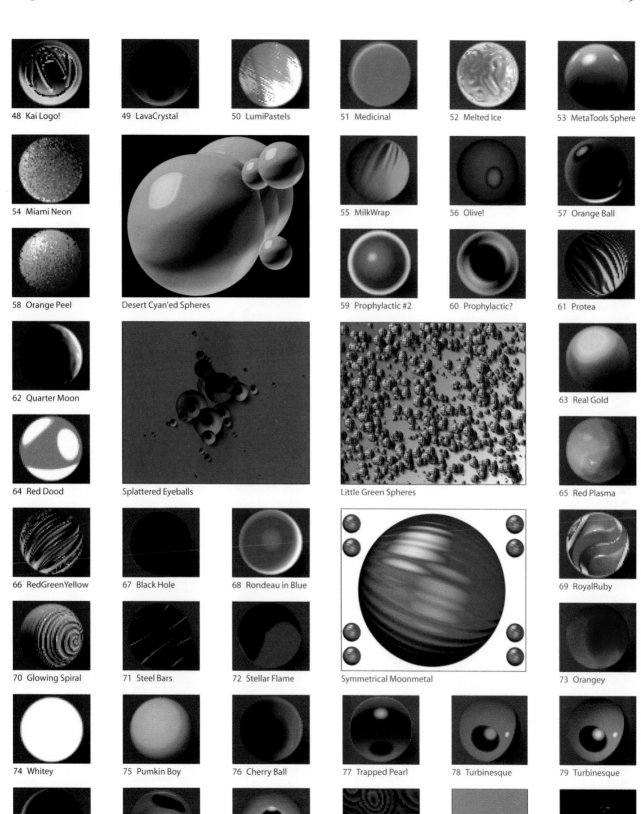

48 Kai Logo!

49 LavaCrystal

50 LumiPastels

51 Medicinal

52 Melted Ice

53 MetaTools Sphere

54 Miami Neon

Desert Cyan'ed Spheres

55 MilkWrap

56 Olive!

57 Orange Ball

58 Orange Peel

59 Prophylactic #2

60 Prophylactic?

61 Protea

62 Quarter Moon

Splattered Eyeballs

Little Green Spheres

63 Real Gold

64 Red Dood

65 Red Plasma

66 RedGreenYellow

67 Black Hole

68 Rondeau in Blue

Symmetrical Moonmetal

69 RoyalRuby

70 Glowing Spiral

71 Steel Bars

72 Stellar Flame

73 Orangey

74 Whitey

75 Pumkin Boy

76 Cherry Ball

77 Trapped Pearl

78 Turbinesque

79 Turbinesque

80 Turkish Sphere

81 Two Blue

82 Wheelo

1 1920s Cubist Noir

2 ?

3 A Lovely Vein

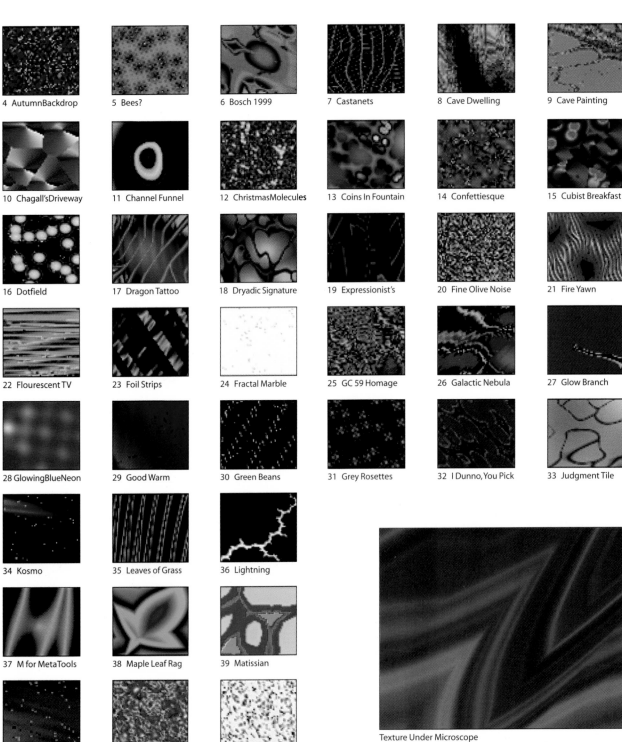

4 AutumnBackdrop 5 Bees? 6 Bosch 1999 7 Castanets 8 Cave Dwelling 9 Cave Painting

10 Chagall'sDriveway 11 Channel Funnel 12 ChristmasMolecules 13 Coins In Fountain 14 Confettiesque 15 Cubist Breakfast

16 Dotfield 17 Dragon Tattoo 18 Dryadic Signature 19 Expressionist's 20 Fine Olive Noise 21 Fire Yawn

22 Flourescent TV 23 Foil Strips 24 Fractal Marble 25 GC 59 Homage 26 Galactic Nebula 27 Glow Branch

28 GlowingBlueNeon 29 Good Warm 30 Green Beans 31 Grey Rosettes 32 I Dunno, You Pick 33 Judgment Tile

34 Kosmo 35 Leaves of Grass 36 Lightning

37 M for MetaTools 38 Maple Leaf Rag 39 Matissian

40 Metal Marble 41 MicrobeRushHour 42 Microbial Thread

43 Molded Contours 44 MultiLevelBubble 45 Overlay

Texture Under Microscope

Textures often take on another look entirely when you zoom in on them closely. Nothing has been done to the preset above to change it except a bit of zooming. The same thing happens for zooming out, although the results look a little less dramatic.

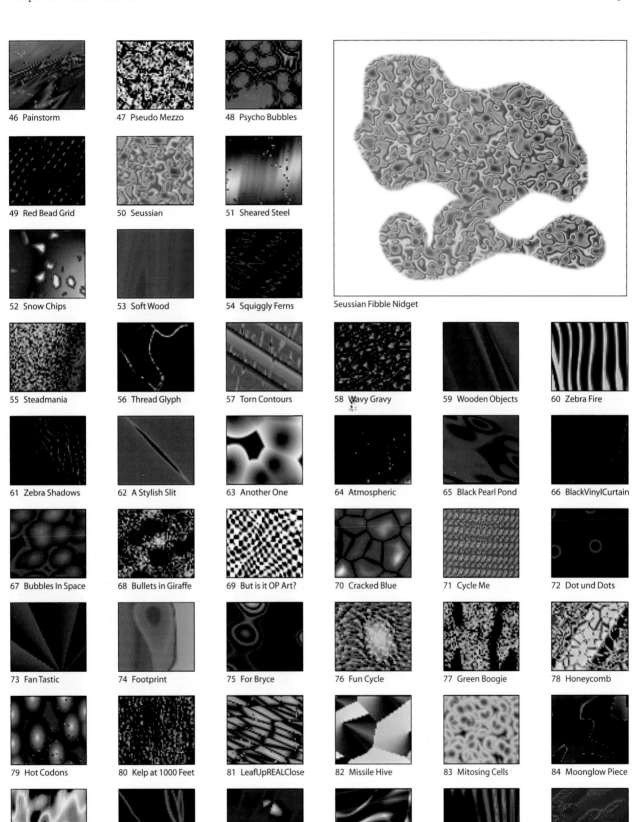

46 Painstorm

47 Pseudo Mezzo

48 Psycho Bubbles

49 Red Bead Grid

50 Seussian

51 Sheared Steel

52 Snow Chips

53 Soft Wood

54 Squiggly Ferns

Seussian Fibble Nidget

55 Steadmania

56 Thread Glyph

57 Torn Contours

58 Wavy Gravy

59 Wooden Objects

60 Zebra Fire

61 Zebra Shadows

62 A Stylish Slit

63 Another One

64 Atmospheric

65 Black Pearl Pond

66 BlackVinylCurtain

67 Bubbles In Space

68 Bullets in Giraffe

69 But is it OP Art?

70 Cracked Blue

71 Cycle Me

72 Dot und Dots

73 Fan Tastic

74 Footprint

75 For Bryce

76 Fun Cycle

77 Green Boogie

78 Honeycomb

79 Hot Codons

80 Kelp at 1000 Feet

81 LeafUpREALClose

82 Missile Hive

83 Mitosing Cells

84 Moonglow Piece

85 More Fire

86 Neon Bunny

87 Nest Eggs

88 Net of the Spider

89 Not Wood

90 Oil on Water

91 Over the Road I	92 Papers Croco	93 Pink Ripples
94 Pinterly Flames	95 Popcorn	96 PurpleBlurblezorgs
97 Rave Planar	98 Reeds	99 Scales in Copper
100 Scales in Jade	101 Sheared Tube	102 Simplesse
103 Space Quadran	104 Stylish Forms	105 Super-CYCLE
106 Tenative	107 The Incredible	108 Thought Bubble
109 Topo in Snow	110 Triangle	
111 Water Durn It	Chunks	Fire/Tiger Wallpaper
112 White Wigglies	113 Wolverine	114 Women in Line
1 Cool Scintilla	2 NeoNeon Glow	3 Blue Green Metal
4 BrushedAluminum	5 Cool Metal Jacket	6 Cool Metal Jacket
7 Cool Metal Jacket	8 Cool Tube	9 Coppertone Cym
10 Dark Sweep	11 Gentle Gold	12 Gold Sweep VI
13 Golden Center	14 Golden Eggplant	15 Golden Leonard
16 Golden Leonard	17 Golden Leonard	18 Golden Sweeps
19 Golden Stripes	20 Green Tube	21 Large Metallic
22 Liquid Purplex		

Gradient Preset Possibility #1

Gradient Preset Possibility #2

Gradient Preset Possibility #3

You can acheive interesting effects by combining gradient presets in different ways. Using the Layer Bin (accessed with Command-Shift-L), the top preset (above) is a combination of a basic star preset and the Blue/Silver preset.

 23 Metal Sweep

 24 Metal Sweep

 25 Metal Sweep

 26 MetalTransparent

 27 Metallic Brown

 28 MetallicReflection

 29 Metallic Torus

 30 Moonlight Green

 31 Moonlight Metal

 32 New Gold 2

 33 Polarized Crystal

 34 Sax and Violets

 35 Silver Blue Cone

 36 Silvery Sheen

 37 Soft Light Green

 38 Southwestern

 39 Steel Reflections

 40 Purple Reflection

 41 The Reflecting

 42 ThinkZincCopper

 43 Titanium Sheen

 44 Warm Tube

 45 WintergreenSheen

 46 Blues and Green

 47 Blues Greens

 48 CMYK Blues

 49 Is this Placid, or

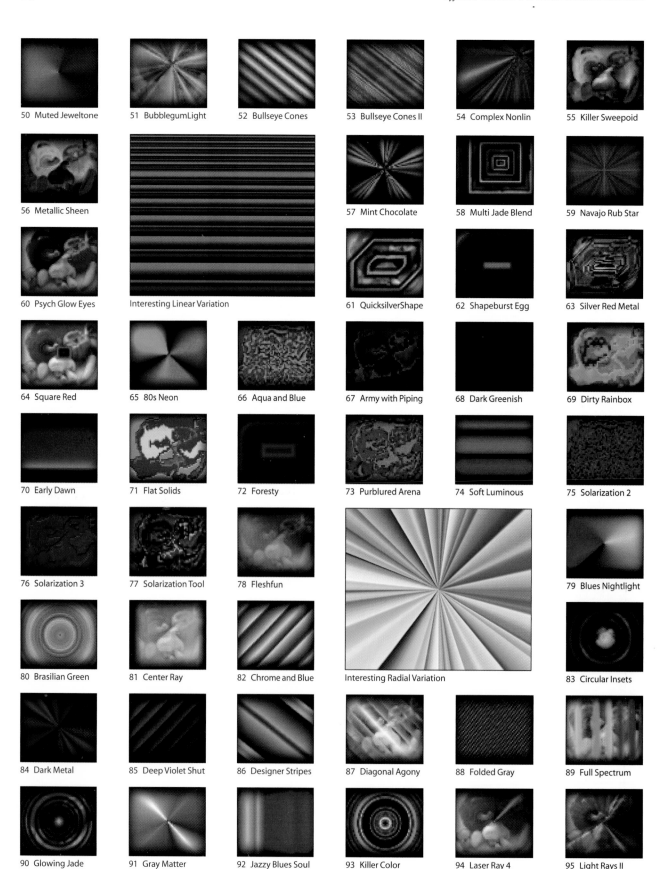

50 Muted Jeweltone   51 BubblegumLight   52 Bullseye Cones   53 Bullseye Cones II   54 Complex Nonlin   55 Killer Sweepoid

56 Metallic Sheen   Interesting Linear Variation   57 Mint Chocolate   58 Multi Jade Blend   59 Navajo Rub Star

60 Psych Glow Eyes   61 QuicksilverShape   62 Shapeburst Egg   63 Silver Red Metal

64 Square Red   65 80s Neon   66 Aqua and Blue   67 Army with Piping   68 Dark Greenish   69 Dirty Rainbox

70 Early Dawn   71 Flat Solids   72 Foresty   73 Purblured Arena   74 Soft Luminous   75 Solarization 2

76 Solarization 3   77 Solarization Tool   78 Fleshfun   Interesting Radial Variation   79 Blues Nightlight

80 Brasilian Green   81 Center Ray   82 Chrome and Blue   83 Circular Insets

84 Dark Metal   85 Deep Violet Shut   86 Designer Stripes   87 Diagonal Agony   88 Folded Gray   89 Full Spectrum

90 Glowing Jade   91 Gray Matter   92 Jazzy Blues Soul   93 Killer Color   94 Laser Ray 4   95 Light Rays II

The Preset Manager for Kai's Power Tools (which works very much the way the Preset Manager does in Vector Effects) is the method you use for importing and Exporting presets. The Presets supplied on the CD-ROM from Kai Krause can be imported into the respective plug-in application.

To access the Preset Manager, click on the - symbol when no preset is currently loaded. The Presets Manager appears. To trade presets with friends and coworkers, select the presets you'd like to give to them and click the Export button. The resulting file will be saved in a format that can easily be imported into another user's Kai's Power Tools dialog box.

Within the Preset Manager, select more than one preset at a time by Command-clicking on the presets you want to select. Shift-click to select several contiguous presets.

Double-clicking on the preset displays that preset in the box in the lower right. Of course, the look and size of that display depends on your selection, just as the preview in the main filter window is.

Click the Done button when you've finished playing around within the Preset Manager.

96 Lightray Overlay

97 Lumina Green

98 Metalloid Xmas

99 Mexicanagrams

100 NBC

101 Ocean Skies

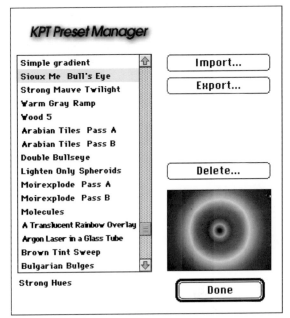
Preset Manager Dialog

CHAPTER 3
BRYCE

In the beginning, Bob created a mountain and some clouds . . .

This line from the original Bryce manual exemplifies the capabilities and philosophy behind Bryce better than any single sentence we've ever seen (especially if your name happens to be Bob). The almost off-handed ease with which Bryce (3.1) lets you create breathtaking landscapes of rolling hills, lush plains, sparkling oceans, starry skies, and yes, even mountains and clouds, is simply amazing.

Bryce's landscapes can be natural or surreal, with customizable terrains, materials, lighting, and atmospheric effects. They can include ground, water, hills, mountains, rocks, and clouds, as well as all sorts of simple and compound objects created from primitive shapes, and can even include imported complex objects made with other 3D modeling programs. In fact, Bryce's ability to create complex objects out of simple primitives enables you to use it almost as a general 3D modeling program (although it currently lacks precision alignment capabilities). See the sample images and the More Than Just Landscapes section later in the chapter.

When Bryce was first introduced in the spring of 1994, it was a runaway hit, taking the Macintosh graphics community by storm and inspiring comparisons to Photoshop and the original Kai's Power Tools for sheer impact and innovative genius. But the genesis of the software program that would become Bryce began years earlier in France, with a gentleman named Eric Wenger (3.2), who combined a longtime love of nature with an affinity for computer programming. Eric

There are new possibilities for people to discover—areas where nobody has been before.

KAI KRAUSE

3.1

3.2   *Eric Wenger*

Wenger's work came to the attention of Kai Krause and the folks at what was then HSC, who then spent months defining, designing, and redesigning the software until it was finally released as KPT Bryce. Version 2 has seen the loss of the KPT prefix but the addition of an amazing host of features and technology, many from MetaTools' latest wunderkind, Sree Kotay (creator of Vector Effects). With this latest version, Bryce reasserts itself as one of the absolute must-have software programs for digital artists.

BRYCE EXAMPLES

Having built Bryce up as such an amazing software package, it's only fair that we show a few of the cool images that have been created with it. This section highlights some of the best stuff that's been done with Bryce since its initial release. We start with several nice landscapes designed with the original Bryce, move into more innovative pieces, and end with some of the more intriguing images developed with Bryce 2.

3.3

This wintry landscape (3.3) created by Eric Wenger and used widely in early Bryce advertising is a great example of how the software comes alive in the hands of a master. Bryce shines (no pun intended) whenever dramatic lighting combines with complex, reflective surfaces. Like virtually all of Eric's materials, this ice was created by using Bryce's deep materials editor, an undocumented room within Bryce that has been mastered by only a handful of people in the world. Fortunately, Bryce 2 makes the deep materials editor (now called the Materials Composer) more accessible. It is still, however, the least intuitive of all of Bryce's rooms.

Because Bryce lets you create new and unimagined worlds, that's what most people spend their time doing. Another one of Eric's images, this 1995 Bryce calendar creation (3.4) shows one such world. The fiery planet in the background features everyone's favorite preset texture from the original Bryce and makes "Xanades Fjord" one of the most dramatic Bryce images to date.

3.4

WHY BRYCE?

A frequent question that comes up when telling someone about Bryce is "Who is this Bryce person, and why is the software named after him?" First of all, Bryce isn't a who, it's a what (and a where). Bryce Canyon National Park in Utah, with its natural beauty, dramatic rock formations, and breathtaking panoramic vistas, is one of Kai's favorite spots. As Kai worked on the development of this new 3D landscape generation program, he began referring to it as "Bryce," in honor of Bryce Canyon. Bryce became the code name for the software and was used throughout its development. Prior to the release of the software, it was given the official name "New World Explorer" to indicate what the software did. Through the beta-testing process and industry gossip, however, so many people had already come to know the software simply as "Bryce" that it was eventually decided to use the original code name for the final retail product, making Bryce the best known canyon in the computer graphics industry.

3.5

3.6

3.7

Phil Clevenger's "Necrofelinia" (3.5), another image from the 1995 Bryce calendar, is one of the more imaginative and disturbing variations on the Bryce theme. Phil created this image by using a cat image (from a digital stock photo CD collection) as a gray-scale terrain map, applying the color Pict of the cat as a material, and repeating the terrain.

Chris Casady, one of our featured artists and a long-time Bryce aficionado, created this definitive underwater scene (3.6) through the clever use of lighting effects and an unbelievable "underwater" texture. In addition to the images that appear in this chapter, Chris and his artwork are featured in Chapter 14, "Special Effects Showcase."

Two variations on a favorite Bryce theme, "Reflections" (3.7) by George Hazelwood and "Orbital" (3.8) by featured artist Pieter Lessing, show off Bryce's reflective capabilities.

"Visage" (3.9), another image by Pieter Lessing, picks up where "Orbital" left off, using spheres for dramatic emphasis and reflecting the colorized image of the woman both in the spheres and on the mercury sur-

3.8

3.9

3.10

face of the "water." Because he is a photographer, Pieter incorporates KPT- or Convolver-modified photos into Bryce landscapes in many of his images. Pieter and more of his images are also featured in Chapter 14, "Special Effects Showcase."

Combining Bryce's reflective capabilities with some water-tricks of his own, Mark Smith has created "Shiny Turkey" (3.10), which nicely illustrated Bryce 2's new Replicate command.

"Stone Age Coffee Cup" (3.11) by Henry Lim shows off one of Bryce 2's more impressive features. It features a spill-proof coffee cup created with Bryce 2's Boolean rendering capabilities. The "chips" in the cup were actually made by partially embedding a "negative" terrain into the cup's surface.

Crossing the line between the real and surreal, Chris Casady (creator of the chapter opening image, "Sedona Strikes") shows us a convincing Brycean canyon, within the setting of an equally convincing Brycean "Movie Set" (3.12). Chris is another featured artist, and his images appear in both Chapter 11, "Patterns, Textures, Papers, and Backgrounds," and Chapter 14, "Special Effects Showcase."

"Magic Meta" (3.13), from another featured artist, Bill Ellsworth, shows a beautiful, completely abstract image created entirely with Bryce. As you'll see in later chapters, many of Bill's images make use of Bryce to create a lot more than just landscapes.

3.11

BOOLEAN OBJECTS IN BRYCE

One of Bryce 2's most powerful new features is its ability to assign Boolean characteristics to objects. (The term *Boolean* is generally used in mathematics or programming to refer to a variable that has only two states, such as true/false, or positive/negative.) In Bryce, there are three different Boolean characteristics: positive, negative and intersecting. By default all objects are positive objects, which add themselves to your scene (that is, they behave normally). Making an object "negative" (via the Attributes dialog box) and then grouping it with a positive object causes the negative object to cut itself out of the positive object, leaving a hole or impression that exactly matches the dimensions and properties of the negative object. Intersect objects create the exact opposite effect, wherein rather than one object cutting itself out of another, only the portions of the two objects that overlap (that is, intersect) are visible.

3.12

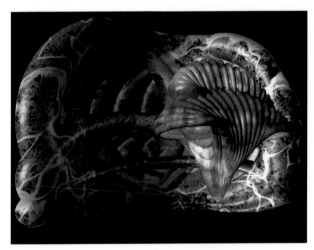

3.13

Finally, believe it or not, "Big Rig" (3.14) was designed entirely with Bryce and comes to us from the amazing artists at ArtEffect Design Studio. Jackson Ting and Robert Bailey have made a name for themselves by doing the impossible with Bryce. This image was the first in what is turning out to be a collection of Bryce images that defy belief. Chapters 13 and 14 ("KPT Can't Do That" and "Special Effects Showcase") cover the work of Ting and Bailey in detail.

HOW DOES BRYCE WORK?

While there are many applications on the market that can generate landscapes, what sets Bryce apart from the competition is its single-mindedness of purpose. Bryce is designed from the ground up to do nothing but landscapes, terrains and panoramic vistas—and to do them in ways that have never been done before.

The key to Bryce's success is in its rendering engine, which uses sophisticated raytracing algorithms to create its final images. (Raytracing is a sophisticated way of creating an image by mathematically shooting virtual rays of light out from a focal point and determin-

3.14

ing where each ray of light would strike if there were actual target objects. Depending on the color, texture, opacity and reflectivity of the imaginary target, pixels are drawn on-screen to reflect the image that would be created.) These proprietary algorithms give Bryce rendering muscle and sophistication to equal or surpass any 3D modeling program on the market.

BUILDING WORLDS WITH BRYCE

While Bryce is an extraordinarily powerful software program with hundreds of different tools, options and possible settings, the process of creating an image is actually fairly simple. Bryce lends itself very well to experimentation and exploration. Once you have created a few simple images, you can dig deeper at your own pace.

3.15

UNDERSTANDING THE INTERFACE

Bryce has arguably the most accessible interface of any 3D program on the market (3.15). The Camera Palette, located along the left side of the screen, contains controls that enable you to pan and zoom, rotate your camera, activate a "fly-around" view, and switch quickly and easily among several preset or user-defined camera views. The five gray globes at the bottom of the Camera Palette are used for setting rendering options and for rendering your Bryce scenes. Below the render globes is a text area that contains information about your scene or whatever interface element your cursor is currently pointing at.

The Create Palette along the top of the interface lets you design Bryce objects with a single click of the mouse. Available objects include water, cloud and ground planes, terrains (for hills, mountains, and so on), rocks, a variety of primitive geometric objects, PICT objects, and four separate types of light sources.

Two other palettes are also available. Clicking on either the Edit or Sky & Fog labels at the very top of the interface brings up the Edit Palette or the Sky & Fog Palette. The Edit Palette contains controls for editing materials, resizing, rotating, repositioning, aligning, or randomizing objects and for editing terrains. The Sky & Fog Palette contains controls for setting the sky mode, the shadow intensity and color, the fog and haze intensity and color, the cloud height and cloud cover, the cloud frequency and amplitude, and

---

Q: What in Bryce 2 is just a killer, knock-out feature?

KAI: Only all of it (laughs)! No, a lot of it, is still at a compromise level. I can still not look at that and say, "The material is really what I'm proud of." No. Sorry, I'm not. It's a temporary measure because the real materials editor has to have time with every material component, and we have to really design it for that. And it's a compromise with what we had before.

But there are some things: Sree's grayscale editor was a brand new element. That was fun. That was pristinely

new. The fact that you can click on something and it does it inverted. But you can click and drag on something, and it will do the inversion continuously, in realtime, while rotating in color. You know, while you take sub-ranges, rotate the color, take a sub-data piece and fly around on it. That makes me happy past the obvious. It's not about making little mountains anymore. It's showing that we're doing here what you see the CIA and AT&T doing in data exploration, in data mining, on big stuff. And you know we are *this* far away from doing it. Right now we're showing it to

the sun (or moon) location. Memory dots enable you to save your favorite skies for future use.

The majority of the interface is filled with your workspace, which acts as a window through which you can see and manipulate your Bryce objects. You can reposition an object by simply pressing on it and dragging it to a new location. A selected object can be resized by pressing and dragging any control handle. Objects can be rotated by holding down the Command key while pressing and dragging a control handle.

Finally, the right and bottom edges of the interface contain palettes for selecting objects or for setting display options.

UNDERSTANDING THE PROCESS

Most Bryce scenes can be created by following a fairly straightforward process. First you design the fundamental objects in the scene (you can easily add more objects later, but you need to start with enough to roughly lay out your scene). You then position, resize, and/or rotate these objects as desired. Compound objects can be created by arranging and grouping primitive shapes. Once your objects are placed in your scene, materials are applied to them using either Preset Materials or the Materials Composer (3.16), the atmosphere is modified using the Sky & Fog Palette, camera angles are set using the camera controls on the Camera Palette, and your scene is rendered.

> **TIP**
>
> **All of Bryce's palettes can be "torn" off and placed anywhere on screen (or on a second monitor) by holding down the spacebar while pressing on the palette and dragging it to a new location. Palettes can be returned to their original location by choosing the Reset Palettes command from the Edit menu or by Option-spacebar-clicking on any palette.**

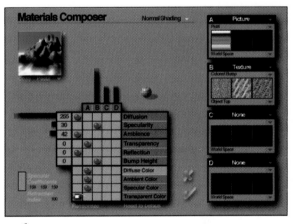

3.16

you in little mountains floating in Bryce. But if we can fly around on the little PowerMac or the smallest Pentium and see data sets like that and look at pieces while clipping, while cutting, with two light switches and shadow—that's great fun for us to be able to do.

So I love Bryce for those forays into new territories; an interface that has this hugging mode with areas that wake up out of nowhere and go away again; all these little new kind of tool things that are prelight, that pulse as they go; the little jokes. When you go to a side or rear view, the controls are not usable. So they become little mirrors, you know. When you click on something, you see a little mirror light on there. Lots of things like that. The integration of the Convolver dot memories in the skies with the randomization. Incredibly useful. I think, if you really allow yourself to get into that, and get over the obvious, there are new possibilities for people to discover— areas where nobody has been before. Period. Six billion hands. Not one of them has been over that little log on the other side of the road. And that, to me, is what it's all about. If some little kid, twelve years old, can be the first human to make that picture, that's worth something.

You know, that's where the Robert and Ting Jackson in L.A. examples come up. The people are patently, absurdly misusing it to do something else, you know. Making a guitar out of little mountains. It didn't seem logical to make little mountains in grayscale to build a guitar, and yet it's a perfectly viable way to do it. And once you're on that side, they now do miraculous new things with it. I love that. It's a good product.

Each of these steps is discussed in greater detail in the following sections.

CREATING OBJECTS

Object creation is undoubtedly the most straightforward step in a very straightforward process. If necessary, click on the Create label at the top of the interface. This brings up the Create Palette (3.17). Once this palette is active, you can create any object by simply clicking on it in the palette. The newly-created object appears within the workspace. To indicate that the newly-created object is selected, the wireframe is red and a gray bounding box surrounds the

---

TIP

By default, all objects in your scene are redrawn in a low-resolution mode when any object is moved. If you hold down the S key, however, the screen is not redrawn until after the object is moved. This has three beneficial effects. First, because none of the objects are redrawn in low-resolution mode, it can actually be easier to visualize how objects will look when making relocation decisions. Second, because Bryce doesn't redraw the screen until after the object has been moved (when it has to redraw anyway), this method is actually faster—you are saving Bryce one redraw pass. Finally, because the screen isn't immediately redrawn, a "ghost" of your object remains (temporarily) in its original location, giving you a better idea of exactly how far you're moving the object.

3.17

3.18

object. Multiple objects can be created one on top of the other, or individual objects can be moved out of the way before additional objects are created.

While most of the icons in the Create Palette are self-explanatory, a few do merit special attention. The water, cloud, and ground plane icons create infinite planes which stretch off into the horizon.

Immediately to the right of the rock icon is the "symmetrical lattice" icon. Clicking this icon creates a terrain object with a mirror image of itself attached at the base. Perhaps "mirrored terrain" would be a better name for it (and a more appropriate icon). Symmetrical lattices are edited using the Terrain Editor, and can be used to create all sorts of symmetrical objects, such as the wheels and tires of the "Big Rig" shown earlier.

To the left of the four light source icons is the Leonardo Oscar icon (the small gold figurine based on da Vinci's classic sketch of the male body). Clicking on this icon produces a dialog box of PICT images that can be placed in your Bryce scene. If the selected image has an alpha channel, Bryce respects that alpha channel, providing you with a nicely silhouetted or translucent image.

RESIZING, REPOSITIONING, AND ROTATING OBJECTS

Bryce objects can be resized, repositioned, or rotated (and more) using either the Edit Palette (3.18) or the selected object's control handles. The Edit Palette gives you more editing options, but the control handles are more convenient and have some options not found in the Edit Palette.

The Edit Palette contains unique controls for accessing the Materials Composer, for resizing, rotating, repositioning, or aligning along the X, Y, or Z axes, and for accessing the Terrain Editor. What makes these controls unique is their interactive, visual style. For example, the Resize control changes shape based on which end of which axis you point to, indicating the direction in which your object would be stretched (3.19). This is just one example of the thought that has gone into the Bryce interface and how accessible Bryce's controls really are. Below every control in the Edit Palette (except for the Terrain Editor icon) is a pop-up menu with additional options for controlling the selected object.

Selected objects can be modified without accessing
the Edit Palette by using any of the object's control
handles (the black or gray squares on the corners and
centers of the object's bounding box). Pressing on
any control handle and dragging to the right
increases the size of the selected object in the direction of the control handle.

Objects can be rotated rather than resized by holding down the Command key while pressing and dragging a control handle. The corner handles let you
rotate the object freely, while the handles in the center of the bounding box's sides constrain the rotation
around the appropriate axis.

In addition to the control handles, selected objects
also display a set of symbols to the right of the
bounding box. These symbols can be used to access
additional options for the selected object(s), including the Object Attributes dialog box, the Materials
Composer, the Terrain/Object Editor, grouping and
ungrouping of objects, and more.

ADDING MATERIALS

By default, a flat gray material is applied to all Bryce
objects when they are created. Needless to say, a
whole bunch of flat gray objects make for a flat gray,
boring world. New materials can be applied to your
objects quickly and easily with the preset Materials
Libraries (3.20), or not-so-quickly and not-so-easily
with the Materials Composer, a more complex dialog
box which gives you absolute control over virtually
every aspect of your materials.

3.19

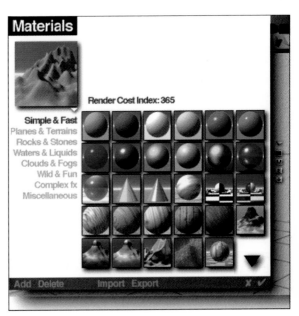

3.20

> **TIP**
>
> When working with complex scenes, it can
> sometimes be difficult to distinguish the
> selected wireframe object from background
> wireframe objects. You can avoid this, however,
> by holding down the D key while moving
> objects. By so doing, you desaturate all back-
> ground wireframes to about 50 percent of their
> normal color, temporarily fading them while
> you reposition the selected object.

For most of your everyday terrain needs the Materials Libraries can do the job. To add a material using the Materials Libraries, first select your object, then click on the down arrow immediately to the right of the Edit label (at the top of the interface). This brings up the Materials Library dialog box.

The Materials Composer is discussed separately in the Deep Inside Bryce section later in the chapter.

ADDING ATMOSPHERE

Adding atmosphere with the Sky & Fog palette (3.21)—the final phase in the creative process—lets you give your world a level of depth and realism unavailable in any other 3D program. The Sky & Fog Palette, accessed by clicking on the Sky & Fog label at the top of the interface, contains six nearly-identical panels for adjusting various atmospheric parameters, a two-toned cloud frequency graph, a light source globe, and a set of memory dots.

The six panels control (from left to right) sky mode, shadows, fog, haze, cloud height, and cloud cover.

The two-toned graph to the right of the six panels is the Cloud Frequency & Amplitude control. Pointing to this panel results in a four-headed arrow cursor, indicating four-way control with this interface element. Dragging left or right to decrease or increase the *frequency* of your clouds results in smaller or

---

TIP

You can also use the Command key in conjunction with the arrow keys to move your camera around your scene in discrete, precise increments. This is invaluable when precise, repeatable adjustments to your camera are required, such as when creating animations of your Bryce scenes.

3.21

larger *cloud formations*; while dragging up or down to increase or decrease the *amplitude* of you clouds results in harder or softer *cloud edges*. (Note that dragging this control down to create negative amplitude values actually inverts your atmosphere, creating clouds where there once was clear sky and clear sky where there once were clouds.)

The gray globe on the right side of the Sky & Fog Palette is the Sun Control. Press on this globe and drag the mouse around to reposition your sun. The angle of the light shining on the surface of the globe indicates the position of your celestial light source. The yellow "sun" above and to the left of the gray globe indicates that your celestial light source is, indeed, a sun. Click on this "sun" to toggle between sunlight and moonlight. Press on the color swatch below and to the left of the gray globe to choose a different color for your sunlight or moonlight. The trail of small dots to the left of the Sun/Moon symbol can be clicked to generate random skies, which can then be loaded into the memory dots or saved as presets. Note that the Sky & Fog memory dots are only useful *within* a Bryce session. If you quit and relaunch Bryce, your Sky & Fog memory dots are lost.

ADJUSTING THE CAMERA

Although we discuss adjusting your camera as the last step before rendering your image, you will undoubtedly be adjusting your camera angles throughout the creative process, especially when trying to position objects precisely. Your camera views are controlled with the Camera Palette (3.22), located along the left side of the interface.

At the top of the Camera Palette is the "Nano" Preview panel, which shows a preview of your scene whenever you click on it. The Nano Preview options menu, located just below the Nano Preview panel, lets you specify various previewing options, including the extremely useful Auto-Update option.

Below and to the right of the Nano Preview is a white circle. Clicking on this circle generates a "fly-around" preview of your scene, useful for getting an overview of your entire scene. This fly-around preview is a great way to find "lost" objects that have been accidentally moved out of your normal views.

Directly below the Nano Preview is the View Selector, which lets you cycle through seven different views: camera, top, right, front, left, back, and bottom. Note that changing these views *does not affect your camera view* (which is the view from which the scene is rendered). These views are used primarily to aid you in positioning objects.

The next set of controls are for positioning your camera. With all of the camera controls, the scene within your workspace is updated in realtime. Of course, because realtime is relative to the speed of your computer and the complexity of your scene, sometimes the update is less than smooth. To get around this, *you can hold down the Option key and the spacebar while pressing and dragging in the workspace itself.* This gives you a much faster patch preview of your scene as you move the camera around the virtual globe surrounding it.

RENDERING

When you are finally finished creating, editing and placing every object; applying every material; and adjusting every atmospheric element and have selected just the right camera angle, you are ready to render a final image for your viewing pleasure.

As mentioned earlier, the five gray globes at the bottom of the Camera Palette are your rendering controls. The large globe in the middle is the actual button that starts the rendering process. The two smaller globes on the left let you toggle your object textures on or off and turn the preview (fast) rendering mode on or off, and the two smaller globes on the right let you resume an interrupted render or clear the screen and begin rendering again.

The rendering process can be interrupted at any time by simply clicking the mouse. Clicking the Resume Render button causes the rendering process to pick up where it left off. The Escape key can be used to toggle between wireframe mode and rendered scene. A small portion of your scene can be selected (by pressing and dragging within the partially rendered scene) for patch rendering (3.23). Patch rendering is especially useful if you just want to see how a particular object or swatch of texture might look, but don't have time to wait for a full render. The

TIP

Zooming to a selected patch is a great time saver; it's similar to using Photoshop's cropping tool to crop out unwanted parts of an image, except that your Bryce scene remains completely intact—you are merely repositioning the camera.

3.22

TIP

The Document Setup command (in the File menu) normally limits you to a maximum rendering resolution ratio of 1:4. You can get around this limit by holding down the Control key while selecting the Document Setup command (3.24). While this enables you to create amazingly detailed renderings, you may need massive amounts of RAM allocated to Bryce (depending on your image).

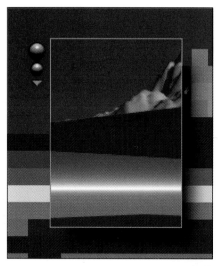

3.23

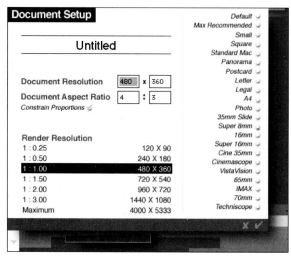

3.24

Patch Render option menu can be used to hide the patch frame and buttons or to zoom the camera so it includes just the selected patch.

MORE THAN JUST LANDSCAPES

Although Bryce was designed and built to be the best landscape generator and renderer available, Bryce users have bent the program to create images never envisioned by Eric or Kai (or anyone else, for that matter). With Bryce 2, MetaTools has added capabilities to Bryce specifically for those users who want to do more than just create landscapes. One of the more powerful of Bryce 2's new features is its ability to import objects created in other 3D modeling programs such as Ray Dream Designer, Strata Studio, or (and here's a match made in heaven) Onyx Software's Trees. Bryce 2's ability to perform Boolean rendering operations also enables you to create composite objects by combining two or more regular Bryce objects.

Henry Lim's "Earth Avatar" (3.25), uses both of these techniques. The human figure is actually an imported DXF file originally created with Fractal Design's Poser, and the hollow cube that he is contemplating was created by placing a negative cube inside a slightly larger positive cube and embedding negative primitive shapes all along the cube's "skin" to make the cutouts.

3.25

CREATING BOOLEAN OBJECTS

Creating Boolean objects in Bryce is a very straightforward process. Simply position two or more primitive shapes so that they overlap to a small or large degree. Click on one object's Object Attributes control (the A at the lower right of the object's bounding box) and specify that that object is to be negative rather than positive. Then select both objects and group them. The negative object is then "cut out" of the positive object.

This technique can also be used to create much more complex and useful Boolean objects. For example, you can "cut" one terrain out of another to create a cave or pit or put a negative cylinder inside of a positive one to create a tube.

IMPORTING 3D OBJECTS

While Bryce can be used to create some incredibly detailed objects, it is often more convenient to either create a desired object in a dedicated 3D modeling program or to use an already created 3D object. To import an object, simply select the Import Object command from the File menu. Use the Open dialog box to locate and select the desired object. (Bryce checks all possible objects to make sure that they are in an acceptable file format before letting you attempt to import the object.) That's all there is to it. Once an object is successfully imported into a Bryce scene it can then be added to any library in the Object dialog box for easy retrieval.

DEEP INSIDE BRYCE

While most of Bryce's capabilities are easily accessible from the primary layer of the interface, two "deep" rooms are available for more complex editing of your Bryce objects. The Terrain Editor has every control you can imagine for customizing terrain objects, and the Materials Composer provides a thorough, if uncharacteristically counter-intuitive, area for creating custom materials.

THE TERRAIN EDITOR

The Terrain Editor interface (3.26) consists of three distinct work areas. The upper left contains a three-tabbed panel filled with all sorts of buttons and options; the upper right contains a grayscale terrain height map within which you can "paint" elevation and other effects directly onto your terrain: and the lower left contains an incredibly cool rotating, real-time preview of your terrain.

Initially, the three-tabbed options panel appears with the Elevation panel (3.27) active. In the Elevation mode, the panel is filled with blue and tan

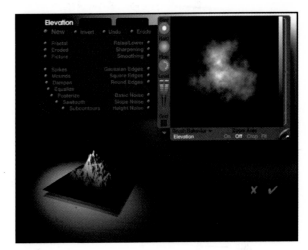

3.26

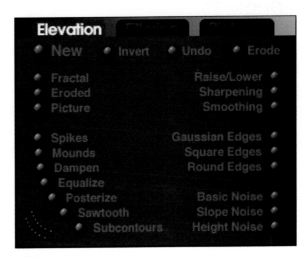

3.27

buttons for various elevation effects. Pressing on any of these buttons and dragging left or right decreases or increases the specified effect globally, applying (for example) erosion or spiking to your entire terrain. These changes are shown in realtime in the grayscale terrain height map and are applied to your 3D terrain preview when you release the mouse button (unless you have the Caps Lock key down, in which case your 3D terrain preview updates in realtime as well).

Clicking the Filtering tab brings up the Filtering panel (3.28), from which you can select one of nine filtering settings; or you can create your own by drawing in the custom filtering swatch (the left swatch in the Filtering panel). The right swatch is a realtime preview of your grayscale height map. Clicking the Apply label applies your filter settings to the actual grayscale terrain height map. *Note:* Some interesting patterned effects can be created by using multiple applications of the filtering presets, combined with the Filtering options menu (just to the right of the Smooth text button).

Clicking the third and final tab brings up the Pictures panel (3.29), a simple panel that can be used to select a grayscale Pict file to use as a terrain height map. The Blend button is used to select the amount of blending from your original terrain to the grayscale Pict file. The Apply label then applies your settings to the actual grayscale terrain height map.

The grayscale Terrain Canvas (3.30) is actually a canvas on which you can paint elevation, erosion and various terrain effects by simply pressing and dragging. The Size, Hard, Flow, Level, and Grid controls along the left side of the Height Map let you select

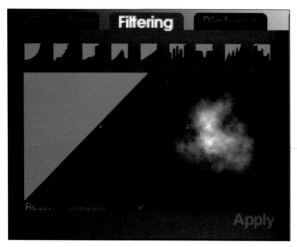

3.28

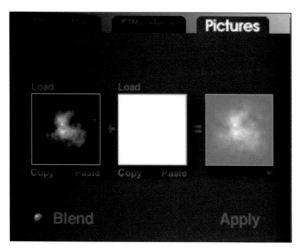

3.29

various options to control your brush's behavior, as does the Brush Behavior pop-up menu.

The four Zoom Area controls let you zoom in to a small area of your terrain and then crop your terrain to include just the area within the cropping square (effectively zooming in on your terrain) or force the entire terrain to fit within the cropping square (effectively zooming out). The rainbow enables you to switch from a grayscale height map to one of several colorized height maps, and the little ball under the rainbow is just a quick and easy way to return to grayscale.

THE MATERIALS COMPOSER

The Materials Composer is the deepest and most potentially confusing aspect of Bryce. Understanding the Materials Composer is the key to creating ultra-realistic materials for convincing terrains and waters.

The Materials Composer interface (3.31) consists of three primary areas: The Interactive Preview in the upper left, the four Texture Components along the right, and the Materials Grid in the Center.

The Interactive Preview shows you what your current settings would look like if applied to an object. Below the Preview is a pop-up menu with preview object choices and to the right of the Preview is a pop-up icon which gives you access to the Preset Materials libraries (discussed earlier). The Interactive Preview is truly interactive, as you can press and drag in the preview itself to move your "preview camera" around, viewing your object from different angles.

Note: If you hold down the Command key and drag up or down in the Preview, you can zoom in or out, and if you hold down the spacebar while dragging, you can pan left or right.

The four Texture Components (3.32), labeled A, B, C and D, contain the subtextures which make up your final texture. Each of the four subtextures is either a three-dimensional texture itself, a two-dimensional Pict, or nothing, as selected from the top pop-up menu triangle. The second pop-up menu contains a list of preset textures that can be used as components, and the third pop-up menu contains texture mapping options, enabling you to specify how your texture is mapped onto the selected object (using object or world space, parametrically, and so on). The three frames within the Texture Component boxes contain (from left to right) the subtexture color and (if available) the alpha channel and bump map.

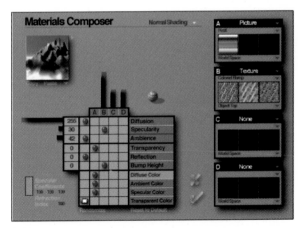

3.31

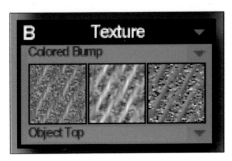

3.32

3.30

The Materials Grid (3.34) is used to specify global settings for lighting, special effect, and color properties. The first set of parameters, Diffusion, Specularity, and Ambience, are lighting properties; the second set, Transparency, Reflection, and Bump Height, are special effect properties; and the last set, Diffuse Color, Ambient Color, Specular Color, and Transparent Color, are (surprise!) color properties. While a little intimidating at first, the Materials Grid is actually fairly straightforward. Here's how it works: You can do one of two things. If you want to manually specify the

THE "DEEP" MATERIALS EDITOR

Eric Wenger originally wrote Bryce for his own use, and only later did it come to the attention of Kai and the company and become shaped into the program you have in your possession. Eric wrote the Deep Materials Editor so that he could really get into the deepest level of custom material generation and manipulation. Its place in Bryce, intended to be as accessible and intuitive as possible, has never really been decided one way or another by MetaTools, so (after much deliberation) it was decided to leave it in if anyone wanted to play with it, but not to spend the considerable design and engineering resources necessary bring it in line with the rest of the program. So it is there if you want to use it, but it isn't documented and MetaTools Tech Support doesn't support it (in other words, you're on your own).

You can access the Deep Materials Editor (3.33) by Option-clicking any panel of any filled texture component. The Deep Materials Editor consists of three texture components (A, B, and C) and a set of global controls. Within each component you can set the noise type (by clicking the Set Noise button, which gives you a sub-dialog box); and assign a mathematically-defined filtering effect (clip aX+b, and so on), change the texture frequency (by pressing and dragging in the frequency

curves panel), and change the output type, color map, and phase amplitude (using the controls on the right-hand side) for individual components and globally for all components. When you have made any desired modifications, clicking the "accept" checkmark return you to the relative "normality" of the Materials Composer. *Note:* This dialog box contains Eric's interesting combination of French and English. "Value" refers to the alpha channel, "color" is color, and "normale" refers to a component's bump map.

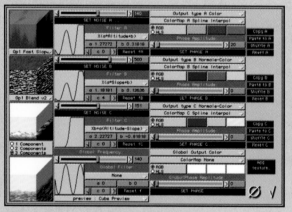

3.33

settings for light or special effect properties, simply click or press and drag on the sliders to the left of these properties. In the same vein, you can press on the color pickers to manually select diffuse, ambient, and other colors. On the other hand, if you want these properties to be determined by one of your subtextures, simply click in the A, B, C, or D columns for any property to specify that that property will be determined by the specified subtexture (A, B, C, or D) in the Texture Component area. Above the A–D headings are four columns that can be adjusted to modify the frequency of individual subtextures. The Frequency Globe is used to modify the frequency of *all* subtextures.

FINAL THOUGHTS

The original Bryce, with its accessible interface, powerful rendering technology and low price, made custom landscape generation available to just about anyone with a Macintosh computer. That alone made Bryce a praiseworthy software package. The new capabilities of Bryce 2, though, especially the improved interface, Boolean objects, importing of DXF and other file formats, and increased speed, really do take Bryce to the next level of power and accessibility. The information we've presented so far should help you to get the most out of Bryce 2. To really make the program scream, though, check out the many Bryce 2 images featured in Chapter 13, "KPT Can't Do That," and Chapter 14, "Special Effects Showcase."

TIP

You can press and drag the preview to rotate it to any angle you want. You can also hold down the Command key while pressing and dragging up or down to zoom in or out of the preview. Option-clicking returns the Preview to its default state.

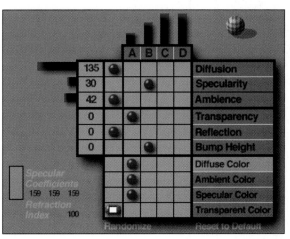

3.34

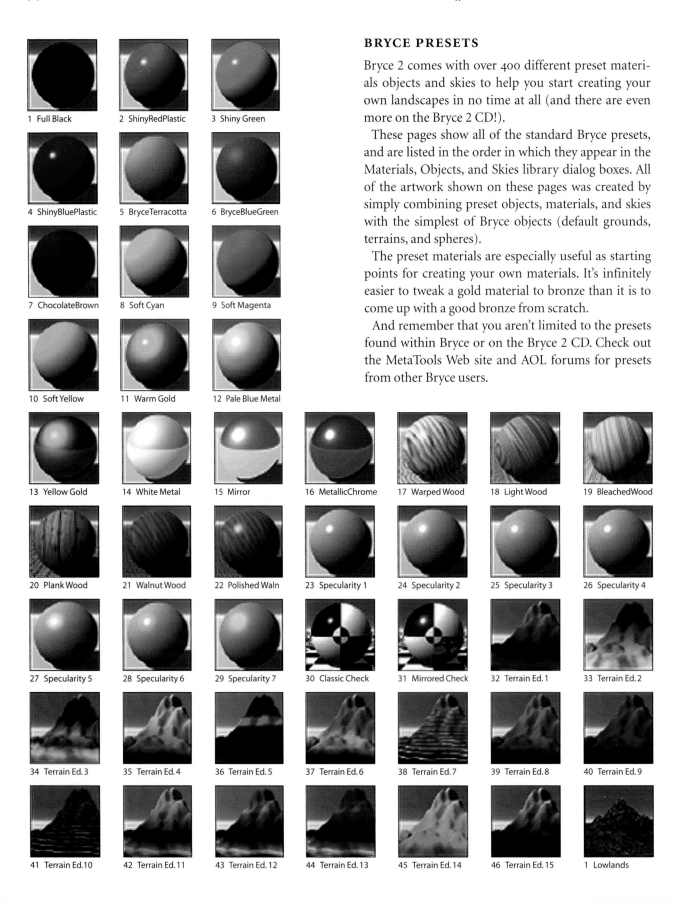

BRYCE PRESETS

Bryce 2 comes with over 400 different preset materials objects and skies to help you start creating your own landscapes in no time at all (and there are even more on the Bryce 2 CD!).

These pages show all of the standard Bryce presets, and are listed in the order in which they appear in the Materials, Objects, and Skies library dialog boxes. All of the artwork shown on these pages was created by simply combining preset objects, materials, and skies with the simplest of Bryce objects (default grounds, terrains, and spheres).

The preset materials are especially useful as starting points for creating your own materials. It's infinitely easier to tweak a gold material to bronze than it is to come up with a good bronze from scratch.

And remember that you aren't limited to the presets found within Bryce or on the Bryce 2 CD. Check out the MetaTools Web site and AOL forums for presets from other Bryce users.

1 Full Black   2 ShinyRedPlastic   3 Shiny Green

4 ShinyBluePlastic   5 BryceTerracotta   6 BryceBlueGreen

7 ChocolateBrown   8 Soft Cyan   9 Soft Magenta

10 Soft Yellow   11 Warm Gold   12 Pale Blue Metal

13 Yellow Gold   14 White Metal   15 Mirror   16 MetallicChrome   17 Warped Wood   18 Light Wood   19 BleachedWood

20 Plank Wood   21 Walnut Wood   22 Polished Waln   23 Specularity 1   24 Specularity 2   25 Specularity 3   26 Specularity 4

27 Specularity 5   28 Specularity 6   29 Specularity 7   30 Classic Check   31 Mirrored Check   32 Terrain Ed. 1   33 Terrain Ed. 2

34 Terrain Ed. 3   35 Terrain Ed. 4   36 Terrain Ed. 5   37 Terrain Ed. 6   38 Terrain Ed. 7   39 Terrain Ed. 8   40 Terrain Ed. 9

41 Terrain Ed. 10   42 Terrain Ed. 11   43 Terrain Ed. 12   44 Terrain Ed. 13   45 Terrain Ed. 14   46 Terrain Ed. 15   1 Lowlands

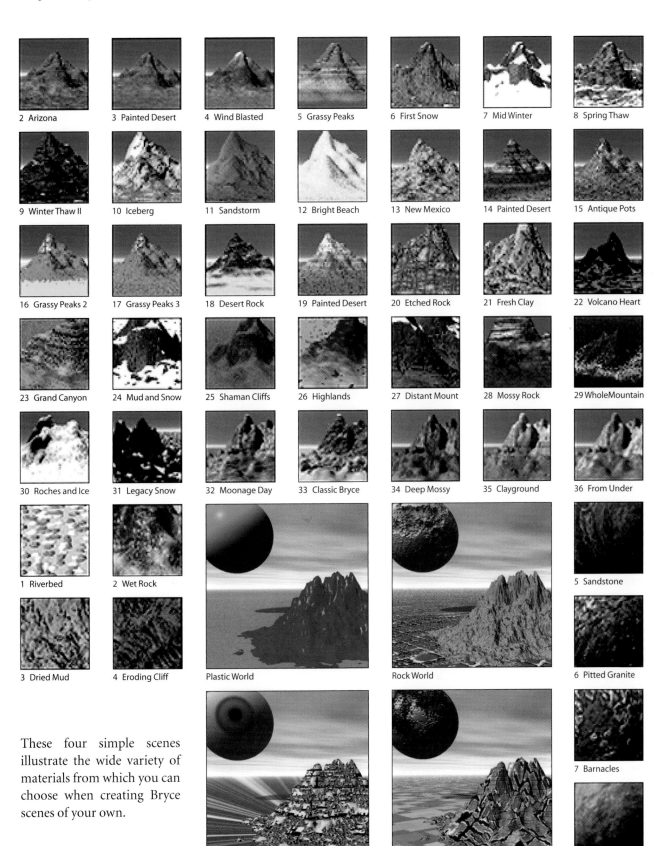

2 Arizona
3 Painted Desert
4 Wind Blasted
5 Grassy Peaks
6 First Snow
7 Mid Winter
8 Spring Thaw

9 Winter Thaw II
10 Iceberg
11 Sandstorm
12 Bright Beach
13 New Mexico
14 Painted Desert
15 Antique Pots

16 Grassy Peaks 2
17 Grassy Peaks 3
18 Desert Rock
19 Painted Desert
20 Etched Rock
21 Fresh Clay
22 Volcano Heart

23 Grand Canyon
24 Mud and Snow
25 Shaman Cliffs
26 Highlands
27 Distant Mount
28 Mossy Rock
29 WholeMountain

30 Roches and Ice
31 Legacy Snow
32 Moonage Day
33 Classic Bryce
34 Deep Mossy
35 Clayground
36 From Under

1 Riverbed
2 Wet Rock
5 Sandstone

3 Dried Mud
4 Eroding Cliff
Plastic World
Rock World
6 Pitted Granite

7 Barnacles

These four simple scenes illustrate the wide variety of materials from which you can choose when creating Bryce scenes of your own.

Weird World 1
Weird World 2
8 Desert Sand

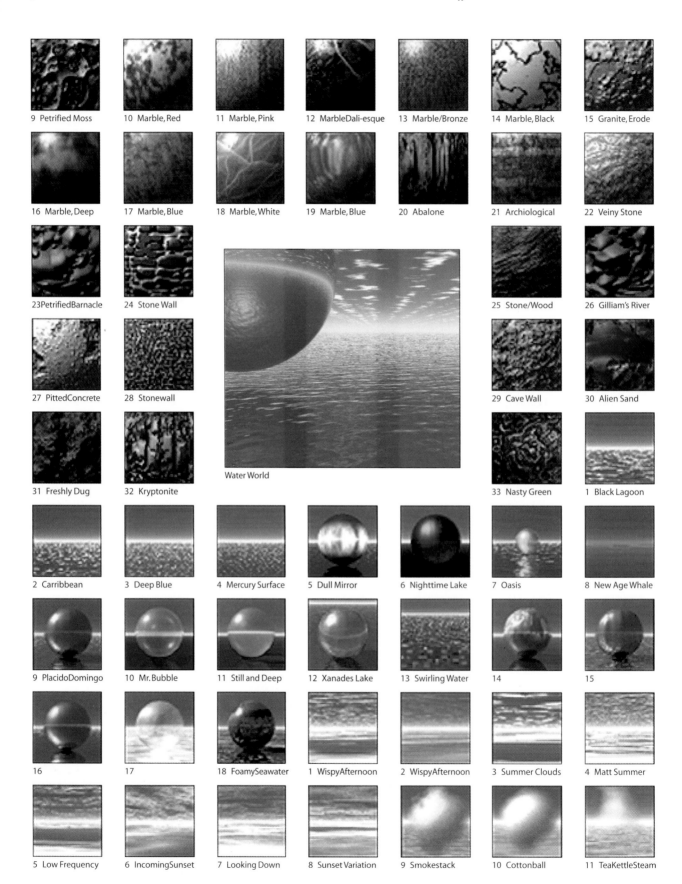

9 Petrified Moss   10 Marble, Red   11 Marble, Pink   12 MarbleDali-esque   13 Marble/Bronze   14 Marble, Black   15 Granite, Erode

16 Marble, Deep   17 Marble, Blue   18 Marble, White   19 Marble, Blue   20 Abalone   21 Archiological   22 Veiny Stone

23 PetrifiedBarnacle   24 Stone Wall   25 Stone/Wood   26 Gilliam's River

27 PittedConcrete   28 Stonewall   29 Cave Wall   30 Alien Sand

31 Freshly Dug   32 Kryptonite   Water World   33 Nasty Green   1 Black Lagoon

2 Carribbean   3 Deep Blue   4 Mercury Surface   5 Dull Mirror   6 Nighttime Lake   7 Oasis   8 New Age Whale

9 PlacidoDomingo   10 Mr. Bubble   11 Still and Deep   12 Xanades Lake   13 Swirling Water   14   15

16   17   18 FoamySeawater   1 WispyAfternoon   2 WispyAfternoon   3 Summer Clouds   4 Matt Summer

5 Low Frequency   6 IncomingSunset   7 Looking Down   8 Sunset Variation   9 Smokestack   10 Cottonball   11 TeaKettleSteam

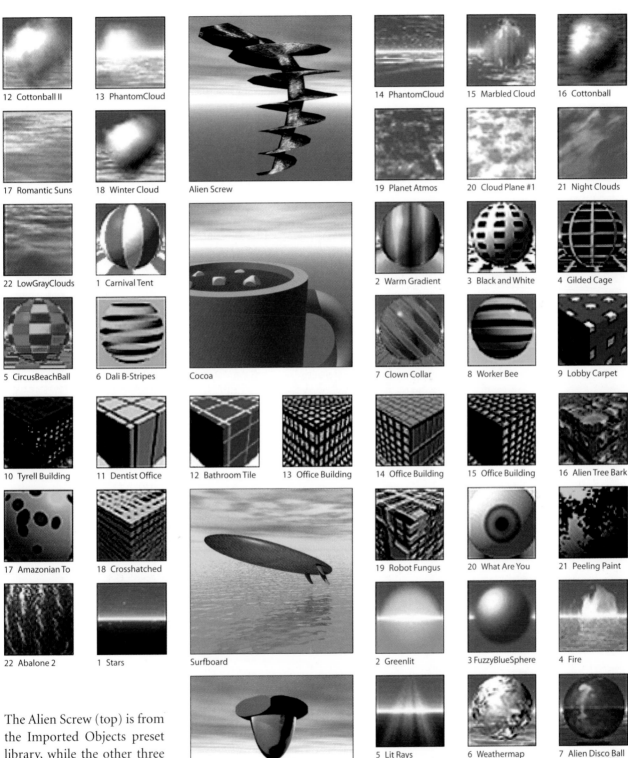

12 Cottonball II

13 PhantomCloud

14 PhantomCloud

15 Marbled Cloud

16 Cottonball

17 Romantic Suns

18 Winter Cloud

Alien Screw

19 Planet Atmos

20 Cloud Plane #1

21 Night Clouds

22 LowGrayClouds

1 Carnival Tent

2 Warm Gradient

3 Black and White

4 Gilded Cage

5 CircusBeachBall

6 Dali B-Stripes

Cocoa

7 Clown Collar

8 Worker Bee

9 Lobby Carpet

10 Tyrell Building

11 Dentist Office

12 Bathroom Tile

13 Office Building

14 Office Building

15 Office Building

16 Alien Tree Bark

17 Amazonian To

18 Crosshatched

19 Robot Fungus

20 What Are You

21 Peeling Paint

22 Abalone 2

1 Stars

Surfboard

2 Greenlit

3 FuzzyBlueSphere

4 Fire

The Alien Screw (top) is from the Imported Objects preset library, while the other three images were created with objects from the Boolean Objects library.

Hourglass

5 Lit Rays

6 Weathermap

7 Alien Disco Ball

8 Oily Bronze

9 Copperbump

10 Jupiter

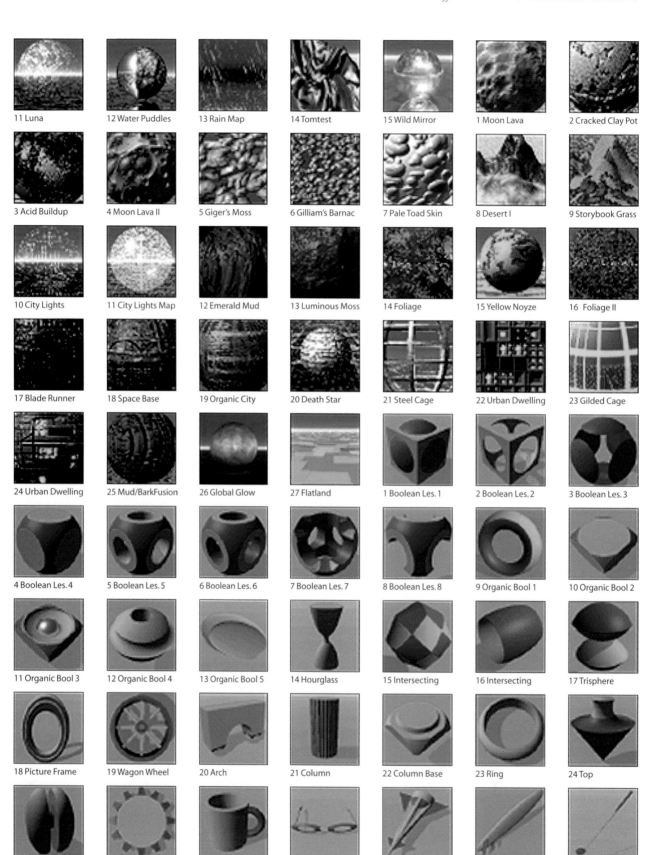

11 Luna	12 Water Puddles	13 Rain Map	14 Tomtest	15 Wild Mirror	1 Moon Lava	2 Cracked Clay Pot
3 Acid Buildup	4 Moon Lava II	5 Giger's Moss	6 Gilliam's Barnac	7 Pale Toad Skin	8 Desert I	9 Storybook Grass
10 City Lights	11 City Lights Map	12 Emerald Mud	13 Luminous Moss	14 Foliage	15 Yellow Noyze	16 Foliage II
17 Blade Runner	18 Space Base	19 Organic City	20 Death Star	21 Steel Cage	22 Urban Dwelling	23 Gilded Cage
24 Urban Dwelling	25 Mud/BarkFusion	26 Global Glow	27 Flatland	1 Boolean Les. 1	2 Boolean Les. 2	3 Boolean Les. 3
4 Boolean Les. 4	5 Boolean Les. 5	6 Boolean Les. 6	7 Boolean Les. 7	8 Boolean Les. 8	9 Organic Bool 1	10 Organic Bool 2
11 Organic Bool 3	12 Organic Bool 4	13 Organic Bool 5	14 Hourglass	15 Intersecting	16 Intersecting	17 Trisphere
18 Picture Frame	19 Wagon Wheel	20 Arch	21 Column	22 Column Base	23 Ring	24 Top
25 Yoyo	26 Gear	27 Mug	28 Glasses	29 Spaceship	30 Surfboard	31 Golf Club

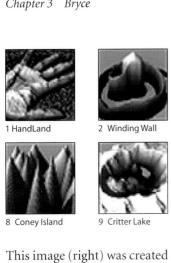
1 HandLand

2 Winding Wall

3 Skulls the Limit

4 Another Good

5 BasicRiverTerrain

6 Big Sur

7 Complex

8 Coney Island

9 Critter Lake

10 Dunes

11 Fractal Mount

12 FunnyAbstract

13 HaveaNiceDay

14 Iceberg Terrain

This image (right) was created by using the Skull terrain from the Mountains and Terrains lib-rary with a blue metallic material, and slightly submerging it in a ground plane. The ground plane was then converted to lava by applying the lava material from the Materials library.

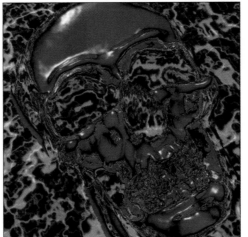
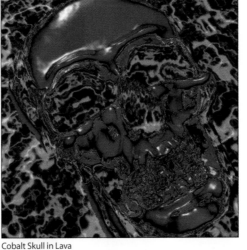

15 Mayan Pyramid

16 Morro Bay

17 Mt. Baldy

18 Sharpies

Cobalt Skull in Lava

19 Stalagmites

20 River Terrain

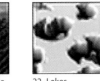

21 Waves/Ripple

22 Lakes

23 CobraPitTerrain

24 TextureExplorer

25 For the TileNut

26 For the TileNut

27 Bryce

28 Apex

29 Breakout

30 Stonehenge 9

1 Stone

2 Stone

3 Stone

4 Stone

5 Stone

6 Stone

7 Stone

8 Stones

9 Tree

10 Tree

11 Tree

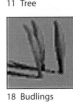

12 Tree

13 Charley Brown

14 Leaf

15 Four Fronds

16 Green

17 Simple Plant

18 Budlings

19 Full Tree

20 Your Parents

Arizona with Cacti

Boolean Initials

Examples of imported trees and carved initials in a rock (both using presets from the Rocks and Trees library), an imported DXF screw (from the Imported Objects library), and a perfect watery sunset (from the Skies and Fog library).

21 Tree

22 Tall Bush

Golden Screw

Indian Summer Sunset

23 Post Fire

24 Tree

25 Tree

26 Tree

27 Tree

28 Treeling

29 Solo Tree

30 Cactus Tree

1 Icosahedron

2 Octahedron

3 Dodecahedron

4 TetraHedron

5 Decahedron

6 Frustoid

7 Octahedron+6

8 Bucky!

9 Rounded Cylind

10 Egg

11 Rounded Cub

12 Pentagonal

13 Soccer Ball

14 Triangular

15 Six Sided

16 Octagonal

17 Deca-Column

18 Super Bucky!

19 Überbucky

20 Four Sides

21 Five Sides

22 Six Sides

23 Eight Sides

24 Ten Sides

25 ThreadedColumn

26 Spring

27 Cube with Bulge

28 Cube Bulge #2

29 Spiral Staircase

30 Slotted Screw

31 I Have No Idea

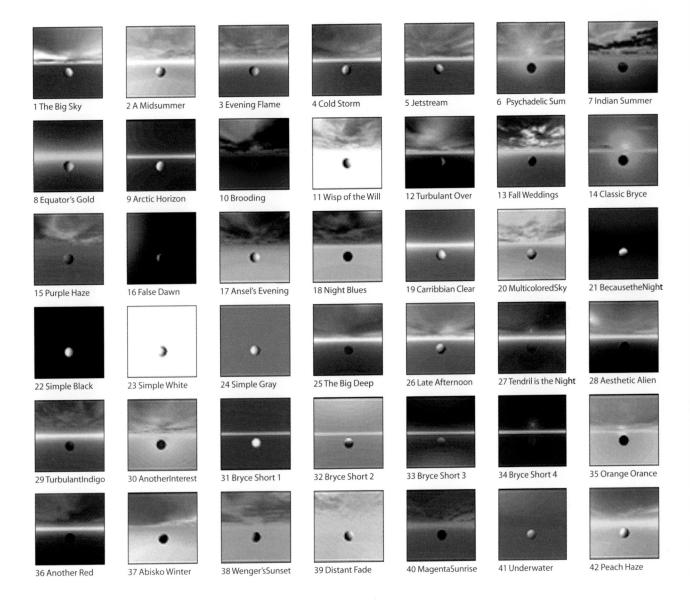

1 The Big Sky

2 A Midsummer

3 Evening Flame

4 Cold Storm

5 Jetstream

6 Psychadelic Sum

7 Indian Summer

8 Equator's Gold

9 Arctic Horizon

10 Brooding

11 Wisp of the Will

12 Turbulant Over

13 Fall Weddings

14 Classic Bryce

15 Purple Haze

16 False Dawn

17 Ansel's Evening

18 Night Blues

19 Carribbian Clear

20 MulticoloredSky

21 BecausetheNight

22 Simple Black

23 Simple White

24 Simple Gray

25 The Big Deep

26 Late Afternoon

27 Tendril is the Night

28 Aesthetic Alien

29 TurbulantIndigo

30 AnotherInterest

31 Bryce Short 1

32 Bryce Short 2

33 Bryce Short 3

34 Bryce Short 4

35 Orange Orance

36 Another Red

37 Abisko Winter

38 Wenger'sSunset

39 Distant Fade

40 MagentaSunrise

41 Underwater

42 Peach Haze

CHAPTER 4
CONVOLVER

Probably the most daunting question we've ever been asked about Convolver (4.1, 4.2) isn't about solving some bizarre, technically advanced problem or even how to accomplish a specific Convolver task. Instead, people want to know what Convolver actually does, and what category of software it falls into. Is it a serious application for enhancing and correcting Photoshop images, or is it just a fun, creative tool for generating special effects? Is it practical or fluff?

Of course, as you'd expect, the answer is yes and no to all of the preceding questions. Named after the *convolution kernel*, the mathematical space where digital special effects are defined, Convolver is a Photoshop-compatible plug-in that can be used to enhance an entire image—or any selected portion of it. It lets you create custom reusable Photoshop filter effects; for example, you can setup a special Unsharp Mask setting that also intensifies the hue and crisps the edges without losing the detail. Its interface provides a unique environment in which you can "play" with your image, gently massaging it until it appears to be exactly what you had in mind. Convolver has three sections, Explore, Design, and Tweak, all contained within the one dialog box. When you use them in that order, Convolver becomes quite powerful, as these different sections enable you to be both creative and task-oriented.

When Convolver first appeared, its practical uses were downplayed in favor of the unique interface and the controversial "star" method of adding new features to the application, which doles out additional

Something that was way over the horizon . . . is now just maybe one step away.

KAI KRAUSE

4.1

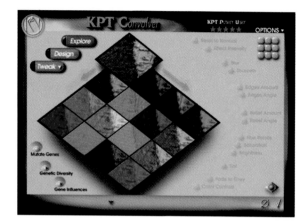

4.2

controls as your time and experience with it increases. (Convolver's stars are discussed in detail later in this chapter.) Eventually, the power behind the "Design" and "Tweak" sections of the interface (explained later in this chapter) became increasingly apparent, and now Convolver is most recognized for its handy compilation of several useful color and texture-adjusting tools.

CONVOLVER EXAMPLES

The following examples show images both in their original states and after Convolver has been applied to them. Many of the images needed to be spruced up in some way, while others were modified to reveal a different side of the photo or to add some sort of special effect.

IMAGE FIXING

This image (4.3) originally was much too blurry. Using the Sharpen feature of Tweak and a few other options, we were able to bring the image into much clearer focus. In the process, the gray tint of the original photo was eliminated as well.

4.3

4.4A   4.4B

4.5

4.6

The original photo of this old-time radio had aged a bit, reducing the luster of the image and of the dial. We used a combination of Contrast and Unsharp Mask to enhance the clarity of the image (4.4).

This image (4.5) was muddy looking and clearly out of focus. A bit of Relief Edges was used in conjunction with Lighten and Sharpen to improve its appearance. More attention was placed on the foreground objects, leaving the background objects a bit blurry.

4.8A   4.8B

SPECIAL EFFECTS

This globe (4.6) was enhanced by adding both Relief Edges and Contrast to the earth portion of the image. The rest of the image was left untouched, increasing the impact of the terrained Earth.

The balloons (4.7) were given new life and plenty of texture using the Relief options in conjunction with blur and Edge Amount.

These blocks (4.8) were enhanced by using multiple contrast, blurs, desaturation, and edge detection.

The ampersand area of this image (4.9) was selected and modified with Convolver, bringing out the texture within the cardboard.

This shell (4.10) was colorized (the background wasn't selected) using a variety of Convolver tools and techniques.

4.9A

4.9B

  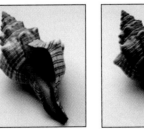

4.7A   4.7B   4.10A   4.10B

4.11A

4.11B

These leaves (4.11) were partially selected and colorized using the Design portion of KPT Convolver.

KPT CONVOLVER FEATURES

Understanding how Convolver works is simple once you're familiar with the three distinct sections of the interface. The sections are usually worked through in order, from Explore, to Design, to Tweak. The following material covers some of the little-known options and features.

TIP

Convolver files should be located in your plug-ins folder (4.12). Convolver should appear in the Filter menu of your software when properly loaded. There are several files that make up the whole of Convolver: Convolver 1.0, Convolver 1.0 Hub, Convolver Image, and Convolver Presets.

METAPHILOSOPHY:

INSIDE THE MIND OF KAI KRAUSE

Q: Of all the KPT interfaces and applications, which is your personal favorite?
KAI: Probably the Amazon Green Room and Goo, and all those things I can't talk about on camera now that we're a public company. Literally, the stuff looking backwards is old stuff for me. It's hard for me to look at that, knowing what I'm on right now. I use Convolver a great deal. I'm very happy with that puppy. There's going to be another integration of that concept that's going to be much more useful. The plug-in limitation there hurts me, so I'd like to think about stand-alone there and

brush it all in and … lose the limitation of being based on current exploration, and do it as a generic concept to fix stuff up. I'd love that. Goo is currently a real favorite just because of the simplicity of the outside and this ultra-killer engine inside. I love those two levels. There are a lot of more complex answers than you could deal with right now. But some other day we'll do another book on that.

Q: What do you see down the road for yourself as far as designing and interface? What do you think could be the

EXPLORE

The best way to start seeing what Convolver can do is to click on the Mutate Genes button. This randomizes the little diamond pieces, changing their appearance drastically. You can do this several times until you find the next "base" image style you'd like to work from. To use that piece as the base image, click on it once; that style appears in the smaller diamond above. To generate a new set of random images based on the new base image, click on the Mutate Genes button again. Rinse and repeat until you've achieved a desirable effect.

To achieve more control in the appearance of the mutations that appear, press the Genetic Diversity button, which displays a pop-up menu (4.13). Choose the amount of variation from this menu.

You can view a full-screen preview by clicking on the top diamond. To change what is displayed in the full-screen preview, Option-drag in the lower window. If this method isn't precise enough, Control-dragging in the window changes the screen to a view of the entire image containing a little floating diamond that determines what the preview is.

TIP

Use the keys "E," "D," and "T" to zip between the modes instantly. You can also click on the "sleeping" interface elements to go to the mode that supports those elements.

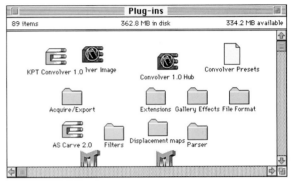

4.12

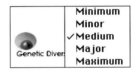

4.13

ultimate potential interface as far as using the computers we have today?

KAI: I don't believe anything we have now is getting anywhere near what it should be like. We're going to have to completely redefine how we interact with machines. I see a lot of researchers and academia play with these interface ideas; and they get lost, I believe, in the things that sound great on paper, such as space mice, and six-dimensional degrees in freedom. That's very contrived. I don't think that's the answer to it. We've learned how to use the mouse, and peo-

ple are very good with that. I do believe, though, that we should make use of the other hand; and so I'm actually, actively working on something that does a bi-handed approach.

Q: Do you consider at this point that the mouse is right now the most limiting factor?

KAI: No. Not by far. No. Maybe the mouse driver on Windows is, because it's a bunch of jerky crap going on; but the mouse as a concept works fine. There's nothing wrong with that. See, at

one point in time we had Xerox PARC. And then in one fell swoop, these guys brought all the principles from WYSIWYG—mouse, pixels, windows, hierarchies, those icons—from the basics of the interface all the way to subtle things such as structure and the iconic representation of events. They brought these in one three-year span, and we're still living with all that. Now that was fine at the time—and, considering when they did it, it was pretty incredible—but I'm saying it's time for another Xerox PARC to do this the other way. Meaning, we

DESIGN

The image to the side (4.14) shows how the two different characteristics interact within the grid squares in Design Mode. For this example, Blur and Brightness were used. The actual percentages only hold up at 33 percent, 67 percent, and 100 percent when the Arrow bar for that characteristic is fully extended on each side. If the Arrow bar is only partially extended, the total effect will be less than 100 percent, and the other percentages will decrease in proportion to that figure.

Several of the effects "go both ways," which, in this case, is a good thing. For instance, when Brightness is selected, the characteristic actually reads "Lighten." Clicking once on Lighten changes the word to Darken.

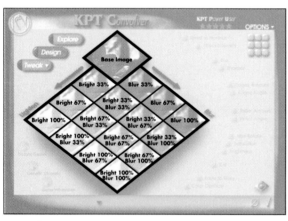

4.14

Effect Level (Normalize, Intensity), Blur/Sharpen, Edge Detection (Edges +, Edges -), Edge Angle (Edges CW, Edges CCW), Relief Amount (Relief +, Relief -), Relief Angle (Relief CW, Relief CCW), Hue Rotate (Hue Warmer, Hue Colder), Saturation (Saturate, Desaturate), and Contrast (Contrast, Fade) work the same way.

To pick a tile to use as a new base image, click on the tile you've chosen as the base image; it replaces the current base image. To move the sampled area around, click on the base image; this changes the tiles into a solid image that you can scroll around. This works in all three modes of Convolver.

You can also move more subtlety in one direction by clicking on a tile and dragging. This process, called "scrubbing," slowly moves between different elements in the preview above. It is perfect for directional options such as edge angle and relief angle.

TWEAK

Tweak doesn't have tiles; they wouldn't make sense, and it's better to see as much of the image as possible when doing these types of fine adjustments.

All the buttons that are shown (with the exception of Reset to Normal) are actually sliders. Okay, now the weird part. They're invisible sliders, handy for your little invisible friends to use, but a bit bewildering at first for the rest of us poor mortals. Clicking on any of

---

are at a completely different level right now. Machines are 2- 3- 400× over the beginning in the early 80s, and even the first Macintosh to the current Macintosh is 175× difference. So it stands to reason that you can reapply yourself to the same problems and resolve them in a whole new manner. Things that we now take for granted were not even an option back then. I can see the difference even just in three years of design, how something that was way over the horizon as an impossibility is now just maybe one step away.

It used to be that the first Bryce pictures were maybe 45 hours to render. Now they're down to 10, 12 minutes to pixelize at that same size—and we're only one more generation away from you flying around on the stuff. And that, of course, is—it's not about getting home 12 minutes earlier. It changes fundamentally how you do what you do, and that's kind of the story when you see the tools that we've done.

those buttons and dragging to the right increases the effect; dragging to the left decreases the effect, as you can see instantly in the upper diamond. If you keep the mouse button pressed after moving the slider in one direction and stopping, the larger diamond updates as well, showing this effect in more detail.

OTHER CONVOLVER OPTIONS

Convolver has numerous other options, accessed from the Options menu (4.15). These include the ability to save *presets*, which are compilations of all the changes made within the application. Those presets can be loaded for any image.

Presets in Convolver are strange beasts; the settings for one document will usually not work for others. However, carefully designed presets can be great "starting points" that require just a little bit of er, uh, Tweaking to get just right.

STARS

Finally, among the most controversial interface elements of KPT Convolver are the stars (4.16) you'll see to the left of the Options menu. After you've used certain features in KPT Convolver long enough, stars start to appear. Each star provides a new capability to Convolver so that new users won't be "overwhelmed" with too many features at once. Many users have stated that they dislike this method of doling out features, claiming it makes them feel like they're not smart enough to understand them any other way. We've found that for most users, however, the slow revelation of each star is both rewarding and useful.

On the bad side, this method can cause problems during reinstallation of the software because the stars have to be worked for all over again.

If you run into this particular problem, or if you can't wait to use the functionality that a certain star gives you, here are the "cheats" for getting your stars quickly and easily.

> **TIP**
>
> Tweak mode seems to be a giant box where all sorts of filters can be tried and played with until a certain effect is achieved. While this is the case with pixel-based software such as Photoshop, it's even more relevant to vector-based software, such as Illustrator and FreeHand. Because both programs accept Photoshop-compatible plug-ins, Convolver works within either.
>
> Perhaps the most important benefit to using Convolver in a Vector application is that it contains plug-ins that aren't individual files in Photoshop, such as Unsharp Mask and Gaussian Blur. Convolver provides a way for Illustrator and FreeHand users to blur and sharpen without ever leaving the vector software!

About Convolver...	
Preferences...	⌘P
Kernel Matrices...	⌘K
Comparison Grid Overlay	⌘C
Reselect Sample...	
Current Selection	
Color – Cool Car	
Edges/Relief – Hand Lines	
Creative Multi Effects – Eye	
Color – Fruit 'n' Cheese	
Detail – Clouds	
Enhancement – License Plate	
Load Dots...	⌘L
Save Dots...	⌘S
Clear Dots	
Animate Dots	⌘A

4.15

4.16

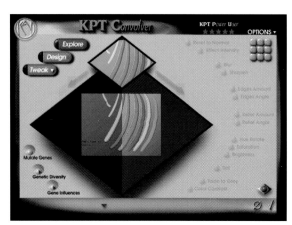

4.17

4.18

INSTANT STARS

You can get all the stars instantly with a little keyboard command. To get all of them at once, press Command-Option-Control-Shift, and double-click on Mutate Genes, and then click once on the Kai logo. There's a little drawback to this method: The stars only work for that particular session. Once you quit Photoshop, they're gone until you re-invoke the key command.

THE FIRST STAR

You should get a particular star regardless of how half-brained you are. Click on each of the modes while in Convolver and adjust *something in each of them* to get the first star, and thus, the first star message (4.17). At this point, no new features are added.

THE SECOND STAR

Click repeatedly on the Top (smaller) diamond in Explore or Design mode to get the second star. Clicking changes the bottom diamond from a one-diamond preview to several diamonds and back. This star enables Split Screen Mode (4.18). When split screen mode is on, one half of the larger preview represents the current settings, one half the original.

THE THIRD STAR

Play with the Tint marble in the Tweak dialog box, and the Third Star will be yours. A Tint Wheel (4.19) pops up and provides a way to visually see tints as you drag.

THE FOURTH STAR

Switch repeatedly between the modes (Explore, Design, Tweak) until the Memory Dots and fourth star appear. Memory Dots (4.20) are used to temporarily hold up to nine settings. To save the current settings to a dot, click on an empty (gray) dot. To recall the settings of a dot, click on a filled (dark brown) dot. If you have a dot selected, it will be red. To empty a filled dot, Option-click on it.

If you think you know how to play tic-tac-toe, go ahead and press Command-T once you have the memory dots in place. Now that you're in "Kai's Power Toe" mode, click to go (you're red, the computer is brown). Don't forget to read the messages along the bottom of the screen.

If you happen to win against the computer, send us a note via e-mail immediately. Tic-Tac-Toe, of course, when played properly, can never be won or lost . . . but if you're really good . . .

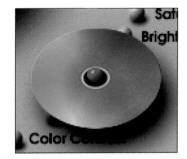

4.19

THE FIFTH STAR

Obtain the fifth star by scrubbing (dragging your mouse in a circle over any of the diamonds in the lower grid). Scrub quickly, and the fifth star, animation, appears. This seems to be the most difficult star to get, and it could take several minutes of scrubbing to achieve it. Animation animates either between memory dot settings (see above) or between random settings. Press Command-A to animate between dots, Command-M to animate between Random settings (determined in Explore's Genetic Diversity and Genetic Influences menus). This is a great way to let Convolver do the exploring for you. Control the speed of the animation with the numeric keypad; 1 is slowest, 0 is fastest.

4.20

THE JOY OF CONVOLVING

Think of Convolver as a little room you go into to do touch-up or special effects on your images. Once you come out, all the changes you'll need to do have been completed. In a way, it's as if all the filters that ship with Photoshop are within one dialog box, and you can do all your filtering in one place.

CHAPTER 5
VECTOR EFFECTS

Vectors Rule, Pixels Drool, goes the saying, and that may be true with Vector Effects (5.1). That's mainly due to the fact that Vector Effects has been widely considered to be the best plug-in set ever for any software package. Not only does Vector Effects contain several "filters" for modifying and manipulating vector objects in programs such as Adobe Illustrator and Macromedia FreeHand, but it also contains several full-blown applications.

VECTOR EFFECTS EXAMPLES

The following images show some of the capabilities of KPT Vector Effects. One of the unique things about Vector Effects is that you can start with the simplest image and end up with one that's incredibly detailed and impressive.

KPT ShatterBox was used to create the individual pieces of the apple in "Shattered Apple" (5.2). After it was "exploded," the Mix Soft feature of Adobe Illustrator was used to create the glass-like effect.

The swirl in the Bézier business card (5.3) was designed by using several KPT Vector Effects filters. A gradient was used to make a blend, then that blend was Swirled using KPT Vector Distort. Finally, the colors of the blend were changed with KPT Color-Tweak (using the Random setting).

KPT 3D Transform extruded text using custom lighting and ambiance colors for the Light, Inc. logo (5.4). The shadow was created with KPT ShadowLand.

The elegance lies in the process, in the flow, in hiding the complexity from the average person.

KAI KRAUSE

5.1

5.2

5.3

5.4

5.5

To achieve the flowing, flag-like appearance of the "Cactus Race" flag (5.5), KPT Warp Frame was applied to a flat rectangular logo.

The Pulse logo (5.6) was created by extruding text ("PULSE") and then using the front panel of the text as a mask for a grid. The metallic edges were copied and pasted in front, but the fills were changed to empty, and the strokes were set to match the front grid.

The designers of "Trivial Floatation" (5.7) extruded the game pieces individually with KPT 3D Transform, then created shadows with KPT ShadowLand.

"Primary Target" (5.8) was created by using Adobe Streamline on a portion of the artwork, then applying KPT ColorTweak to the round "target" area.

Bill Niffenegger designed this vase (5.9) to show off most of the capabilities of KPT Vector Effects. Almost all the filters are used in one way or another.

5.8

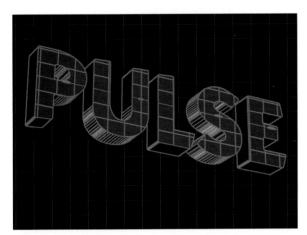

5.6

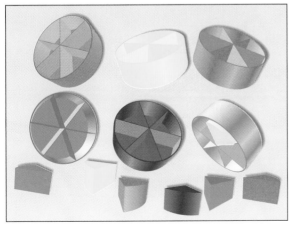

5.7

5.9 *Copyright © 1995 by Bill Niffenegger, Cloudcroft, NM*

THE ESSENCE OF VEX

KPT Vector Effects, or "Vex" as it's referred to by MetaTools insiders, has its own set of interface attributes and options that most of the plug-ins follow fairly consistently.

Most of the interfaces have several sliders, a preview area, and the standard "OK" checkmark and cancel "Ø." By default, the background (call it the "blackground" and everyone will think you really know your KPT lingo) of the dialog boxes takes over the entire screen, though this can be changed from the preferences option located within the Options menu. Clicking on the Kai logo displays a full-screen preview (not the dialog box size, but the full size of your screen. (This means that if you have a screen with 1180 × 832 resolution, the preview will have a sufficient amount of detail.) Pressing Command while clicking on the Kai logo causes the logo to "watch" your cursor and admire your artwork. Pressing three modifier keys at the same time (we can't tell you which ones, because we are Commanded to Control

our Options in this area) while clicking on the Kai logo brings up a very hip breakout game (5.10). Win the game and press Option, and you'll find yet another little Easter egg.

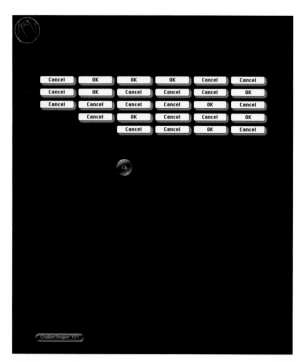

5.10

Smithers
Shiny Silhouette
Sree's Nightmare #1
Sree Still Can't Sleep
Sree's Night Terror
1973
Something's not quite ri
Still Not Right
Not Quite Left
That Healthy Green Glow
Just Plain Ugly
Nuclear Radiation #4
Fuzzy Nights
So quiet
Not So Quiet
Just Plain Loud
Even Louder
Loud, yet Quit
The Deep Bevel Returns
Deep Undercover Bevel
Special Bevel #4
Flatland...NOT
Flatland...KNOT
Preset #74
Lights
X axis only
Y axis only
X, Y, and Z
straight on bevel
Bevel with depth
metallic 1
perspective 1
Center light source
blue highlights/ambients
text 1
Text 2'
psycho highlight
psycho ambient
psycho colors 1
perspective 2
Perspective 3
psycho colors 2
Perspective 4
Perspective 5
Perspective 6
Perspective 7
Perspective 8
Perspective 9
Perspective 10
Perspective 11
Perspective 12

5.11

Within each of the filters with a preview, you can zoom in and out by clicking the Zoom In or Out buttons; or you can use the key commands you use in the host application. For instance, pressing Command-Space lets you draw a zoom marquee within the preview window, enlarging the image to the area of that marquee. The Hand tool works in a similar fashion.

Vector Effects is slider-happy. Wherever you see a word in a rectangular box, that's really a slider in disguise. Click on it and drag left or right. Prefer entering numbers to a slider? Command-click on any of those boxes. If you'd like to see these sliders work "live" on the preview (that is, update *while* you're dragging, not just after you finish), engage the Caps Lock key. Press Option to reset any of these sliders back to their default values.

Presets abound in Vector Effects. To view the list of presets for a particular plug-in (5.11), click on the little triangle at the bottom left of that plug-in's interface. To view the presets as graphic previews (5.12), hold down the spacebar while clicking. You can keep these graphical presets turned by going to Preferences (in the Option menu) and checking the Graphical Presets box.

We've included several presets for Vector Effects on the KPT SS CD-ROM, in the Presets folder.

KPT 3D TRANSFORM

To create good 3D effects in Illustrator or FreeHand, you need either Adobe Dimensions (too slow), Ray Dream's Add Depth (too obscure), or Vector Effects' own 3D Transform (too cool) (5.13). Basically, 3D Transform does most of what you want when it comes to three-dimensional effects (extrusion and perspective, for example).

Some of the less obvious features of the 3D Transform dialog box are the perspective slider (used for making your point of view seem closer or farther away from the extruded object) and the beveling system. The Bevel Size slider controls the width of the bevels. The Bevel Depth slider controls their depth (for example, how far back they go). Oddly enough, you don't have to extrude your artwork at all to use the bevels feature; just increase the size of the bevels (5.14) and voilà! Instant 3D objects.

> **TIP**
>
> If you're working on a fast enough system, pressing Caps Lock turns on the "instant" feature. As you drag any slider, the preview is updated instantly. This is quite useful for those minute slider adjustments. Speaking of minute adjustments, pressing Shift while dragging a slider gives you more control over the slider.

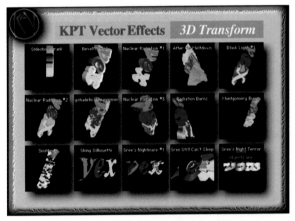

5.12

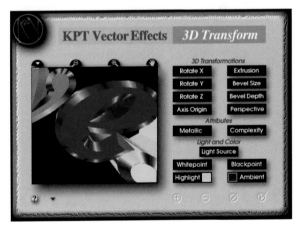

5.13

5.14

5.15

While KPT 3D Transform seems like a natural for working with text, many effects can be applied to other vector artwork with stunning results. When using the filter, you never have to apply both bevels and extrusion; by applying just one, you can achieve differing effects (5.15).

You can extrude not only backward (toward the back of your monitor) but also forward by entering a negative number into the Extrude box (remember that numeric values can be entered by Command-clicking on the desired slider). This way you can create effects such as extruded floor plans (5.16). Be careful when using negative extrusion; you might end up with shapes that are "behind" the viewpoint, which is kind of like picking fights at random at a postal workers convention. It's just something you shouldn't do.

The Metallic slider provides a way to add metallic effect to your art. Unfortunately, you can only apply this effect to curved surfaces. A quick workaround for this problem is to find all the straight segments and give them a slight bend (5.17). Because of the way metal attributes are applied, objects with heavy curves will have more variations than flatter paths.

You can enhance metallic surfaces created with KPT 3D Transform by adding a flare to any of the 3D surfaces. Here (5.18) you can see the difference one little flare makes when added to the metal text we've created.

METAPHILOSOPHY:

INSIDE THE MIND OF KAI KRAUSE

Q: Vector Effects has the most toned down, average interface you've ever designed.

KAI: I love the way you said that: "This is the most average interface ever designed!" I'm the most humble person in the universe.

Q: But when you look at product reviews, certain people have said that it's the best interface to come out of MetaTools, the most usable of all of them.

KAI: I know exactly what some people will say there, and it depends on who you are and how you get to it. When I look at effectiveness, "Number of whining replies" is only one way to measure that. So there certainly are a lot more people who would give me a lot more raspy feedback if I did a funny shaped little lens that moves around. If I do a piece of rock for Spheroids, I'll get a lot more surface replies saying, "that's a little strange." But whether they worked or not is actually another count. The count is who actually ends up with it? What do they do with it? And do I draw in who normally would not do this?

METATOOLS INSIDE INFORMATION

During the beta test phase of Vector Effect, beta testers came up with unique names for the individual parts and the entire set of "Vector Defects." KPT Seedy Transform, KPT Leon, and KPT SkatterFrogs were just some of the terms used to describe the plug-ins as they worked their way toward final development.

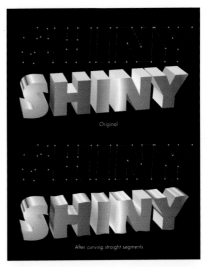

5.17

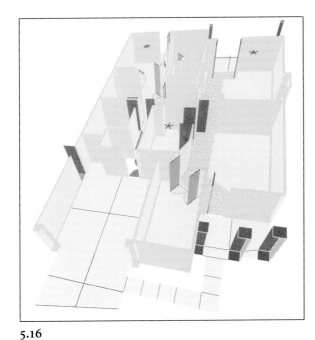

5.16

5.18

That is really is my focus. With Vector Effects, I really was being quite pragmatic. I said, "The Illustrator crowd hasn't really done the funny, happy KPT stuff in pixels in Photoshop before." So they skipped the first couple generations of getting used to all the funny goofiness. By the time KPT 3 came around, I don't think people were so surprised anymore—when they saw that version of the gradients, for instance. It's perfectly toned down by today's standards. In fact, every CD-ROM by now looks like we do it.

In the very beginning, with KPT 1, we had 20 open interfaces with soft-drop shadows and layers; and, literally, this was not the way to do it. It was highly illegal at the time to break all the rules like that, to take every little checkbox and Chicago font and put an alias piece of text in there. But if you notice, since then there isn't a CD-ROM that doesn't look like that. I mean, Microsoft took that look a long, long time ago. I wish I could have patented the look of drop shadows ten years ago (laughter).

But Vector Effects was a good example for something else: Turquoise spheres and whatever else is not what the interface design is about—and I wanted to prove it. It doesn't matter if it's round and turquoise, if it's square and blue, or triangle and red, or black and white and square with text and no icons and no color and nothing. The elegance lies in the process, in the flow, in hiding the complexity from the average person. I don't quite accept the statement that [the Vector Effects interface] was "the most successful one" just because maybe it hit the right crowd the right way, and they're having a good time with what it does.

KPT COLORTWEAK

KPT ColorTweak (5.19) adds color controls to vector software. And these aren't just any color controls. There are controls within Vector Effects to manipulate colors in almost any way imaginable.

Randomize, one of ColorTweak's best features, is hidden away in the Options menu. When this option is "on," each of the active sliders (sliders that have been moved from their default positions) dole out random values to selected paths (5.20). The amount of variation is directly proportional to the slider amount.

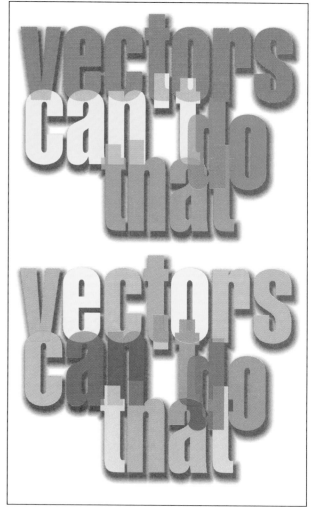

5.20

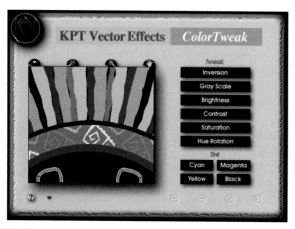

5.19

Q: What do you think is the best feature of Vector Effects?

KAI: The variety of Vector Effects is what makes it useful. You get one of each; it's the Swiss Army Knife. You can check the colors here. It corrects little problems there. It lets you do some things that look like the stroke effects. And then there's some pretty big stuff. You know, I like the simplicity [of the way] you can do 3D extrusion with the beveling and the metallicity on there. A lot of unused areas that haven't really been explored yet are in the mixture of doing these things in Vectors, ripping them out and then bringing them to Photoshop.

Q: Has Vector Effects gotten you to use vector software more?

KAI: People like to put me in little bins. I'm easily seen as the pixel guy; I'm seen as the Macintosh guy. Frankly, I'm not that religious about any of these things. I mean, I've got the Pentiums and the SGIs and all the other stuff. Yeah, I do still prefer the Macintosh, but it's not a religious issue like that. Same with the Vectors versus Pixels. It's all about a tool box, and it's having unique solutions for the different chores. It's silly to use a screwdriver as a hammer or a saw as a vice, you know. It's absolutely absurd. And there are some things you want to do on the Vector world in the Quark/Illustrator side of things, and there's other things you want to do with Pixels where it's very hard to bring them together. And what's fun about Vector Effects, actually, is the ability to take a little bit of this and put it over here and do something in Vectors, and bring it back in Photoshop and vice versa. I can only encourage people to do that.

Another feature hidden within the Options menu is the "Live" option (5.21); when activated, it changes the dialog box into a "palette" that shows changes made within it as they take place.

KPT EMBOSS

KPT Emboss (5.22) is sort of a one-shot filter. If you've ever copied your art, pasted it behind your original art, offset it a bit, lightened it a little, then repeated the process, moving the second copy in the other direction while darkening it, you've done embossing the hard way.

One of the best features of Emboss is Soft Emboss, which creates a brief (just a few steps) blend between the frontmost path and the light and dark edges. This gives the edges an almost curved, bevel appearance (5.23). This feature is invaluable because KPT 3D Transform doesn't enable you to create curved bevels.

5.22

5.21

5.23

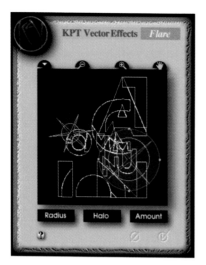

5.24

KPT FLARE

From the name, you'd think KPT Flare (5.24) would produce the sort of lens flare effect so prominent in Kai's Power Tools. But instead, this filter creates little sparkles of light that seem to pop out at you from your illustration. It's the perfect filter for making stars, glints of light, and backdrops for science fiction television shows.

Because KPT Flare fully interacts with the selected paths, lightening and darkening the original path colors, it actually performs quite well as a custom logo generator. We show one such logo right here (5.25). It was made primarily with KPT Flare by selecting only the frontmost objects at a time. Très cool.

5.25

KPT INSET

KPT Inset is a "better" version of the offset path filter with a preview to boot! One of the strengths of the filter is a method for creating "bold" or "heavy" versions of your favorite typefaces (5.26). Just convert your typeface to outlines and offset the path via KPT Inset. Instant "FuturaUltraLightSuperBlack."

KPT NEON

Neon tubes in vector software were a mystery to both Ted and Steve until they read something in Ted's *Macworld Illustrator 6 Bible* about creating neon tubes by blending different stroke weights. While that works just fine, it's still a lot more work than you would have to do were you to use KPT Neon.

5.26

5.27

5.28

So Neon creates neon tubes; big deal, right? Well, it also does something else to make those neon tubes a little bit more real. It makes overlapping separate paths, producing almost "real" physical tubes (5.27). This is quite different from the glowing function of KPT ShadowLand, discussed below.

KPT POINT EDITOR/KPT RESIZE AND REPOSITION

These are the obligatory un-fun filters in the Vector Effects package. In fact, KPT Point Editor is so much un-fun that we couldn't think of any really great way to demonstrate it here, except by twirling it with the Twirl Lens fx (5.28). Actually, both Point Editor and Resize and Reposition (which doesn't even have a preview!) have their practical uses, but those uses are rather dull.

KPT SHADOWLAND

As a three-part filter, KPT ShadowLand (5.29) is stacked full of options and possibilities. Only one of the three parts, Soft Shadow, creates a shadow in the typical sense. The other two parts are much more special-effects oriented.

The most effective way to use the soft shadow portion is to change the From color to a slightly darkened version of the background color by adding a small percentage of black while keeping the To color the background color. If that slider is pushed far enough, the resulting shadow (5.30) is both subtle and distinctive.

Halosity (the "bad breath" filter) can be used to create a halo, but it is actually more useful to create glows around artwork. A few pages back we mentioned that although Neon and Halosity were somewhat similar, there was an important difference between them. The halos produced by ShadowLand *interlock*, which lets the filter simulate lighting; as physical objects (neon tubes) cannot produce this effect. For great results, combine Neon with ShadowLand for Neon that really glows (5.31).

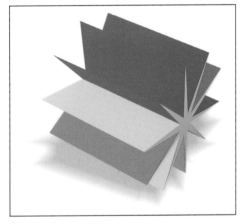

5.30

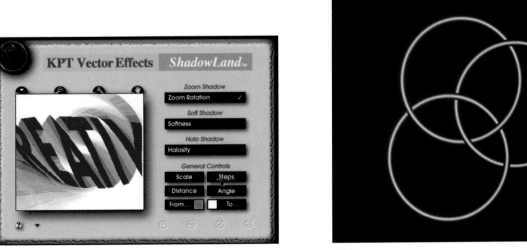

5.29

5.31

Zoom Shadow is a fantastic special effects feature, but it only really works when the Connect Steps option (in the Options menu) is turned on (5.32). When the option is off (5.33), the resulting artwork can look jaggy and stairstepped; just the opposite of the intended effect.

5.32

5.33

KPT SHATTERBOX

This filter (5.34) should come with a tagline: Sure to Strike Fear in the Hearts of RIPs Everywhere. ShatterBox is a quantum leap forward in vector software. Unfortunately, it's a leap past FreeHand (which doesn't have the chutzpah to handle it) and straight to the maximum of what Illustrator can handle. ShatterBox, you see, creates paths. Not hundreds of paths, but thousands! Illustrator starts groaning around 20,000 paths, begins moaning after 35,000, and goes into death spasms around 50,000 paths. ShatterBox can be the death of Illustrator.

Anticipating potential disaster, the brilliant engineers who worked on the Vector Effects suite of plug-ins limited the sliders to a respectable, but not deadly, amount of 50 "lines" that would be used to shatter selected paths. Of course, that didn't mean that there would end up being 50 pieces; in fact, there were several hundred! How does this happen? Take, for instance, any two lines used to divide an object. If the two lines do not cross, they'll create three objects; if they *do* cross, four objects. It's easy to see how several hundred paths can be created with only a limited number of lines used to break them. You *can* go over the "limit" of 50 lines by Command-clicking on the slider and entering a larger value, and also by increasing the Global slider, but it isn't recommended.

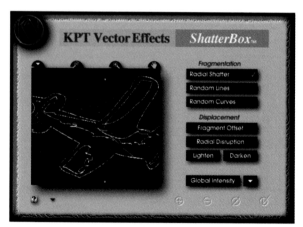

5.34

Be careful when using the Fragment Offset slider, as slight values can cause something as basic as text (5.35) to become destroyed (5.36). Larger values turn the text into the vector equivalent of shrapnel (5.37).

KPT SKETCH

The KPT Sketch plug-in slightly alters the location of points on a path and creates an overlapping path with a new stroke attribute. And the result is, well, sketchy at best.

You can achieve a hand-drawn effect by setting up KPT Sketch to resemble pencil drawings (5.38). To do this, use a small amount with the Pen style and repeat the filter several times. Then change the paths to a light stroke weight and a light gray color. Change the strokes to paths and apply the Mix Hard filter to all the paths. This gives the look of several overlapping pencils.

5.35

5.36

5.37

METATOOLS INSIDE INFORMATION

Vector Effects is the creation of the astounding Sree Kotay, who initially planned on marketing a set of vector-based filters as Sree's Cool Tools. John received an e-mail shortly before Macworld in 1995 telling him that someone was getting ready to launch a plug-in product using his online name, "Cool Tools." John exchanged e-mail with Sree about possible trademark problems. John thought that the product sounded interesting, and invited Sree to meet with him and Kai at Macworld. Kai and Sree connected, saw the potential of working together, and John offered Sree a deal: MetaTools (well, they were HSC at the time) would publish his filters, and Sree would be well compensated. In the end, both parties benefited greatly: Vector Effects was given what is widely considered to be an excellent interface, while MetaTools gained both a top-selling product and a top-notch engineer. Since that time, Sree has been a key engineer on Kai's Power Tools 3 and Bryce 2

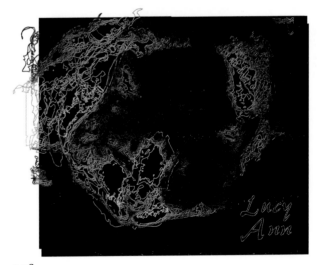

5.38

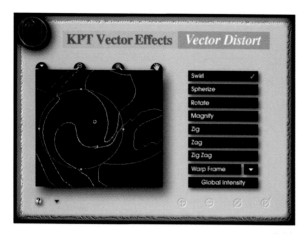

5.39

5.40

KPT VECTOR DISTORT

KPT Vector Distort (5.39) has a scary acronym but a fun and usable interface that combines some of the best aspects of all the Vector Effects filters. Each distortion within KPT Vector Distort can be any one of several different types, and those types can be combined by creating new distortions (technically called influences) and giving each influence a different distortion characteristic.

One of the pseudo-hidden features of KPT Vector Distort is the little Warp Frame slider in the lower right of the dialog box. Pressing on this slider lets you access all the KPT Warp Frame presets (see the KPT Warp Frame section, next). Then you can control how much of any KPT Warp Frame is applied to the artwork: a tiny bit (5.40), a lot (5.41), or a negative amount (5.42).

KPT Warp Frame is one of those plug-ins that MetaTools could have sold separately and charged megabucks for, and people would've lined up to pay—especially those people who had already paid big money for a competing product that was so buggy and flawed it makes System 7.5.3 look sterling.

Possibly the best thing about KPT Warp Frame is not what it does, but what it *doesn't* do. And what it

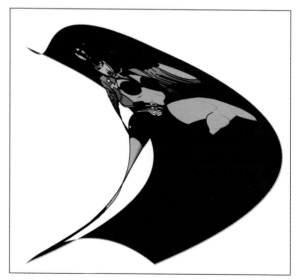

5.41

doesn't do is add any extra points. Figure 5.43 shows the original paths, and 5.44 shows the "after" Warp Frame paths. Note that no extra points were added. Now how much would you pay?

There are a few Options worth mentioning—like the fact than when the Option key is pressed, and more than one point or handle is selected (via shift-click or marquee drag), the points/handles mirror each other across the center as they move. You can also pull your handles right off the screen to adjust your frame. To select those handles, zoom out (Command-Option-Space-click) until you can view them.

The Options menu lets you turn off either the side or top/bottom handles, or both. You can also double the sets of curves, though the results can end up being pretty outlandish.

OUTLINED THOUGHTS

KPT Vector Effects is a great starting point for digital artwork. Combining Illustrator's vector attributes with Photoshop's (and Kai's Power Tools') pixel-pushing power, you can creating outstanding artwork with ease.

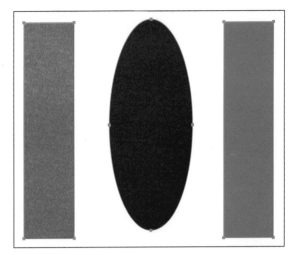

5.43

5.44

5.42

1 Above Slightly

2 Above More

3 Dead On

4 Below Slightly

5 Below More

6 On End

7 On End 2

8 Perspective

9 Beverly Crusher

10 BeverlyCrusher

11 El Terminado

12 SlightlyAggravated

VECTOR EFFECTS PRESETS

Vector Effects presets can be viewed both as a list of presets, or graphically by pressing the spacebar before clicking on the Presets menu. If you'd like to switch so that graphical presets are displayed without holding down the spacebar, go into the preferences of any Vector Effects filter and check the Graphical Presets checkbox.

Many of the graphical presets, such as KPT 3D Transform, allow you to view not just the basic frame of the preset, but also your specific selection as if that preset was applied to it. To view a preset with your art applied to it, press the Command key when the cursor is over a specific preset. To always view presets in full color, engage the Caps Lock key.

After choosing a preset, the name of that preset appears along the bottom of the dialog box. However, once you make one tiny little change to the preset, the preset name will disappear. To save your current settings as a preset, you'll have to click the + button and give the preset a name.

13 ReallyAggravated

14 Slope O Rama

15 Basic Depth

16 Hello There :)

17 Entering Orbit

18 Entering Orbit

19 Hi There :)

20 Basic Depth 2

21 Basic Depth 3

22 Basic Depth 4

23 Rotate 45

24 Rotate 45

25 Rotate -45

26 Rotate 90

27 Rotate -90

28 Simple Bevel

29 SimpleBevel#2

30 Sweep Left

31 Sweep Right

32 Sweep Extrude

33 Sweep Extrude

34 Monster Truck

35 Get Real, Bob

36 Beverly Sills

37 LeaveittoBeaver

38 Reflection

39 Reflect Right

40 Reflect Left

41 Reflect Up

42 Reflect Right

43 Reflect Left

44 Diagonal Bevel

45 Diagonal Bevel

46 Don't Even Ask

47 Homewrecker

48 Scary Bevel

49 Distort Zoom

50 Wall 'O China

51AndHisDogSpot

1 Simple Twirl

2CoolRadialSmear

3 Zoom Twist

4 Popup Left

5 Popup Right

6 Distant Shadow

7 Fast Shadow

8FloatingElectricity

9 Drop In!

10 Fallout

The Just Plain Loud preset was created by changing the colors of both lights. Lighting can have a dramatic impact on the way images are colored. Equally important is their original color before lights are applied.

The Metallic slider does not really make objects look more metallic when they have varying light sources, but it can create dramatic results quite easily.

Just Plain Loud

11 Soft Up

12 Soft Down

13 Soft Right

14 Soft Left

15 Zoom Twist 2

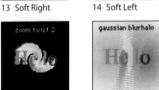
16 Gaussian Blur

17 Zip Out

18 Flyout

19 Flipulation

20 Upward Spiral

21 Kaleidestrobe

22 Intersection

23 Red Hot Spiral

24 Superman

25ComingRightUp

26 Double Twist

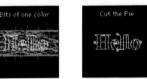
27 Preset #2

1 Bits of One Color

2 CutPaperCollage

3 Cut the Pie

4DarkStainedGlass

5 Destructo

6 Sassemble

7 Doorbell, Igor

8 Glass Shatter

9 Glass Shatter

10 Glass Shatter

11 Instant Cubist

12 IntotheHorizon

13 Medicine Man

14 Morning Face

15 Mosaic Tiles

16 Mutilation

17 Ocean Waves

18 Puzzle Pieces

19 Rain Fractures

20 Running With

21 Santa Monica

22 Shards and Bits

23 Shread To Bits

24 Slivers

25 Sprouts

26 Stained Glass

27 Striated Wood

28 Striated Darken

29 Striated, Light

30 Sunny Side Up

31 Sunrise Sunset

32 Tree Bark

33 Tri Angular

34 Whoosh

1 135°

2 180°

3 225°

4 270°

5 45°

6 90°

7 A Little Swirl

8 A Little Swirl

9 A Lot of Swirl

10 A Lot of Swirl

11 Bad Trip

12 BigConvexLens

13 Bubble Field

14 Concave Lens

15 ConcaveVortex

16 Cyclone

17 DownTheDrain

18 Flag Waving

19 Flag Waving 2

Limitcheck #1

Explosion

Cheeze Doodles

When you name your presets, try to be as descriptive as possible. The MetaTools engineers who designed these presets obviously had a lot of fun naming them, but many of the names, while whimsical, also accurately represent the eventual result.

20 FunhouseMirror

21 Half Warped

22 Inner Warp

23 Ins and Outs

24 Losenge

25 Max Zig Zag

26 Pond Ripples

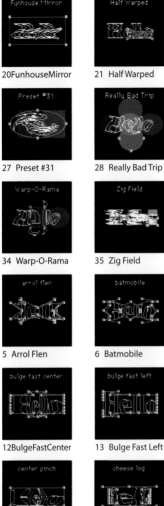

27 Preset #31

28 Really Bad Trip

29 Simple Vortex

30 Tales of the Stock

31 The Mumps

32 Twist and Bloat

33 Twister

34 Warp-O-Rama

35 Zig Field

36 Zig then Zag

1 A Big Pinch

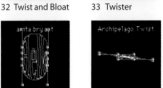
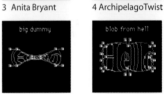

2 A.E.N.

3 Anita Bryant

4 ArchipelagoTwist

5 Arrol Flen

6 Batmobile

7 Batmobile 2

8 Batmobile 3

9 Big Bulge

10 Big Dummy

11 Blob from Hell

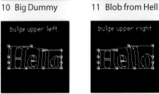

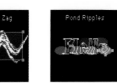

12 BulgeFastCenter

13 Bulge Fast Left

14 BulgeFastRight

15 BulgeLowerLeft

16 BulgeLowerRight

17 BulgeUpperLeft

18 BulgeUpperRight

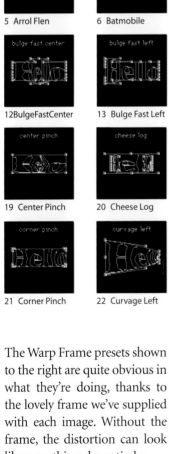

19 Center Pinch

20 Cheese Log

23 Curvage Right

21 Corner Pinch

22 Curvage Left

Too Much Pressure

Blob #7

24 Destination

The Warp Frame presets shown to the right are quite obvious in what they're doing, thanks to the lovely frame we've supplied with each image. Without the frame, the distortion can look like something else entirely.

25 Expand Center

26 ExpandoEdges

Mangled

Toast?

27 Fastbell Left   28 Fastbell Right   29 Fast Flare Left   30 Fast Flare Right   31 Fast Slope Left   32 FastSlopeRight   33 Flare Left

34 Flare Right   35 Flip Left   36 Flip Right   37 Flip Up Left   38 Flip Up Right   39 Floor Da Leeze   40 Happy Wide

41 Happy, Happy   42 Heavy Load

43 Hell   44 Homewrecker

45 Homewrecker   46 Homewrecker

Windy #2

The Windy preset shows what can happen all too easily with KPT Warp Frame: pseudo 3D effects that don't look quite right. At first glance, the image appears like a square sail on a ship. A second glance reveals that there's a bit of trouble with the text, as the purple "effects" is not being rendered correctly.

47 L'arc de Triomphe   48 Loopy Curvy   49 Lozenges   50 ManuscriptPage   51 MellowSqueeze   52 ModerateCarve   53 NotSoModerate

54 Nothing Preset   55 Oscar Meyer   56 OverhangWarp   57 Pointy Lil' Head   58 Preset #3   59 Psychogroovadelic   60 Ripple Bulge

61 Ripple Bulge   62 Ripple Left   63 Ripple Right   64 Sausage Bomb   65 Slice Left   66 Slice Right   67 Slice Down

68 Slice Up   69 Slope Left   70 Slope Right   71 Smooth Left   72 Smooth Right   73 Smooth Right   74 Soft White

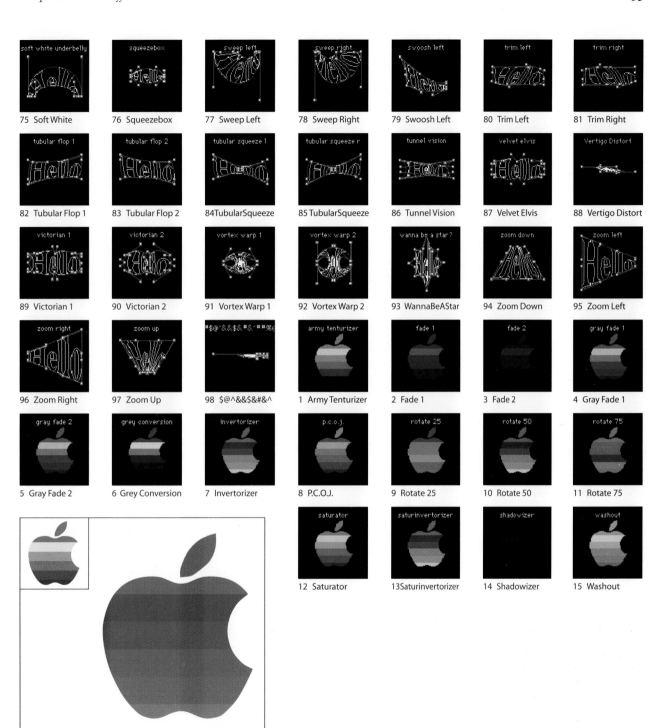

75 Soft White   76 Squeezebox   77 Sweep Left   78 Sweep Right   79 Swoosh Left   80 Trim Left   81 Trim Right

82 Tubular Flop 1   83 Tubular Flop 2   84 TubularSqueeze   85 TubularSqueeze   86 Tunnel Vision   87 Velvet Elvis   88 Vertigo Distort

89 Victorian 1   90 Victorian 2   91 Vortex Warp 1   92 Vortex Warp 2   93 WannaBeAStar   94 Zoom Down   95 Zoom Left

96 Zoom Right   97 Zoom Up   98 $@^&&$&#&^   1 Army Tenturizer   2 Fade 1   3 Fade 2   4 Gray Fade 1

5 Gray Fade 2   6 Grey Conversion   7 Invertorizer   8 P.C.O.J.   9 Rotate 25   10 Rotate 50   11 Rotate 75

12 Saturator   13 Saturinvertorizer   14 Shadowizer   15 Washout

Partial Inversion #2

The ColorTweak presets create results that vary widely depending on the colors of the original object. Blends are especially susceptible to bizzare behavior, especially if the Random checkbox is engaged.

CHAPTER 6
FINAL EFFECTS

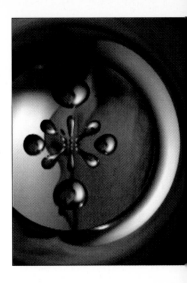

I n August of 1995, MetaTools acquired the rights to Final Effects from UDAC, a Swedish software development company (6.1). Final Effects was an amazing little program for creating sophisticated video special effects such as rain, snow, starbursts, bubbles, and shattering particle effects such as smoke and fire. Well, any plug-in program that created cutting-edge special effects was right up MetaTools' alley; and after meeting with Jens Enquist and Jerry Pettersson, the creators of Final Effects, and thoroughly examining their product, John and Kai knew that they wanted to take it—and video special effects in general—to the next level.

After acquiring Final Effects, MetaTools' engineers worked side-by-side (figuratively speaking) with Enquist and Pettersson in Sweden to polish the program and prepare it for its initial U.S. release as KPT Final Effects (now simply Final Effects). This polishing involved enhancing the capabilities wherever possible, tweaking the controls, and making sure that it integrated smoothly and efficiently with its host application, Adobe's After Effects.

TWO FLAVORS OF VIDEO EFFECTS

Initially, there was only one version of Final Effects and it only worked with one host application, Adobe's After Effects. When Adobe opened Premiere to plug-in extensions, the engineers at MetaTools created a streamlined version of Final Effects to work within Premiere.

We're very interested [in devising] a playful way to get into cutting-edge effects.

KAI KRAUSE

6.1

Images courtesy of Craig Lawson

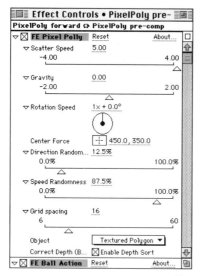

6.2

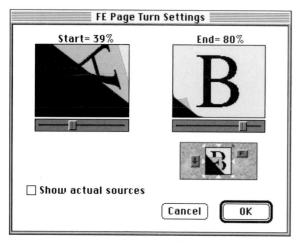

6.3

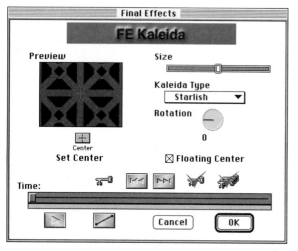

6.4

FINAL EFFECTS

The original Final Effects is an amazingly powerful and sophisticated set of special effects for professional video editing and compositing. Final Effects only works within Adobe After Effects, the industry leader in the field of "desktop" video effects. Final Effects consists of 28 separate filters, including three different particle generators for creating such sophisticated effects as fire, smoke, and explosions.

FINAL EFFECTS AP

Final Effects AP (the "AP" is for Adobe Premiere) is a streamlined version of Final Effects, possessing about half of its big brother's filters (including only one of the three particle generators). This is because Premiere is primarily a multipurpose video-editing and compositing application, while After Effects concentrates on special effects. The filters that do appear in Final Effects AP are virtually identical to the equivalent filters in Final Effects.

NO UNUSUAL INTERFACES (YET)

At this point, neither After Effects' nor Premiere's APIs (application plug-in interfaces) enables the kind of innovative graphical interfaces for which MetaTools is famous. So, for now at least, your interaction with these products is limited to dialog boxes that are very usable, but not exactly exciting, such as those shown here (6.2, 6.3, and 6.4).

These dialog boxes contain all the controls you need to specify precise values for every parameter of your effects. One important thing to remember is that you are not limited to the parameter values within a slider's (or dial's) range. If you Option-click on the control, you are presented with a numeric entry box that lets you enter numbers much larger or smaller than the "normal" range, thereby exaggerating an effect. This is a great way to create unique-looking special effects with Final Effects.

FINAL EFFECTS EXAMPLES

These video sequences provide a small showcase of some of the types of cool effects that can be created with Final Effects. They are included along with several additional examples on the CD-ROM bundled with this book. All were created by Craig Lawson and the folks at Digital Alchemy, who work closely with MetaTools on most of the company's other video projects, such as demo tapes for the press and for trade shows and other events.

The first sequence shows the effects of the Scatterize filter (6.5).

The second sequence illustrates the amazingly cool and amusing Flo Motion filter (6.6).

This third sequence demonstrates a great effect that can be created by combining the Spherize filter with the Flo Motion filter (6.7). One of the things that Kai always talks about when he discusses creativity and the kinds of artwork that catches his eye is taking that "extra" step. Many intriguing and never-before-seen effects can be created by simply combining two (or more) effects.

Another example of a great combination, this final sequence combines an Interform sequence from Kai's Power Tools with a Lens effect from Final Effects (6.8).

This lengthy sequence from MetaTools' Rob Sonner (6.9) illustrates several different filter effects. We start with the MetaTools logo wrapped around a sphere and placed on a multicolored background. In the

6.6

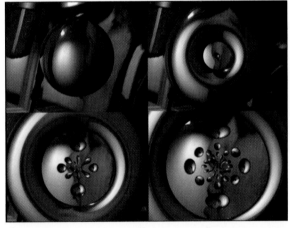

6.7

6.5

6.8

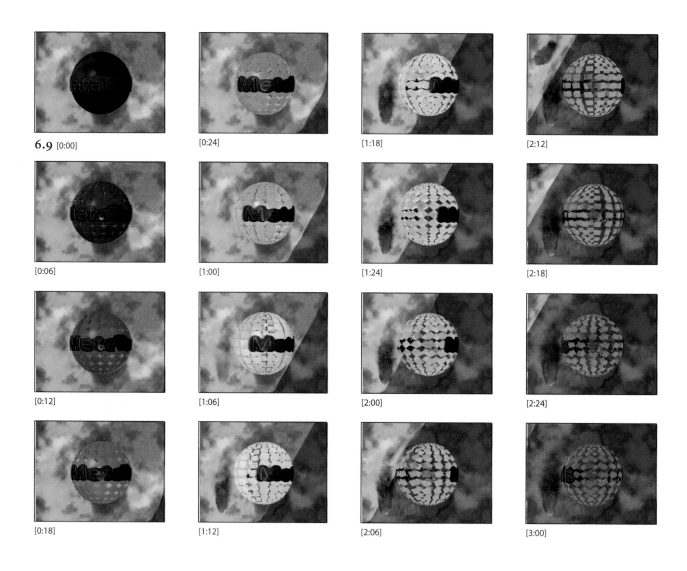

6.9 [0:00]   [0:24]   [1:18]   [2:12]

[0:06]   [1:00]   [1:24]   [2:18]

[0:12]   [1:06]   [2:00]   [2:24]

[0:18]   [1:12]   [2:06]   [3:00]

METAPHILOSOPHY:

INSIDE THE MIND OF KAI KRAUSE

Q: What's the story behind Final Effects?
KAI: It's a big area to go into. We bought a small company in Sweden, connected to the University of Uppsala. [There are] several hundred people there, and a small contingency of them do technology transfer, the big research stuff, and that's how we got in. Very, very lovely folks. They're going to come out here at some point, too.

And so, at this point, I haven't really done the integration that Sree did at phase one. We've taken it, we've brought it to a larger audience, but I haven't done the design, I haven't done the interfaces. They would want me to. I would love to. But also I would like to do it outside of the footprint of merely being connected to just Cosa, or just Premiere, or just Director. We're talking about [the fact] that you can see an interform. You can do stand-alone stuff that starts animations. And [with] Goo, [a] little baby product like that, we can make things fly and move around and do animation strips in a little program.

second frame shown here (which is actually the sixth frame in the sequence), the sphere has begun to rotate and break up.

In the third frame, we can see the lower-right corner of the background begin to peel up. By the fifth frame, the darker pattern behind the original background is visible. At this point, the sphere is obviously changing colors; and we can see through the spaces between the pieces of the sphere. In the seventh frame, we see a particle-generated flame burning in the lower left; and in the eighth frame, we can start to see the back of the MetaTools logo as it rotates around the sphere.

The rest of the frames take all of these effects to their logical conclusions. As the flame burns brighter and produces particle-generated smoke, the MetaTools logo (6.10) rotates all the way to the back of the sphere, and the initial background is peeled completely away.

TIPS AND TECHNIQUES

Here are some tips and techniques for creating popular or innovative effects using both Final Effects and Final Effects AP.

What it means to me is we can bring nearly professional-level software down to the kids. I mean, you watch the NBC Evening News, and all the NBC logos with the sparkling particle effects are done by a couple of kids in Burbank with a couple of PowerMacs with a little program like that. And they use it very much. I think Final Effects is the first cut in us bringing that down. You'll see a lot more of that type very soon. We're very interested [in devising] a playful way to get into cutting-edge effects.

SMOKE

One of the most difficult aspects of creating convincing smoke is getting the speed (or flow) of the smoke right. In most cases, you won't want your smoke to move as though it were being sucked into a vacuum cleaner (which is, unfortunately, the way Final Effects smoke often looks). What you need to do is set your velocity and gravity at very low and raise the longevity to a high setting (such as 3 or 4). Sometimes you may also want use a low setting for turbulence. Keep in mind that if you set longevity to 3 or 4, the time marker must be slightly beyond the three- or four-second point in the animation so you know how your smoke really looks. If you longevity is set at 4 and the time marker at 3 seconds, particles won't have started dying out and your smoke won't look right.

6.10

TIP

The FE Sphere filter can wrap any 2D image or movie around a rotating 3D sphere. This can be used to "cut out" unwanted portions of your image if it contains an alpha channel. One of the cool advantages of using an alpha channel in this fashion is that as your sphere rotates, you can actually see through to the back of the alpha-channeled image. In this sequence, the MetaTools logo is actually split into two layers. The back layer renders the backside only, and the front layer renders the front only. Because an FE Sphere effect can include reflections, this can make your effect that much more realistic.

Unless you want to see the smoke beginning, you may want to set up the layers so that the smoke that appears in your composition is mature. To do this, make sure that if your longevity is 4, the only part of the smoke layer that appears in the comp is the portion *after* four seconds. This ensures that the smoke appears consistently throughout the final animation.

TIP

To make realistic fire and smoke, use several layers for both the fire and the smoke. Each layer should consist of the actual fire/smoke plus a layer using more fire/smoke as a luminosity mask. Additional layers perform darken or lighten channel operations. See the Fire and Smoke tips at the end of this chapter for more details.

Don't forget that you can make a sequence run in reverse by time-stretching the layer(s) and entering a negative time-stretch value (-100 percent, for example). This can be used to extinguish flames or make explosions run in reverse, forming artwork or a company logo out of broken pieces.

6.11

Use either the "Lens Fade" or "Faded & Shaded Sphere" particle types to get good smoke. You will usually have to use multiple layers with different particle types to create realistic smoke. In this sample image, Faded Spheres are used as the background smoke and Shaded & Faded Spheres are used in the foreground with slightly different Particle Systems II settings for each layer. You usually have to do a lot of tweaking and experimenting to get smoke looking exactly right. It can also be helpful to use a picture of real smoke as your layer image and sample colors from that (using Original-Original in the Color Map pop-up menu) (6.11).

FIRE

Flames are very similar to smoke, so a lot of the techniques described previously apply here. Getting realistic flames requires a good combination of velocity, gravity, longevity, and turbulence, along with the right colors (using a picture of flames such as the "Fire Map 3" file in the Final Effects tutorial can help dramatically). The proper particle type is also important. Surprisingly, you can use a wide range of particle types, depending on the kind of fire you want. Again, you will need multiple layers with varying settings. In the previous sample image, the background is made of up pixels from the "Fire Map 3" file in the Final Effects tutorial; the middle layer uses textured polygons (the "Fire Map 3" file is used as the source image); and the foreground layer uses pixels again, but with settings significantly different from the background. Spheres, stars, motion polygons, bubbles, and drops can all can also help create realistic flames.

EXPLOSIONS

To create convincing explosive effects, you need Pixel Polly. Here are some great tips to get the most out of this filter.

If you want to stop Pixel Polly from breaking apart until a given time, set scatter speed, gravity, and rotation to 0. At the frame *before* you want the explosion to occur, set another duplicate keyframe; and on the following frame, change the scatter, gravity, and rotation to the desired levels, creating several hundred polygons.

We highly recommend that Final Effects AP users Option-click on the sliders/dials to make sure that they're set to exactly 0. If they're even slightly off, your image will break up.

If you want to have Pixel Polly *im*plode rather than *ex*plode, use time remapping. Precompose your Pixel Polly layer, import it into your current composition, then apply time remapping and make the Pixel Polly animation run backwards! This also works with Particle Systems and any of the other filters.

And don't forget about negative gravity. If you want to have shards look as though they're being tossed up, set gravity to negative initially, then keyframe it and change gravity to positive. The shards will be tossed up and then fall back to the ground.

Another tip for Premiere users: If you want to explode an object over a background, and you want the background to stay intact, you need to prerender the explosion. Put the object you want to explode over a black background (6.12), apply Pixel Polly to it, and then render it out to a QuickTime movie. Import the QuickTime movie into the project that has the background you want, lay it on top of the background in one of the superimposed channels, and then key out black (using the Transparency command in the Clip menu). Doing so makes the black background in the QuickTime movie transparent, and your object will explode over the normal background.

FIREWORKS

The key to creating *sparkling fireworks* is to set a large *x* and *y* size and a very short longevity. The *x* and *y* size values should increase over a short time to get a burst effect and then stay at a given size for a little bit, producing particles that last for a very short time.

For example: Set the particle type to "Star," the birth/death colors to white (white is ideal, but you can experiment with other colors), and your birth

rate to 14 (or whatever you think makes your burst look dense enough). Set your *x* and *y* values to about 5 at the beginning. One second into the animation have them increase to 35; at two seconds, have them increase to 40. If you have the Production Bundle of Final Effects, use the Glow command from the Stylize menu to give your particle a bit of a halo (this helps but isn't necessary). Finally, render and enjoy. You may want to have two or more layers generating particles with different colors to get another effect.

Flare fireworks are even easier (6.13). Just set a really high birthrate (20, for instance) for two or three frames, then change the setting to 0. This instantly creates a whole bunch of particles. Set the longevity for 1.5 or 2 (or experiment to find what looks best to you) and then render.

6.12

6.13

MISCELLANEOUS TIPS

Setting the FE Lens filter very low and performing some judicious color tweaking can add a "vintage TV" look to your video sequences (6.14).

If you miss the Video Cyclone filter from the older versions of Kai's Power Tools, you'll be happy to know that the Color Offset filter can produce similar effects—it's great for producing cool animated backgrounds. You can also combine this technique with the Kaleida filter and Flo Motion for some very cool, psychedelic effects (6.15).

Whenever you use the Light Burst filter, be sure to render that layer at one-quarter resolution for previewing; otherwise, your previews will take forever. Also, be aware that you'll have to spend a tremendous amount of time on your final, high-resolution renders if they involve Light Burst effects. (Light Burst effects can be up to 20 times slower than other effects to render.)

The Ball Action filter (6.16) can create very cool dispersal effects, especially with a decent amount of rotation (à la the *Lawnmower Man* movie).

When using Page Turn, be sure to set your producer point completely off of the page (in the gray work area) for both the beginning and ending of the effect. Multiple Page Turns, timed correctly, can produce the effect of the wind turning over the pages of a book.

For a nice transition with any of the appropriate Final Effects filters, use a dissolve based on luminosity rather than a standard video dissolve (which merely changes layer opacity values) (6.17, 6.18).

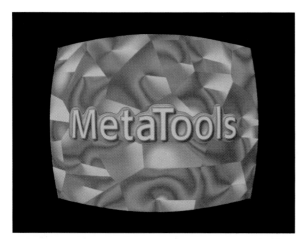

6.14

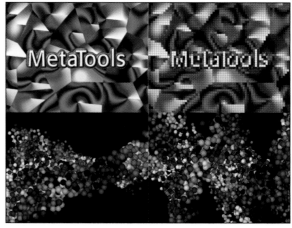

6.16

6.15

To create a *Brady Bunch* type of grid effect (with different sequences playing in different areas), use the Griddler filter to break up your image, then use Tiler to break the "griddled" image into separate boxes.

Use Pixel Polly or Particle systems as a track matte or alpha channel. Just make the particles/polygons white and the background black and precompose them. You can generate some interesting effects this way.

ANIMATED WOW

While all of the MetaTools products discussed in this book have a high "wow" factor, something about animating your effects makes them immensely satisfying. We suppose that animated wow will always be cooler than static wow, and Final Effects and Final Effects AP are as wow as animation gets. The tips and techniques that we've discussed so far, combined with a sense of adventure and exploration, should produce effects unlike any that the film, video, and multimedia industries have ever seen.

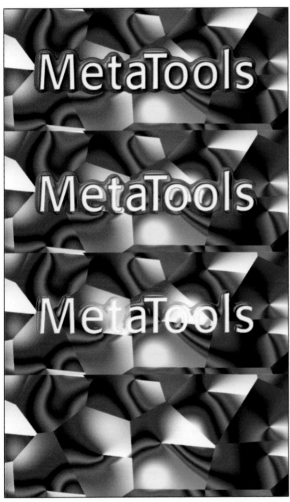

6.17

6.18

CHAPTER 7
POWER PHOTOS

After MetaTools (as HSC Software) wowed the digital imaging world with programs such as Kai's Power Tools, Convolver, and Bryce, the initial reaction to the news that the company would be producing a series of Photo-CDs may have been less enthusiastic than what they were used to. Historically, Photo-CD collections haven't been known for triggering gasps of delight and wonder from the people who buy them. This is primarily because they have always been composed of excess (that is, leftover) photography: stock photographs purchased from professional photographers and compiled into a set of Photo-CDs for consumer and professional use. What sets MetaTools' Power Photos series (7.1) apart from the crowd is: a) the forethought and professional expertise that goes into creating each image, and b) the built-in alpha and Transflectance channels, which make compositing with Power Photos a breeze.

You'll discover three key advantages to using Power Photos over any other set of Photo-CDs on the market. First, the images themselves are uniquely interesting and visually appealing. Second, all images are of consistently high-quality and maintain consistent perspective and lighting for optimal compositing. Third, all images have built-in alpha channels, and many have built-in Transflectance channels, which can be used as combination opacity and reflection masks.

A very good bang for the buck , good quality, and lots of it.

KAI KRAUSE

7.1

As early as 1986, digital artist Stephanie Robie (7.2) was frustrated at the lack of quality images in commercial Photo-CD collections. She wanted interesting, high-quality images that could be composited together with a minimal amount of tweaking. Unfortunately for Stephanie (but fortunately for all of us, as it turns out) nothing like this existed. She discussed the possibility of creating a such a product with her friend Val Gelineaux, an accomplished photographer, and the seed that would become Power Photos was planted. Stephanie's husband Dave joined the pair as the digital image-manipulation wizard, and they officially formed PhotoSpin in the summer of 1994. The trio then met with the folks at MetaTools, who recognized the value and innovation of PhotoSpin's approach, and KPT Power Photos was presented to an appreciative public in the spring of 1995. Bob Morrison (former MetaTools VP of Sales) joined them in the fall of 1995 as their business development expert, completing the PhotoSpin foursome .

7.2 *Stephanie Robie*

POWER PHOTOS EXAMPLES

In this section, we'll look at some images that rely on Power Photos. These images were created by combining some of the 1,600 Power Photos currently on the market. Effective images can often be created by simply combining several different Power Photos, as in this image used in early Power Photos ads (7.3).

If you would like to see more of the available Power Photos, check out the Power Photos I–IV slide show included in the MetaTools Product Info section on this book's CD.

The first two images on the facing page are from Stephanie Robie, the digital artist who got the whole Power Photos ball rolling. The whimsical "Row-Bee" (7.4) is a play on Stephanie's last name and was created by combining a bee from Power Photos Volume 8: Bugs and Butterflies with an overhead shot of a person rowing.

"Butterfly and Paint" (7.5) illustrates how easily an image can be created by simply using individual Power Photos (the sky is from Volume 1: Natural Backgrounds and Textures, the peeling paint and street sign are from Volume 3: Urban Textures and Backgrounds, and the butterfly is from Volume 8: Bugs and Butterflies) and a little creativity and ingenuity.

"Nostalgia Device" (7.6) is from MetaTools artist and interface design specialist Athena Kekenes and uses six different nostalgia-oriented Power Photos images in the "windows" of this UI element prototype.

7.3

"Night Butterflies" by Donna Troy uses two different Power Photos image libraries (Volume 4: Sky, Water, and Landscapes and Volume 8: Bugs and Butterflies) to create an interesting juxtaposition of colorful butterflies, a dark night sky, and a dramatic moon. After gathering the base images, Donna composited them all together normally in Photoshop, then spent quite a bit of time with Convolver meshing all of the pieces together.

"City of Angels" (7.8) is from Greg Carter and uses Power Photos (Volume 3: Urban Textures and Backgrounds) for *all* of the graffiti on the freeway overpasses. This incredible image shows what a master digital artist can accomplish with Power Photos.

7.5

7.4

7.6

7.7

7.8

METAPHILOSOPHY:

INSIDE THE MIND OF
KAI KRAUSE

Q: Have you played at all with the Transflectency channels in Power Photos? **KAI:** It's a bleeding alpha channel. Give me a break! It's a useful thing, yeah, no doubt. But frankly, you can't make reflectivity until you know where the information is. It doesn't work that way. But, why people haven't done that a long time before, I don't know. It's a useful, cool thing. I have my own crack at what I see for new variations. The beetles was cool, I like that right there. I love, for instance, the value of the very first one: 11 CD-ROMs for a hundred bucks. Can't argue with that, you know. It was a very good bang for the buck, good quality, and lots of it. There it is. As opposed to other guys doing—mass-blanketing the planet with really, really mediocre stuff. So I like the approach to that.

HOW POWER PHOTOS ARE CREATED

To begin with, the images used in the Power Photos series are not "leftovers." Before any pictures are taken, the themes and artistic emphasis for the entire collection are decided upon through a joint collaboration of the MetaTools product management team and PhotoSpin, the company responsible for most of the Power Photos images. The subject matter for each set of images is determined by weighing the artistic and aesthetic merits of each possible subject; the need in the market for such images; and the availability of suitable locales, models or props. Past themes for Power Photos volumes have included Foods, Sports and Recreation, Hot Rods, Nostalgia, Junkyards, and Spring and Summer Holidays. Some themes that haven't been used yet (but which we may see in future versions) are Tattoos, Reflections, Children's Faces, Winter Scenes and Textures, and Fire and Smoke.

After the themes have been agreed upon and the objects selected and prepared for photographing, each picture is taken from the same angle, and with the same or compatible lighting and shadows, so that creating a composite of several Power Photos images does not necessitate manually fixing such elements as shadows and highlights.

Once the photos have been taken, they are drum-scanned at extremely high resolution and then proofed on-screen. If necessary, photos are retaken and rescanned to ensure the highest quality. (PhotoSpin is moving towards a purely digital photographic process; and by the time you read this, virtually all Power Photos will be captured digitally.)

Once all of the photographs have been digitized, the images are then color corrected and sharpened (usually in Photoshop) and the Transflectance channels are created. These are separate alpha channels that include information you can use to create transparent or reflective effects. While the useful and unique themes and the high quality of the images are great features of Power Photos, it is the Transflectance channels that really sets this product above all other Photo-CD collections.

LOADING TRANSFLECTANCE CHANNELS

To ensure cross-platform compatability, all Power Photos images are stored on hybrid Mac/PC CD-ROMs in ISO 9660-compliant, LZW-compressed RGB TIFF format. Complying to the ISO 9660 format limits image information to RGB data plus a single alpha channel (used in Power Photos for the image silhouette). For this reason, the Transflectance channels have to be stored as separate grayscale TIFFs and then "loaded" individually.

Not all images have Transflectance channels. Generally speaking, if an image does not contain significant areas of opacity or reflection, a Tranflectance channel probably hasn't been created for it. If you are working with an image and want to know if it has a Tranflectance channel, simply do a file search for the seven-digit numeric portion of the filename. This code is based on the volume number (the first three digits) and the image number within that volume (the last four digits). Transflectance channels have the exact same seven-digit numeric code, plus the letter "T" at the end. For example, the bee image used in "Composite #1" (7.9) is named 0080026.TIF (volume 008, image 0026). A search for "0080026" would reveal this file, plus another file named 0080026T.TIF. This is the Transflectance channel for the bee image.

7.9

Any time you want to composite two images together and use one object's inherent transparency (such as that of the Bee's wings) or potential reflectancy, a Transflectance channel is the only way to go. Because the Transflectance channels have to be stored separately from the image, you'll need to locate both the image that you want to work with and its corresponding Transflectance channel file. Once you've located the desired Transflectance channel, open both it and the actual color image in Photoshop. To ensure that the Transflectance channel exactly matches the color image, *do not alter the size or resolution of either file before loading the Transflectance channel.* Activate the Transflectance file (if necessary), select all, and copy this grayscale image. Activate the color file. Make sure that the channel palette is active and create a new channel. Paste the grayscale image into this new channel. If you wish, rename this new channel "Transflectance" or something similar. You are now the proud owner of an image with a Transflectance channel. Once the Transflectance channel has been loaded, you may resize or adjust image resolution as desired. This procedure is discussed in more detail in the following section, Compositing with Transflectance Channels.

COMPOSITING WITH TRANSFLECTANCE CHANNELS

As we mentioned earlier, the Transflectance channels can be used as either opacity masks or reflection masks. In this section, we create some very simple image composites to illustrate the advantages and ease of using Transflectance channels. The first two composites use the Transflectance channels as opacity masks, and the last one uses them as reflection masks.

THE "TRANS" IN TRANSFLECTANCE

Using Transflectance channels as opacity masks (or transparency masks, if you prefer, because approaching opacity/transparency from either angle has the same end result) is a simple and straightforward process. To create the surreal composite bee image shown earlier, which we like to call "Bee with Translucent Wings Inside Bay Window of House with Cloudy Sky," we used the cloudy sky from Power Photos I / Volume 1: Natural Backgrounds and Textures/file 0010003.TIF (7.10), the giant bee from Power Photos II / Volume 8: Bugs and Butterflies/files 0080026.TIF and 0080026T.TIF (7.11), and the bay window from Power Photos III / Volume 14: Frames/files 0140024.TIF (7.12).

7.10

7.11

We began by opening each of these files in Photoshop, loading the Transflectance channel for the bee as described earlier (see Loading Transflectance Channels, previously), and saving the resulting images onto our hard drive as Sky, Bee, and Window. We then activated the Bee image, chose Load Selection from the Selection menu, and loaded the Transflectance channel (channel #5). Next we copied this information, switched to the Sky image, and pasted the Bee onto that image. Because of our Transflectance channel selection, the areas within the bee's wings are fairly transparent, allowing us to see through them to the background sky (7.13). We repeated this process for the window image, loading the silhouette channel (channel #4) instead of the Transflectance channel (because the image consists solely of completely opaque or completely transparent areas), copying the opaque portions of the window, and then pasting that data onto the Bee/Sky image.

This second image of a teddy bear wearing a pair of retro eyeglasses (7.14) was equally easy to create (although we had to visit several DMVs and county libraries to find a woman who still wore these glasses). The teddy bear is from Power Photos II / Volume 6: Kids Toys & Backgrounds/file 0060048 .TIF (7.15) and the eyeglasses are also from Power Photos II / Volume 9: Nostalgia/files 0090044 .TIF and 0090044T.TIF (7.16).

7.13

7.12

7.14

7.15

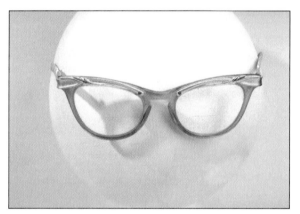

7.16

7.17

We created this image exactly the same way that we started creating the previous image—opening all three files in Photoshop, loading the Transflectance channel for the eyeglasses, and saving the resulting file as Glasses on our hard drive. The teddy bear was saved simply as Bear.

We then activated the Glasses file, selected the Transflectance channel (channel #5), and copied that information to the clipboard. After that, we simply activated the Bear file, pasted in the glasses, resized them a little bit, and saved the resulting image.

THE "FLECTANCE" IN TRANSFLECTANCE

While the transparent aspects of Transflectance channels are fairly accessible to anyone who is moderately familiar with Photoshop, casual users may never be able to understand how to use Transflectance channels to create reflective effects on their own. If only there were a book that explained the process in simple, easy-to-follow steps—wouldn't that be great? Well, this may seem like an amazing coincidence, but that's what we've done for you in this book! Well, here's how you use Transflectance channels as reflection masks.

To use Transflectance channels for opacity effects, we first selected the Transflectance channel, copied it, then pasted that information *onto* another image. To use Transflectance channels for reflective effects, we pretty much do the opposite, pasting image

7.18

information *into* the Transflectance channel of the target image.

To illustrate this technique, we started with two images, one of a tropical beach (7.17) and the other of a 1950s hood ornament (7.18). The plan here was to get a convincing reflection of the tropical beach onto the hood ornament (as if we had hopped into a time machine, traveled back to the fifties, bought a new car, driven it under the Pacific Ocean, and just emerged from the ocean and pulled up on this lovely beach). Here we simply copied the tropical beach image, activated the hood ornament image, loaded the Transflectance channel as a selection, and then pasted the tropical beach image into that selection. This gave us an interesting combination of the two images (7.19), but not really a convincing reflection. To create the effect that we're looking for, we needed to perform a simple channel operation before bringing in the tropical beach image.

Starting from scratch again, we copied the tropical beach image into memory. We then switched to our hood ornament; but before pasting in the beach, we created a sixth channel (a reflection channel) by performing a calculation to combine the Silhouette channel with the Transflectance channel using a Difference blending mode (7.20). We then loaded this new channel as a selection and pasted the tropical beach image into it, which gave us this final image (7.21). Once created, this reflection channel can be tweaked as desired to give you just the reflections you want.

IT CAN'T BE THAT EASY . . .

. . . but it is. The images we've created so far are, of course, very simple examples of working with Transflectance channels; but they illustrate the ease with which you can composite images together with convincing transparencies and reflections.

This ease of use is the key to Power Photos. The reflection effect we just created is an excellent example, as finding the two images, cleaning them up, and creating the reflection mask by hand would have been inordinately time-consuming. With the high quality and built-in Transflectance channel, it was a fairly painless process, giving us more time to tweak the reflection or add other effects.

7.20

7.19

7.21

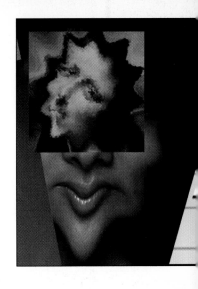

CHAPTER 8

GOO, GAMES, AND MORE

A fter years of trying to add an element of fun to software designed primarily to help people work, MetaTools has finally created some software designed specifically to help people have fun. And we guarantee that when you get your hands on some of this stuff, you are in for a treat. Kai and company are approaching the "fun" angle from two different directions. With Kai's Power Goo, MetaTools has taken their philosophy of "we thought it was cool, so we put it in the software—*you* figure out what to do with it" and created an entire product that is "cool," "fun," "wow," *and* powerful. The online games, on the other hand, fit within a defined genre more so than Kai's Power Goo; but even they have layers of philosophical "left-of-centeredness" that help them to transcend the "just games" label.

Goo is a product that almost immediately generates an emotional reaction when you play with it.

JOHN WILCZAK

KAI'S POWER GOO

Kai's Power Goo (or simply "Goo") (8.1) is MetaTools' first venture into the consumer software market; and from the initial response they've gotten from early Goo users (Goosers?), it looks as though MetaTools has another monster hit on its hands.

Kai's Power Goo is a simple-to-use—but deceptively powerful—piece of software. The first in what will probably be a highly successful line of "creative entertainment tools," Goo combines an intuitive and accessible interface with some pretty amusing results and does so acceptably well on low-end consumer

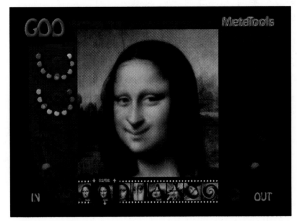

8.1

GOO HUMOR

One of the actual reasons for choosing "Kai's Power Goo" as the name for this product was all of the opportunities for "goo" puns in marketing materials (as evidenced by the "Just Goo It" buttons passed out at the Electronics Entertainment Exposition in Los Angeles in May, 1996). The Goo Explorer's Guide contains a tongue-in-cheek glossary of "goo" terms such as "Goober" for someone who has had their picture gooed, or our personal favorite, "Moo Goo Kai Pan," the definition for which manages to include references to cows, Kai's Power Goo, Kai himself, and Chinese food. The name of the product is a spoof of "Kai's Power Tools," and we won't be at all surprised to see the next version referred to as "Goo Too." The phenomenon isn't isolated to the MetaTools marketing department, either. Ask anybody at MetaTools how they are doing, and the likely response is "pretty goo." Hang out at the office around noon, and you might be invited to "goo to lunch" with them. Personally, we think it's sad to see some of the most creative minds in the industry reduced to this; but there isn't much we can goo (uh, make that "do") about it.

machines (Quadra or 486 with 16MB of RAM, although a Power Mac or Pentium is recommended).

WHAT IS GOO?

Simply put, Goo is a software program for creating image- or brush-based, animatable distortions of photographs or other images. To be more precise, Goo contains about two dozen different distortion effects, ranging from brushes that let you push or pull portions of your image as if the image itself were liquid, to image-based effects such as twisting, spiking, and glass lens distortions. After any distortion, the resulting image can be loaded into keyframes to create incredible smooth (and amusing) animations that can be exported to QuickTime (Macintosh) or AVI (Windows) files. Check out our "Goovie" samples on this book's CD-ROM.

Because it's infinitely more fun to "goo" people you know, MetaTools has worked very closely with scanner and digital camera manufacturers to ensure that Goo can easily acquire images directly from such devices. Once loaded, these images can be distorted and saved in several popular still file formats as well as the QuickTime or AVI formats for Goo animations.

SPECIAL EDITION INTERVIEW WITH JOHN WILCZAK

Here MetaTools CEO and cofounder John Wilczak shares his thoughts on the future of the company.

Q: What are MetaTools' Web plans?
JOHN: Well, first of all, understand that MetaTools is already deeply involved in the Web. Our graphic tools are already some of the most popular graphic tools used to create Web sites today. When you look at the graphic sets of products that people use, you look at Photoshop, Illustrator, maybe Freehand, but you're also looking at Kai's Power Tools, Con-

HOW DOES IT WORK?

Kai's Power Goo consists of six "rooms" or screens where you do all of your work—or play, as the case may be (8.2). The Goo room is where you create your image distortions; the Fusion room lets you composite any two images; the In and Out rooms let you import, save or print images; the Options room lets you set your application preferences; and the Help room provides you with online Goo instructions and advice.

Creating a distorted image with Goo is about as easy as anyone could wish for. To select an image, click on the IN text label to access the IN Room (8.3). From here, click on the appropriate button to acquire your image (depending on whether your image is stored in a digital camera, on a Photo-CD, or saved as a file on your hard drive). You can also always just use an image from one of several supplied image libraries. Once the image is loaded into Goo, the real fun begins.

Clicking on either of the two palettes on the left side of the interface brings up a set of clearly labeled buttons (8.4, 8.5). Click on one of these buttons to select the type of distortion you want. If you selected a button from the first palette, your distortions will be brush-based; simply press and drag within your image area to distort your image. Some of the distor-

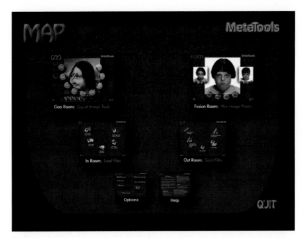

8.2

8.3

volver, Vector Effects, and I've seen a number of Bryce Images up there. The kinds of people who are using us for their Web sites: *Hot Wired, MTV Online,* and other major players in the industry. They're already using our products, so we're already on the Web. Our tools are part of the graphics tool box that people use to create a certain look and feel. Beyond that, we have a series of development projects in-house related to the Web. We announced at E3 our realtime interactive online games with America Online, which are built for the Web as well.

Q: Online games?
JOHN: We believe that it's going to be a long time before there is going to be enough bandwidth to do "twitch-level games." But there are a variety of things that people can play online that can be quite enticing. What we've done is create a unique environment that gives people very compelling strategy games. In the America Online environment, with almost half its business being related to people chatting in forums or private e-mail, and what they call "instant messages," now you have the ability to have a chat with

somebody, and play a compelling strategy game along with them. This is about community building and about having a fun experience at the same time. The way we created our business model for this is that Kai has created these incredible user interfaces that are fun to interact with in these games. The games themselves— we could play point to point, but other people can watch in and be spectators in what I like to call "arena play." Other online people can watch and learn strategy moves, etc. But they can also heckle the players and chat if they want to,

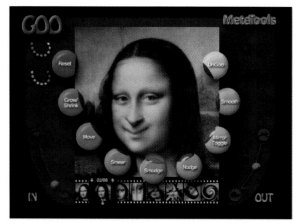

8.4

tions offered include enlarging or shrinking portions of your image, moving image areas around, and smearing and smudging you image as if you were finger painting (in fact, an early candidate for the product name was "Digital FingerPaint") (8.6). If you selected a button from the second palette, your distortions will be image-based. You can, for example, twirl or rotate your image; add static; or squeeze, stretch or spike your image (8.7). Press and drag the effect slider in the lower-left corner of the interface to change the direction and/or intensity of the effect. Mix and match distortions until you are satisfied with the crime against nature that your warped little mind has created.

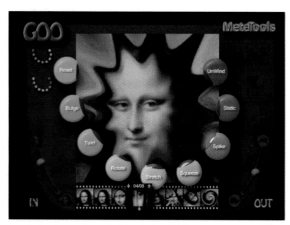

8.5

TIP

You can access two "hidden" effects, Zig Zag and Bump, by holding down the Control key while dragging the effect slider when the Squeeze or Stretch buttons are active.

which is kind of fun. Probably the most important thing is, we're giving the games away for free. Because what we are telling people is, we think this is good enough that, if you like them, we want to give you the games for free, and go ahead and play with them. People will vote on what they want to use online and on the Web environment, and we think these games are good enough that consumers will find them compelling and interesting. Of course, we are going to sponsor tournaments. Up at our own Web site, we are going to be posting

pages about what the games are about, the strategies in playing the games. We will have guest players there all the time that people can challenge and play with and talk to, etc., etc. So again, this gets back to a core philosophy of MetaTools, and that is to do community building.

Q: Now that MetaTools is branching out, going more cross-platform than ever before, MetaTools is probably, eventually going to lose the perception of a lot of graphic artists and professionals of that cool software company that has those

really neat products that not that many people have. And that people that did have them think that all Kai's Power Tools, Vector Effects, those types of things were, very cool products. Whereas Goo is such a consumer-level product it might be not considered as part of that exclusive group. **JOHN:** I would say quite the opposite. We went to the N.A.B. (National Association of Broadcasters) in April, and showed Goo to the highest end professional video people, the people who do broadcast video every day. We could have easily sold a couple thousand copies of Goo at

8.6

8.7

TIP

You can have Goo randomize your keyframes for playback by Control-clicking on the Projector button.

TIP

To create more gradual transitions between keyframes, leave an empty keyframe or two between one distortion and the next.

that show to those professionals, because they immediately recognized the power of what is there, and they recognized that it's also fun. Goo is a product that almost immediately generates an emotional reaction when you play with it. When I bring up Mona Lisa's face, and I say, "You know I've always looked at this kind of little smirk on Mona Lisa and I'd like to see a smile on." And I go [zip-zip] in realtime, and then I make her wink, and I generate a realtime digital movie. It touches people watching the demo emotionally; it makes them laugh. I think there's a "coolness fac-

tor" about that. Enable people to experience creativity. That's what Goo is all about. I'm really excited about what Goo means to the consumer market, because it also means potentially, we're going to start some kid or some 20-, 30-, 40-year old on the road to becoming a professional graphics designer, and maybe, a digital movie maker. And I think that we'll find that over time; I think that's really exciting.

Q: The predominant focus of MetaTools products in the past has been plug-in based. That's shifting to stand-alone appli-

cations. Are the current crop of plug-in products: Convolver, KPT, and Vector Effects, going to evolve into stand-alone applications in the future, or are they going to remain as accessories for other larger, monstrous applications?

JOHN: We look at the marketplace and believe that, fundamentally, our strategic relationships with major players in the industry: Adobe, Macromedia, Autodesk, and others; these relationships are important to MetaTools. That's why people call us the Switzerland of digital imaging, because we've made products and help-

TIP

The keyframes can be put to good use even if you don't want to create an animated movie. Clicking on any empty keyframe saves the current image into that keyframe. Clicking on a full keyframe loads that image into the image canvas. This means that you can use the keyframes to save your image in various states, enabling you to go back to a previous version of your image if you make a mistake. To clean up your keyframes, you can Option-click on them, removing the images stored therein.

To save or print your image, click on the OUT text label to access the OUT Room (8.8). From here you can save your image to disk, print it, save the entire Goo project, or export a Goo animation, all simply by clicking on the appropriate text label.

If you want to create an animated Goo movie, simply click on keyframes (at the bottom of the interface) as you progressively distort the image. To clear a keyframe, either Option-click on it or click on the arrow at the bottom of the frame. To clear several keyframes, press on the arrow at the bottom of the keyframe and drag across the keyframes that you want to clear.

To preview your movie, click on the camera icon in the upper right of the interface. To adjust the playback speed, press on the speed control (in the lower right) and drag towards either the rabbit or the turtle.

In addition to the two sets of distortion buttons, Goo also offers a Fusion room (8.9), where you can create composites of two different images. Composites of several images can be created by saving a two-image composite to disk and then loading it back into the Fusion room for further compositing.

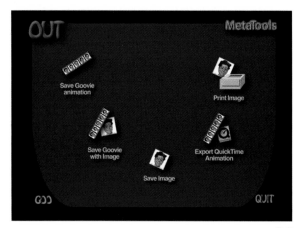

8.8

ed evangelize the API's, so that many different graphic applications could use our tools. We fully intend to continue moving those plug-in applications, and I call them "plug-in applications" because in many cases the amount of code that's in one of our plug-in packages is more than what is in the host application. I mean, when you take a look at Kai's Power Tools 3.0, Gradient Designer is an application plugged in to Photoshop. Texture Explorer is an application plugged in to Photoshop. There are a number of others in there as well. We are going to

evolve those tools to support those platforms. I think it's also right to say that as we develop our own applications, because, as we believe, there's so much virgin snow out there, there's so many new places to develop technology for people, that in a large part, that is where you will continue to see MetaTools develop our applications: in virgin snow. We'll put stakes in the ground, and hopefully people will take a look and say, "They did this right."

GAMES ON AOL

While most people outside of MetaTools have been unaware of this particular project, the Quality Assurance department has been anxiously awaiting a chance to spend a few days (or weeks) playing games for a living. As of this writing, MetaTools is finalizing development of three games to be played over the phone lines via America Online. These are all intriguing strategy games, one of ancient origin and the other two much more recent developments. MetaGo is based on the game of Go and features all of the depth and breadth of this classic strategy game. MetaHex is based on the little-known game of Hex, developed in the 1950s by a Danish poet (according to our sources). The final game, MetaSquares, is based on Squares, a new and thoroughly unique game devised by Scott Kim and presented for the first time in its MetaSquares incarnation.

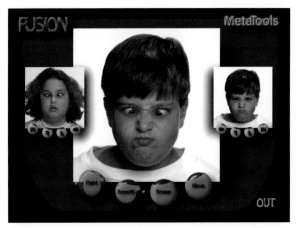

8.9

METAGO

MetaGo (8.10), as mentioned earlier, is a faithful conversion of the classic Strategy game of Go to the online environment. Players alternate placing their stones (white for one player; black for the other) on the game grid. Whenever a stone (or contiguous group of stones belonging to one player) is completely surrounded by stones belonging to another player, the surrounded stones are "captured" and removed from the board. At the end of the game, points are awarded for captured stones and for controlled board "territory." It is a simple game to learn to play but an almost impossible one to master.

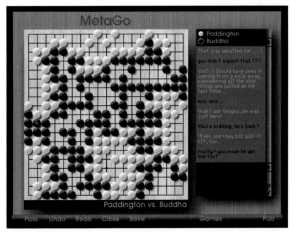

8.10

METAHEX

Another very simple game, MetaHex (8.11) is played by two players (as are all three of the online games), one of whom plays white and owns the left and right sides of the board, and the other of whom plays black and owns the top and bottom of the board. Players alternate claiming hexes, which get marked with the claiming player's color. The goal of the game is to make one unbroken string of hexes connecting your two sides of the board. Players may claim any unclaimed hex whether or not it is adjacent to (or even anywhere near) their other hexes. Obviously, perception and foresight are invaluable traits for success at this game.

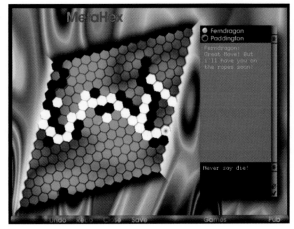

8.11

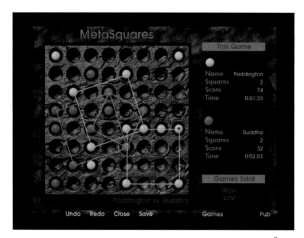

8.12

METASQUARES

MetaSquares (8.12) is also simple to learn in principle but has layers of proficiency. Ian's advice about looking for rotated squares is excellent, because it helps players foresee and then thwart any attempts by their opponents to create "regular" squares. MetaSquares requires more defensive play than either of the other games. Again, two players with different-colored markers take turns claiming points on a grid. Whenever four markers form a perfect square, the game draws the lines and award points based on the size of the square and the number of squares created with a single move. The player with the most points at the end of the game wins. The secret to scoring a lot of points is to use a single move to complete several squares, especially if they are reasonably large squares. The danger, of course, is that your opponent will see the pattern forming and will block the vital grid point, ruining several of your moves.

THE METATOOLS GAMING PHILOSOPHY

One of the overriding themes of any discussion of MetaTools' philosophy on software design and direction is that of community building. MetaTools' strong online presence is designed to provide a community for digital artists and other MetaTools customers—a place where they can exchange ideas, find assistance, and share common experiences. When the decision was made to move forward into the gaming arena, Kai and John knew that they did not want to create "just games." MetaGo, MetaHex, and MetaSquares all reflect this desire. As strategy games, they provide plenty of opportunity for interaction outside of the actual game itself. Players can "chat" while playing; spectators can discuss the game amongst themselves or with the people playing; and aficionados of the games can exchange mail or post messages to the boards, examining moves and strategies at length. As the interfaces for the games demonstrate, these are more than just games—they're conduits for social interaction.

The creators of these three games also felt it was important for players to discover the benefits of shifting their perspective. Ian Gilman, the lead programmer and original designer of the online games, elaborates:

"One of the things people who play these games will learn is to look at each possible move from more than one perspective. In MetaHex, for example, the best offensive move is often the best defensive move, too (or vice versa); a hex that blocks your opponent's path will usually be a good stepping stone for you. MetaSquares also requires shifting perspectives, but in a different way. Beginners will usually only look for regular squares created by vertical and horizontal lines. As they play, though, they'll need to start seeing squares that are rotated. Probably the best advice for new players is to remember that the lines of a square have to be perpendicular to each other, not necessarily to the sides of the board. One of the great things about these games is that they appear simple, but in reality have many levels to them.

"This shifting of perspectives is a theme that can be seen not only in these games—which can be viewed as either as simple games or as devices for promoting community-building within the online environment—but also in most of most of MetaTools' other products—which have continually challenged users to change their way of thinking about what they can do with software and how the design of that software can affect their creativity and productivity.

AMAZON!

For some time now, there has been a tremendous buzz in the industry about "Amazon," MetaTools' *alleged* Photoshop-killer, Live Picture-killer, operating system cum development environment, or whatever (depending on who you talk to). While we obviously can't go into details about exactly what Amazon is, we *can* tell you what it isn't. It isn't a "killer" of any type, nor was it ever intended to be. (In fact there isn't really an "Amazon" per se. Amazon is the term used internally for a collection of software technologies and design ideas that are in the works.) Kai and John have worked long and hard to develop very close business relationships with Adobe, Fractal Design, Apple, and other key industry players. (In fact, when MetaTools was in the process of going public, analysts had a heck of a time finding any "competitors." It seems that just about every company that could be considered a competitor was actually bundling MetaTools products with their own stuff!) Kai's attitude is that Photoshop (for example) is a good product with a huge installed base, and there isn't any reason to try to usurp its position in the market. Instead, MetaTools focuses on the unique and mutually beneficial symbiosis between host application and plug-in and on designing products that, in many ways, create their own market. Kai's Power Goo is a good example of this, as it is the first in a new line of "creative entertainment tools" from MetaTools.

At some point in the future, the technology known as Amazon may (or may not) make its way to the market as a product in itself; but for now, Amazon is a "technology mine," a sort of Xerox PARC for Meta-Tools' imaging wizardry. Again, Kai's Power Goo is a good example of this. Goo began as just one of the many amazing image-manipulation brushes in Amazon. In fact, early on, Goo was named "Kai's Liquid Image" after one of the brushes (the Liquid Image brush) in Amazon.

During one of our conversations, Kai demonstrated the Amazon technology for us. Again, we cannot go into detail; but suffice it to say (and this is not mere marketing hyperbole) that the technology in Amazon is as far ahead of current graphics applications as the Macintosh is ahead of the old Apple II. The good news is that all of this amazing stuff will be available

> **TIP**
>
> To access a cool Easter egg, bring up the About Box/Credits, make sure the Caps Lock key is down, then hold down the Control key. Enjoy!

to us in the form of affordable, accessible, and fun creative tools from MetaTools. The bad news is that it will be made available only when the time is right, and that time may be a long way off.

METATOOLS ON THE WEB

Kai and company have been online almost as long as long as there has been a "line" to be "on." One of the reasons for Kai's notoriety as a Photoshop guru was the posting on America Online of Kai's Power Tips, a vast collection of all sorts of Photoshop tips, tricks, and techniques from one of the undisputed masters of digital imaging. John and Kai built on this base by forming and promoting a robust AOL forum for fans of MetaTools' products and artwork. MetaTools has always had a strong relationship with America Online, as evidenced by the introduction of the online games currently available exclusively through this service. MetaTools still retains a strong presence on America Online and will continue to do so for the foreseeable future.

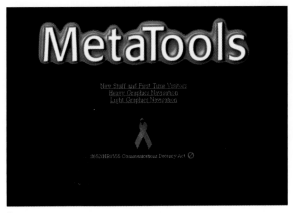

8.13

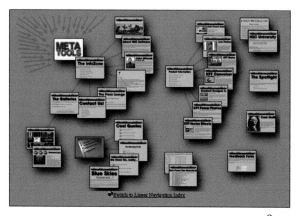

8.14

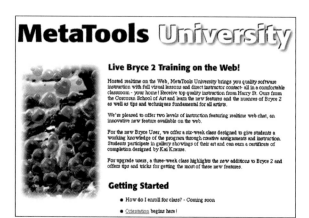

8.15

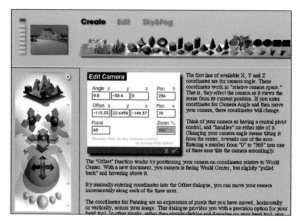

8.16

As the popularity and accessibility of the Internet and the World Wide Web increased over the past few years, the folks at MetaTools realized that the Internet would provide an unprecedented opportunity for them to make their tools, images, and philosophy available to an ever-wider audience. In the summer of 1995, the MetaTools Web site (http://www.metatools.com) officially opened for business (8.13, 8.14). In the year that it's been up, the MetaTools Web site has become the primary source for software patches, updates, software demos, images, and information, with about four times as much usage as MetaTools' AOL Forum. MetaTools is working to bring full-featured chat and messaging capabilities to its Web site, making it a self-contained forum for all things having to do with the company's products, events, and philosophy.

In addition to all of the things that you'd expect to find at the MetaTools Web site, there are also some unexpected goodies. By the time you read this, the company should have implemented procedures to enable you to purchase MetaTools products directly from its Web site. These products include featured filters created specifically for exclusive distribution via the Web site. While final specifications have not yet been completed, the plan is for a "Featured Filter" to be periodically highlighted on the Web site. This filter will not be a part of any other product. Rather, it will be a cool and/or useful filter, small stand-alone application, or other product custom-created for distribution via the MetaTools Web site. This alone promises to make the Web site an exciting place to visit. MetaTools' technical support will also be available in real-time once the full-featured chat and messaging capabilities are implemented. Another unexpected treat is MetaTools University, an online facility for real-time, interactive training on Bryce 2, KPT, and other Meta-Tools products (8.15, 8.16). There will also be a plethora of links to other Web sites for quick and easy access to host application information, private art galleries, philosophical meeting places, and expanded online gaming options.

When you visit the Web site, there are a couple of places you won't want to miss. The first is the image galleries, especially Kai's Image Gallery (8.17). A lot of never-before-seen images from Kai are displayed here; among them are some of his early works. The latest version of Kai's Power Tips (which is frequently updated) is also available exclusively on the MetaTools Web site. The MetaTools University is also a must-see, especially if you have questions about techniques for using MetaTools software or are just interested in advancing your knowledge and increasing your abilities. MetaTools University also has non-MetaTools-specific information, such as general Web page design tips, because a lot of people use MetaTools products when creating their Web pages (8.18). Finally, be sure to check out the 4 Corners area, where you can dive into several different areas of MetaPhilosophy (8.19). The discussions and contemplations in these areas are usually profound, often amusing, and almost always approached from a fresh philosophical angle.

LOOKING AHEAD

In any industry that experiences rapid growth and technological advances similar to the computer software industry, looking ahead is likely to produce predictions of dubious value. And if the software industry itself isn't volatile enough, trying to predict what Kai will think of next is like trying to predict the final topic of a Robin Williams stream-of-consciousness monologue. While we were in the process of writing this book, both Kai and John were kind enough to share with us some of their future plans. Because of the nature of the business, we obviously cannot share specific product plans or timelines; but we can paint a picture of MetaTools' future in fairly broad brush strokes.

As can be expected, new versions will be forthcoming for virtually all of MetaTools' major products. As of this writing, Bryce Pro, the fully animatable version of Bryce 2, is under development and should be available soon. Also as of this writing, Power Photos IV is out, with lots more to come in that series, and a Windows version of Final Effects for Premiere has also been released. Kai definitely wants to release a

8.17

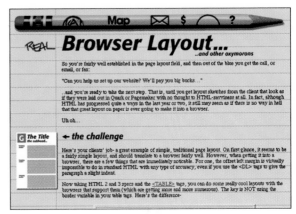

8.18

8.19

new and even more robust version of Convolver (although this hasn't progressed beyond the "Gee, I'd really like to do a new Convolver" stage, so don't pester anyone about it), and development of a new cross-platform version of Vector Effects is already in the works.

Kai's Power Goo is the first in what will undoubtedly be an exciting line of consumer-oriented products. A big part of Kai's overall vision has always been to make the coolest possible tools available to the widest possible audience. Goo is the latest step in that direction, with many more "creative entertainment tools" sure to follow. We can also expect that a lot of the technology showcased in these products will become integral parts of the MetaTools products for professional artists (and vice versa, as shown in the use of streamlined versions of Vector Effects' Twirl and Kai's Power Tools' Glass Lens capabilities in Goo).

Finally, MetaTools will continue to expand its presence on the Internet. The company has ambitious plans for the MetaTools Web site and the MetaTools University and ideas for even more online games.

Whatever the medium, it's a safe bet that Meta-Tools will be on the cutting edge with new ways of working—and playing.

PART 2
STUDIO SECRETS

CHAPTER 9
TYPE MAGIC

Type is such a basic design element that it is often overlooked. But the following pages (and the opposite page's "Type Magic" title, created exclusively for this book by Travis O'Hearn) show that type can be the centerpiece of any illustration. If the first thing viewers first look at in pictures is people, the second thing is type; it gets—and needs—attention.

"ARCADA" BY JOSEPH LINASCHKE

1. Linaschke started with heavy type in a grayscale document to use as the basis of the Illustration "Arcada" (9.1). "Relatively thick letters tend to work best," notes Linaschke.

2. Linaschke then created several new channels, and placed the following in each:

- Channel #1: Copy of the original image
- Channel #2: with Minimum applied to fatten up the letters
- Channel #3: Gaussian blurred and offset slightly
- Channel #4: Offset in the opposite direction
- Set Difference of #4 and #5, Invert, use Levels to darken
- Set Difference of #5 and #6, use Levels to Lighten
- Channel #7: Modify Curves to an "M" shape, Gaussian blur slightly

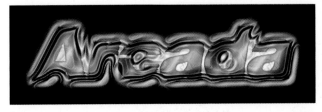

9.1

- Channel #8: Run Find Edges Charcoal (or use the Find Edges fx Charcoal setting)
- Channel #3: Gaussian blur slightly

3. After creating these channels, Linaschke copied the contents of #9 into a new Photoshop-format document called "Displace map.photo." Then he created more channels:

- Channel #2: Run Displacement filter using the file created previously as the displacement map.
- Channel #11: Inverse, minimum just a bit, Gaussian blur a bit.

4. At this point, Linaschke changed the mode of the file to RGB and filled the RGB channel with black. Then he created a new layer and loaded a selection (Channel #10).

5. Linaschke went to channel #9 and copied (using the selection from #10), then pasted in the RGB channel.

6. After pasting, Linaschke loaded #11 as a selection and floated it. Then he created a new layer for the floating selection.

7. Linaschke then tweaked the colors using Levels so that the whites were more of a gray for better results with the next step which uses Gradient Designer's Procedural blends. "The way Gradient Designer's Procedural Blends works is by applying color 100% into the 50% gray areas, and less into the darker and lighter areas," he says. "So, since

9.2

9.3

you probably want your logo/type to stand out, before you run the coloring filter adjust the levels on Layer 2 so that the whites are more middle gray. You may want to use the eyedropper to measure amounts here. How much highs and lows you leave intact is up to you."

8. To make the colors fold into the image, Linaschke ran KPT Gradient Designer (9.2) on Layer 2. He's included a preset (shown) on the *Official KPT Studio Secrets* CD-ROM that he used, though you can use any gradient you'd like. Just make sure the Procedural Blends option is selected.

9. Finally, Linaschke loaded #12 as a selection and used Levels to darken the selection, making the edges appear darker. "This should help define the logotype edges. That's it!!! You should now see a bubbleous puddle of metallic goo with your logo or type wrapped perfectly around it. Cool, eh?!"

"TYPE MAGIC" BY TRAVIS O'HEARN

The "Type Magic" illustration (9.3) (see the first page of this chapter for a larger, more detailed view) was created using Vector Effects first, then enhanced with Kai's Power Tools, and finally touched up with KPT Convolver. It's a classic case of how the various KPT tools are used at different stages of an illustration.

OVERVIEW

1. O'Hearn started his illustration with a simple pencil sketch, to get the feel of the layout before going digital.

2. The five major elements were considered individually: The word "Type," the two ovals, the word "Magic," the top hat, and the background. O'Hearn decided that the two words and the hat should be created in Adobe Illustrator before moving into pixels.

3. Because the end illustration would be about 25MB, O'Hearn set out to compose each portion separately from the others, "to reduce the time spent waiting for some of the more basic tasks in Photoshop, like selecting."

"TYPE"

1. The word "TYPE" was set in Adobe Illustrator, with the letters converted into outlines.

2. To give the letters a more organic feel, O'Hearn roughened them 1 percent, 10 per inch (9.4).

3. O'Hearn opened the Illustrator file in Photoshop as a grayscale image to keep the overall file size small.

4. After creating two duplicates of the original image, O'Hearn changed the channels into a high-light mask and a shadow mask.

5. O'Hearn converted the image into RGB, and then filled the letters with a custom texture from Texture Explorer 3.0. "Texture Explorer not only lets me experiment with different textures, but the ability to zoom in and out indefinitely can create new textures in and of themselves."

6. Finally, O'Hearn applied the highlight and shadow masks to the letters, giving them a subtle 3D effect (9.5).

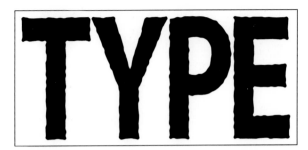

9.4

9.5

THE HAT

1. O'Hearn wanted the hat to be more of a back-ground element, something that you might notice only after looking at the illustration for a while. He used KPT Vector Effects' 3D Transform to Extrude a dark circle in Illustrator.

2. Because 3D Transform is better at creating the exterior surface of 3D object than its interior, O'Hearn took the cylinder he had created and masked it with an oval, giving the illusion of the inside of the hat.

3. O'Hearn created the brim by creating a slight extrusion (not visible in the final picture) on a larger circle, and then placing that circle behind the masked "interior."

4. Finally, O'Hearn scaled up the hat so that only the upper portion of it would be visible (9.6).

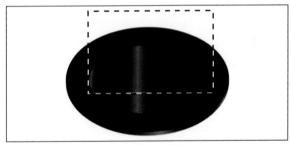

9.6

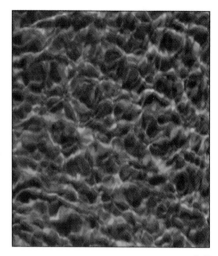

9.7

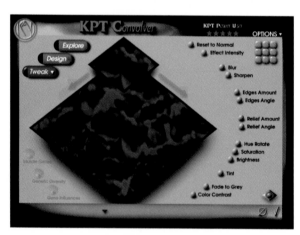

9.8

9.9

THE BACKGROUND

1. O'Hearn decided against using Texture Explorer for the background of the image early on. "I wanted a natural, organic feel that I knew TE wouldn't quite create for me. So Instead of using a texture in this manner, I dug into KPT Power Photos, finding a texture-based background (9.7) that I liked."

2. Unfortunately, the image that O'Hearn liked was too light. He used KPT Convolver to darken the image and color it a little differently (9.8).

THE EGGS

1. "I wanted an object to separate the words 'TYPE' and 'Magic', so that the two words could each stand on their own, yet be connected," O'Hearn states, "I eventually decided on two objects, not side by side, but aligned vertically."

2. O'Hearn created a custom Sphere with KPT Spheroid Designer, using three light sources (9.9). To achieve the oval shape (as opposed to perfectly circular), he made an oblong elliptical selection.

3. With the oval still selected, O'Hearn duplicated it below.

MAGIC

1. "I wanted the word 'Magic' to really stand out from the rest of the illustration. I sorta went overboard with it, but the end result is stunning." O'Hearn typed the word into Illustrator, converted it to outlines, then used KPT Warp Frame to give it a slightly bowed look.

2. O'Hearn then extruded "Magic" with 3D Transform (9.10), using a high perspective setting. "When you combine the curved appearance from Warp Frame with straight-back extrusion and 100 percent perspective, the result is that the art appears to have a slightly bowed look."

3. O'Hearn then opened the Illustrator file in Photoshop, where he selected the face of the word Magic, and applied a gradient from KPT Gradient

Designer. He took advantage of the Layer Bin to create 3 overlapping gradients with various Glue settings (9.11).

Finally, O'Hearn assembled each component piece by piece into the final illustration.

"S'S" BY RAY TERRILL

Ray Terrill created "S's" (9.12) for a typography article cover page. "I wanted to explore just how far you could go with one basic shape," he says. And that he did, using not just a capital "S," but one typeface as well.

"Vector Effects sparked the idea of the unlimited possibilities that could be created with one base object," notes Terrill, "After that, I knew that Kai's Power Tools and Convolver would finish the illustration, getting rid of the vectory sort of feel it had to it in Illustrator."

"S" AS IN "VECTOR"

1. Terrill started by placing an Adobe Garamond SemiBold letter "S" smack dab in the middle of the page and converting it into outlines. He experimented with several different positions and duplicates before he arrived at the final layout (9.13). He used the long diagonal bar of the "S" to create both a division to the page and a red highlighting bar. At this point he was ready to move onward, confident of both his color scheme and his base design.

2. Next, Terrill started using various Vector Effects filters to achieve the different effects for specific S's. First he applied KPT Neon to the red bar, while retaining the red fill of the shape. Because KPT

9.11

9.12

9.10

9.13

Neon zaps the fill color, he made a copy of the path, pasted it behind the art, and applied the first pass of KPT Neon to that back-most path. The first time, he applied KPT Neon at 100 percent Brightness with a width of about 30 points. For the next pass, Terrill changed the color of another pasted path to a blue and applied KPT Neon at 60 points. For the last pass, he pasted another path in the back, changed the color to Yellow, and the width of the neon tube to 200 points.

3. The second application of Vector Effects was to the large "top" of the "S" that appeared along the bottom of the page. Terrill selected it and applied the Distort⇨Roughen filter at 0 percent with three segments each inch. This was necessary to supply more detail to the path without manually inserting points. He then applied KPT Sketch to the path by repeatedly using the Color Stroke option and applying varying amounts. All those paths generated by KPT Sketch were the same color. Terrill wanted some of them to vary in color, so he selected some and applied KPT ColorTweak to them, using the Random option with only the Hue slider changed slightly.

4. The third application of Vex was to the black "S" that forms the "insignia" of the entire piece. The "S" was selected and KPT ShadowLand's

Zoom Shadow was applied. How did Terrill get the different colors? He says, "Most users of Vector Effects don't realize that you have total—I mean total—control over your colors in several of the big filters," Terrill says. "In ShadowLand, you can choose both the "from" and "to" colors; you can make each color a variation of the original object color, or you can use totally different colors. I opted to use different colors in this section of the illustration." Terrill used 16 steps (the default) without the Connect Steps option on to achieve each of the three spinaways that come out of the left side of the black "S."

5. To give the image more depth, Terrill added the black outlines later in Illustrator by using the KPT Inset filter repeatedly, then applying another filter, Doodle Jr. (available only with the Macworld Illustrator 6 Bible) to mutate the paths slightly.

6. The last pieces to be added to the illustration before it was rasterized in Photoshop were the little trail of multicolored S's and the big black "tail" placed at the very back of the Illustration. The Illustration was then masked off into a rectangle for faster rasterization in Illustrator.

"S" AS IN "PIXEL"

1. Rasterizing the Illustrator document in Photoshop into a 20.1MB RGB file took over two hours, due to the complexity of the original vector artwork.

2. The upper right corner of the image looked silly in white, so Terrill copied a large chunk of the image and pasted it into the white corner. He then applied Vortex Tiling and Convolver to the paste pixels to offset them a bit.

3. To fill the "S" in with color, while keeping in mind that the goal of this image was to use only the S's he began with, Terrill copied the entire image and pasted it inside, darkening those pixels with Levels.

4. To give the dark lower left some texture, Terrill used KPT Spheroid Designer to create several "Random Spheres." In order to vary the appearance and size of the spheres within the selection, he checked the Use Mutation box in the packing menu

9.14

and picked Color and Rotation in the Mutation menu. That's all fine and dandy, but what really makes this image stand out is the "glass" marble look. This shows in the amazing glass spheres (a different set is shown in figure 9.14).

5. For the remainder of the Illustrator, Terrill used KPT Convolver on different selections of the image, choosing Relief and Hue changes, that "drastically changed the appearance of the image, from the sullen, flat reds into a green undertone that really suits the image much better," he notes.

"$75" BY TED ALSPACH

Ted Alspach created "$75" (9.15) by using Vector Effects with Illustrator and then bringing the image into Photoshop, where he added texture.

FAKE CHIPS

1. In order to keep the complexity of the chips to a minimum (just extruding the text in 3D Transform alone would take hours),Ted designed them so that only the edges were extruded. In other words, the green disc—along with the "Painted" edges—were copied and extruded alone in KPT 3D Transform, away from the detailed top of the chips.

2. To create the "lid" (the tops) of the chips that had detail at exactly the right angle, Ted brought the tops into 3D transform; but they weren't extruded. Instead, he used the exact same settings, from X, Y, and Z to Perspective, but changed the Extrude amount to 0.

3. Once again, to keep the complexity to a minimum, the original chips were not beveled when they were extruded. Instead, a darker band of green was used around the outside edge to simulate a bevel. A lighter band was used on the inside to simulate the opposite bevel.

4. The little "bez" images looked quite flat initially, so Ted used KPT Emboss ever so slightly to emboss them.

5. To stack the chips, Ted simply copied them up and offset them just a bit until they appeared to be stacked.

6. After rasterizing the chips in Photoshop, Ted applied Pixelfx to the edges to give them a sort of texture. He uses the Pixelfx lens quite often when objects are looking too flat or vectory. It's a quick fix, not nearly as detailed or interesting as what can be achieved with Texture Explorer, but it can be just as fulfilling to the end illustration.

AMUG COVER ART BY DONNA TROY

The thick-textured-goo AMUG logo (9.16) was created by Donna Troy for an AMUG magazine cover.

1. The original art was created in Adobe Illustrator. Troy first drew the letters in stick fashion with the Pen tool. Then she selected all the letters, filled them with Red, and applied KPT Neon at 100 percent Brightness, and 20 points.

2. On a layer below the text, Troy then drew several short squiggly lines with the Freehand tool. She filled those lines with random color via KPT

9.15

9.16

ColorTweak, and applied KPT ShadowLand's Halosity shadow to them. Troy explains, "The fundamental difference between Neon and Halosity is that Neon groups all the created paths together, while Halosity, and all of the shadow options, blend the paths together as they're created," notes Troy. "In this way, it appears that the squiggles get thicker at the same depth. Using Neon would've caused one entire squiggle to be in front of another, and so on."

9.17

9.18

3. After rendering the image in Photoshop, Troy achieved the textured, thick paint effect by Applying Convolver's Relief function to the entire image.

JOHN STEWART'S "FLARE"

"Flare" (9.17) by John Stewart is a logo created for a comic book character. John's aim was to get a look that was "onyx surrounded by gold." Using the large number of options in Vector Effects, he was able to achieve this look in Adobe Illustrator.

1. Stewart set the type in Illustrator, then converted it into outlines. He knew he would need two pieces—one for the outside outline and another for the interior color—so he made a duplicate of the type and grouped it.

2. Stewart Applied KPT Inset to the duplicate at -7 points and then made a compound path of both the outline and the inner paths. This created the "frame."

3. Next, Stewart took the frame into KPT 3D Transform and added one-point bevels. To achieve the muted metal quality, he changed the white and ambient lights to a light and dark gold color and lowered their intensity.

4. Because the black section had to be placed "between" the extruded outline and the bevel, Stewart had to do the extrusion separately, but only after the bevel was created. Until that point, he would not have any art that he could use to duplicate the extrusion exactly where the bevel ended (all KPT 3D Transform bevels appear on the outside of the artwork). Stewart copied the beveled art, United it, and then cleaned up the stray points generated by Unite. He then extruded this art to form the base. All three base pieces are different sizes at this point (9.18).

5. The three pieces were brought together, but the front of the outline wasn't shiny yet; it was still a solid goldish color. Stewart gave it a shine by implementing the following steps.

THE GOLD FACE

1. Stewart moved the front plate of the outline exactly 100 points above the rest of the art. By moving it an exact distance, he could place the finished piece back into position more easily.

2. Above the front plate, Stewart created a blend consisting of about seven rectangles, with colors sampled from the extrusion of the finished art.

3. With the blend selected, Stewart applied Vector Effects KPT Vector Distort to the blend, using several different Spherize and Swirl influences. The result (9.19) appears much more organic than a standard Illustrator gradient.

4. Stewart masked the blend with the front plate, then moved the front plate back down 100 points to form the final logo.

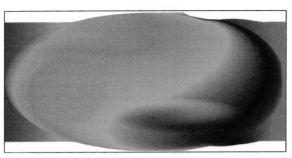

9.19

THE ULTIMATE TYPE MACHINE

Vector Effects is the ultimate type machine, and when combined with Kai's Power Tools and Convolver, the typographical possibilities are endless.

The House of Asterio

By Todd DeMelle

based on the short story by Jorge Luis B

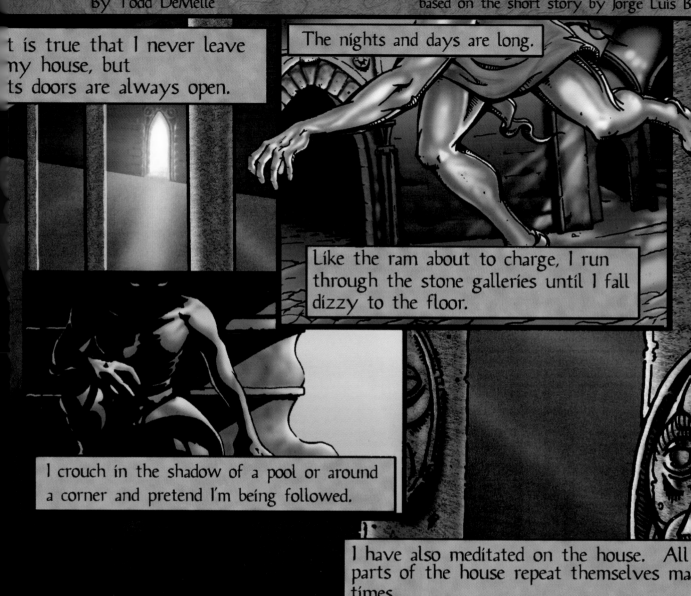

It is true that I never leave my house, but its doors are always open.

The nights and days are long.

Like the ram about to charge, I run through the stone galleries until I fall dizzy to the floor.

I crouch in the shadow of a pool or around a corner and pretend I'm being followed.

I have also meditated on the house. All parts of the house repeat themselves ma times.

Everything is repeated many times, but two things in the world seem to only once: above, the intricate sun; below, Asterion.

CHAPTER 10
MIXING AND MATCHING MEDIA

Creating a killer image—whether for viewing in print, on-screen, or on the Web—often requires the use of several tools. For any given project you may mix and match filter effects within any KPT application, use features across the entire MetaTools product line, or (as is often the case) use *all of the above* in combination with both bitmap- and vector-based products such as Photoshop and Illustrator. The techniques in this chapter focus on the ways in which artists have combined digital resources for a variety of target media from ink to pixels.

"ARTWORKS STUDIO"

Joseph Jones created this logo (10.1) for his own business by using both Vector Effects and Kai's Power Tools. Because this logo would be used in both print and on screen, it required special consideration throughout the design process. It also required both pixel and vector processing. Jones started with a rough pencil sketch (10.2) of the artwork.

EXTRUSION OF THE GEAR WITH VECTOR EFFECTS

1. "Initially I was going to attempt to extrude my original Illustrator line art (10.3) in Adobe Dimensions, but I found this task easily controllable and much better suited for Vector Effects," Jones says.

10.1

10.2

10.3A Final flat line art: Copy implemented in KPT Vector Effects

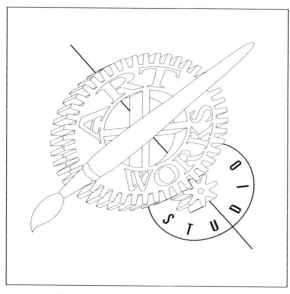

10.3B Final line art for Photoshop: Gears were extruded using 3D Transform

2. Jones extruded the gear with Vector Effects' 3D Transform. As a rule, if you have a fast system, you can view all the changes "live" in two ways. Jones would normally view the artwork in full color (Command-3), and have the Caps Lock key pressed. The Caps Lock key shows the effects of the sliders as they are being dragged, as opposed to displaying changes only after the sliders have been released.

3. To ensure that the text matched the gear, Jones selected it and used 3D Transform with the same settings he used to extrude the gear, except with no extrusion. You can ensure that these values will be the same by saving them as a preset during the "extrusion" phase. "I had attempted this seemingly simple effect in other type manipulation and vector applications, but Vector Effects ended up being the best tool for the job," he notes.

GIVING LIFE TO THE BRUSH

1. To achieve the subtle blends in the wood handle and the chrome effect (10.4), Jones used both Gradient Designer (for the soft blended wood tones and chrome-like colors) and Texture Explorer (for wood grain and the chrome shape variations).

2. Careful inspection of the brush reveals that Jones added an extra touch of realism by adding a pseudo-reflection at the bottom of the brush. For this, he needed to select the main portion of each section of the brush separately and apply a different gradient to each of those portions.

3. "I utilized some of the most complex texture mapping, lighting effects, and channel work to get the brush to look as good as possible," Jones states. He used various gradients applied in Grayscale mapburst mode to achieve the end results.

4. The bristles required a different technique entirely. Jones hand painted the bristles and then used Texture Explorer and added the multicolored paint. He used a custom gradient as the source for the texture. If you look very, very closely, you'll see the remnants of a Texture Explorer-like design.

The texture used in the gear is examined in the following chapter.

"ARGON ZARK! (PAGE 27)"

This comic book page (10.5) created by Charley Parker has strong undertones (some would say overtones) of Kai's Power Tools, utilizing several different filters. The comic book was designed primarily to be viewed on-screen, although, as you can tell, the printed version works quite well.

10.4

PANEL ONE: EVERYTHING'S DISTORTED!

1. The first two panels used the same background as that used for the "page 19" comic (10.6). Hard to tell, eh? That's because Parker took some liberties with the background of each panel to provide the distortion effect he was looking for. The original background was created in Bryce, except for the flowers and foliage, which Parker painted in.

10.5

10.6

10.7

2. Parker manipulated the first panel background (10.7) by telescoping the entire image with KPT Video Feedback.

3. "I made various circular selections to which I applied KPT Twirl and/or Photoshop's ZigZag filter," says Parker.

4. Parker created Argon's vest and glasses, filled them with custom textures in KPT Texture Explorer, and then adjusted them slightly with Photoshop's Dodge and Burn tools.

PANEL TWO: CYBERT TRIES TO GET LUCKY

1. Parker rotated the background from "page 19" 90 degrees for panel two (10.7).

2. He then manipulated the background with KPT Planar Tiling in the Perspective Tiling mode before rotating it back 90 degrees. A technique often used by digital artists is to transform an image in one way or another (anything from Scaling, to Polar to Rectangular, to Rotating, as in this instance), then performing some sort of effect (Planar Tiling in this instance) before reversing the previous transformation. This results in effects that take a "filter" through an entirely different process, giving the artists much more flexibility than dealing with the filters on a standard linear basis.

3. The shadows (behind Cybert and the server) were hand-drawn selections darkened with Photoshop's Hue and Saturation's Lightness slider.

4. Parker used a different texture from Texture Explorer for Argon's vest in panel two.

PANEL THREE: DON'T LOOK NOW, ARGON, BUT . . .

1. Parker rendered the monster "Badnasty-JumpJump" in color, then overlaid it with a KPT Texture Explorer texture at 60 percent opacity.

2. The Background behind BadnastyJumpJump was selected, and Parker filled it with another Texture Explorer texture.

3. Argon's vest is once again another texture. "In fact, Argon's vest is a different KPT Texture Explorer texture in every panel throughout the entire strip," Parker says.

ILLUSTRATOR A DOG?

Brian Strauss created "Old Dog" (10.8) to highlight some of the features in Vector Effects. He also wanted to create an illustration that combined pixels and vectors.

THE CAVE PAINTING

1. Strauss found an image to be the basis of "Old Dog" while doing some miscellaneous Web surfing. This image (10.9) was downloaded from a French cave art Web site.

2. After working with the file for some time, Strauss decided that he couldn't use it in its current state. He traced over the original image with a Wacom tablet, modifying it slightly as he went.

10.8

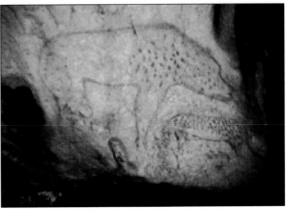

10.9

10.10

10.11

10.12

3. The background of the "painting" was taken from a scanned-in photo of a boulder. Strauss merged the two together to achieve the final base image (10.10).

PIXELS TO VECTORS

1. Strauss used Adobe Streamline on the entire image, changing it from pixels to vectors in just a few minutes. The default settings in Adobe Streamline almost always need to be massaged before an acceptable result can be gained. In this case, Strauss went through several attempts at different settings before an acceptable image was created.

2. In Adobe Illustrator, Strauss cut away the left side of the wolf (using Illustrator 6.0's Knife tool) and started working with the right side only. He made a few modifications and prepared to extrude the artwork (10.11).

3. Strauss only extruded the outline of the wolf with Vector Effects. This resulted in fewer paths than would be created otherwise with 3D Transform if all the paths had been extruded.

4. The other, central paths were transformed with 3D Transform without extruding them, employing the same settings used for extruding the frame, but with the Extrude slider reset to zero.

5. Strauss applied KPT Emboss to the central paths to achieve a lumpy, cracked look.

6. To fill in the few white areas that Streamline left, Strauss created a KPT ShatterBox background that he placed behind the dog. This completed the vector portion of the dog (10.12).

7. Finally, Strauss combined the two halves in Photoshop to produce the final image. In order to get the Illustrator half into Photoshop, Strauss rasterized the Illustrator file in Photoshop at the same size and resolution of the Photoshop portion, in RGB mode (which matched the RGB mode of the Photoshop half). Strauss then copied the Illustrator half into the Photoshop half document, which he had enlarged using Photo-shop's Canvas Size function.

HTTP://WWW.BEZIER.COM

One of the first things Ted did with KPT 3 was to use Texture Explorer and KPT Seamless Welder to create a tile for the background of his Web page (10.13). (Ted had just learned about the tile function in HTML and decided to take full advantage of this capability.)

1. Ted started by going to KPT Texture Explorer and, well, exploring until he found a pattern he liked. He notes "I ended up zooming out about 20 times on a particular texture until I got the look I wanted."

2. Because the texture was a little too intense for the background, especially if the text was going to be black, Ted used KPT Convolver to adjust the tint and the contrast of the texture. "Doing all the adjusting in one dialog box isn't just easier, it saves time as well," he says.

3. The tile was selected, and KPT Seamless Welder was applied to make the edges less apparent.

4. Finally, Ted made several variations of the original tile in different hues. He ended up using the same texture for different "areas" within his Web site. Shown here (10.14) is part of the Illustrator-related area, which has a different color than the pink background of the Bézier site.

HITTING THE DIGITAL TARGET

The most successful images are born from a clear vision of whether they will ultimately be displayed in print, pixels, or both, as well as the creator's willingness (and ability) to cross toolsets and formats in their preparation. Many of the artists featured in *Official Kai's Power Tools Studio SECRETS* have had the foresight to prepare their images for both screen and print using numerous filters and vector-bitmap technology marriages. The results extend KPT boundaries even further.

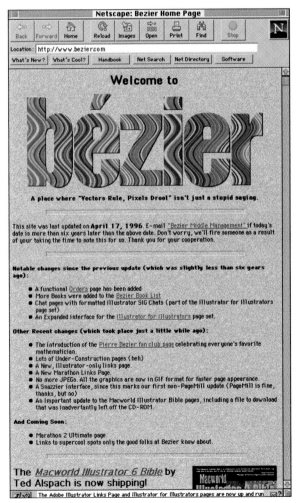

10.13

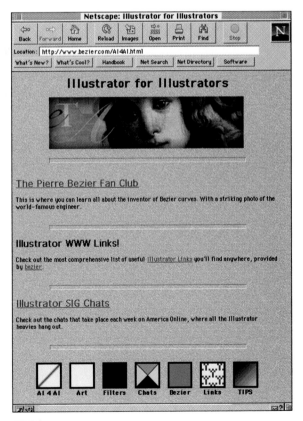

10.14

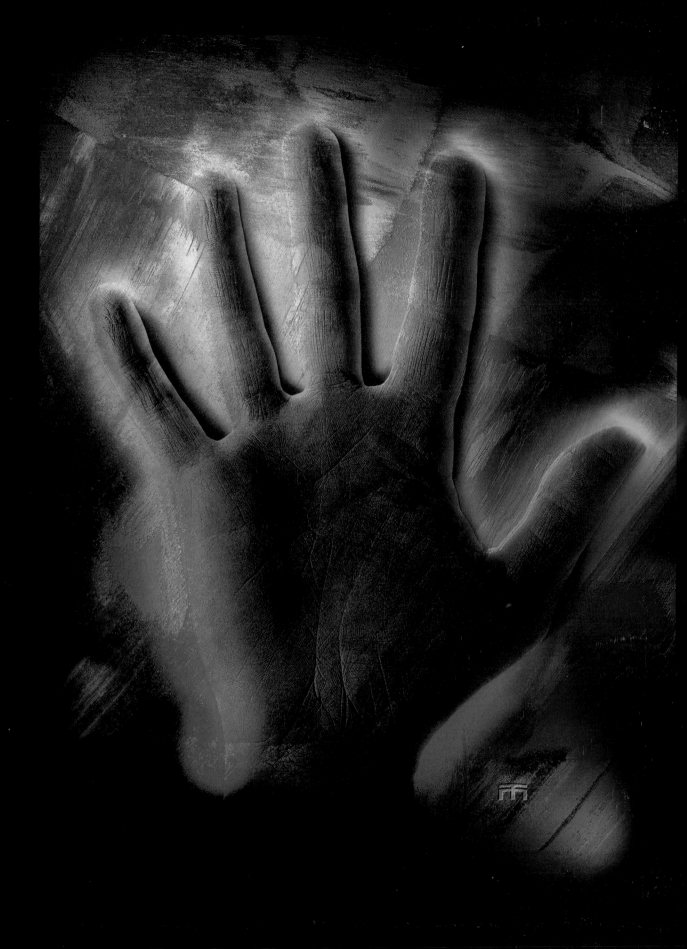

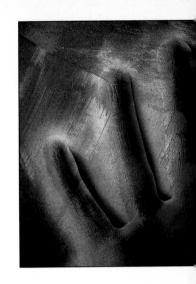

CHAPTER 11
PATTERNS, TEXTURES, AND BACKGROUNDS

P atterns, textures, and backgrounds are the elements of illustrations that give life, providing depth and realism. Bryce, Kai's Power Tools, Vector Effects, and Convolver each can create and manipulate these elements—some in ways so subtle you wouldn't notice them if we hadn't pointed them out to you (and we wouldn't have noticed them had the artists not pointed them out to us).

"INFLAMMATORY RESPONSE" BY EDMOND ALEXANDER

Edmond Alexander created "Inflammatory Response" (11.1) to show a common occurrence in veterinary medicine close-up. Extremely close-up. Alexander describes it as "foreign invaders (antigens) attaching to specific receptor sites on a cell membrane. Arachiodonic acid is released as the inflammatory response begins and your pet starts scratching and chewing at his skin." Ick.

SPHEROIDS EVERYWHERE

1. Alexander used KPT Spheroid Designer to create most of this illustration. A single light source set to a high highlight value was used for all the spheres.
2. Although the single highlight source remained the same for all spheres, other lights (specific to each sphere) were added or modified as needed.

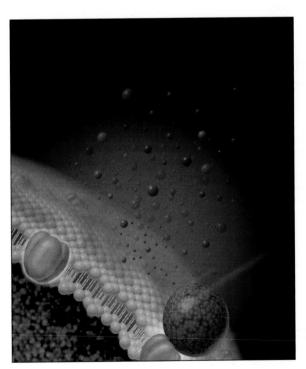

11.1

HAND PAINTING
Michael Tompert

147

11.2

3. Instead of using a bump map for the frontmost (magenta) sphere, Alexander created a document filled with spheres that was similar to 11.2.

4. Alexander designed another spheroid-based sphere (11.3) around this sphere-filled document. He used a sphere with no opacity and a strong light source to create a larger sphere in KPT Spheroid Designer. He then cut out the corners using the Elliptical Marquee tool in Photoshop and placed the sphere in his evolving document.

BILL ELLSWORTH'S TEXTURAL VISIONS

When you look at most of Bill Ellsworth's illustrations, you might wonder what drives a seemingly normal person to create such abstract, unusual images. It turns out that Ellsworth just loves playing with the array of MetaTools products; and the results, while atypical, are also both intriguing and pleasant to look at.

"96-2-9"

Ellsworth created this image (11.4) by taking a not-too-interesting Bryce image and selectively distorting paths with Photoshop's Wave filter. Then he used Twirl in various smaller areas to create twisty distortions, Spheroid Designer to add little spheres as a form of texture in some of the broader areas, and Gradient Designer to provide texture and color to objects that might otherwise appear flat and lifeless. Texturizing these "flat" areas can convert an otherwise sterile-looking image into one with life and vibrancy. "To add a little more interest to the surface," he says, "I [added] a couple Knots that I created with Lloyd Burchill's great Knot generating program, available at http://hyperarchive.lcs.mit.edu/HyperArchive/Archive/gst/grf/knot-35.hqx." It is the amazing compilation of these "little" details, from the knots to the twirls to the various tiny spheres used for texture that give Bill Ellsworth's images such personality.

11.3

"96-2-19"

Ellsworth create this stunning image (11.5) from basic shapes he generated with KPT Video Feedback. He selected small and large areas of the image with the Lasso tool and also used the Video Feedback filter on those areas. "I used Convolver to create an overlaid patina of mother-of-pearl," he adds. Ellsworth then finished off the image with Spheroid Designer by adding tiny, almost-similar spheres to create a sort of bubbled texture in various areas.

At first glance, this image appears perfectly symmetrical. The longer you look at it, however, the more asymmetrical it becomes (even the center is off-center).

11.4

"96-2-25"

Ellsworth says he created the texture of this image (11.6) by scanning in "a crummy photograph of an old painting of mine and applying Adobe's Lighting Effects, KPT 3's Gradient Designer, and Convolver to make it a bit more interesting." The image in the background is made up of Knot pict images (described previously) modeled in several different ways:

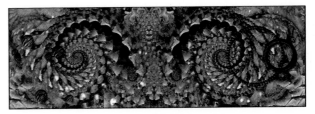

11.5

Glass Lens had been applied to give some of the art a curved, extruded look with a tiny amount of highlight. It is this effect that makes the objects in the lower right appear to be floating above the rest of the image.

Spheroid Designer's ability to create an almost ridiculous number of spheres in a given area was taxed as Ellsworth spread these spheroids across the entire image, concentrating them more tightly in some areas than others.

Texture Explorer, in conjunction with selections made by Ellsworth, was used to simulating the almost tie-dyed color scheme of the surface. A different, darker and more mottled texture was used for the areas that are kind of "under" the main surface.

Convolver was used with just a touch of "find edges" and "relief amount" to change the flat, gooey texture into one that resembles a brittle plastic. The spheroids were affected in much the same way, so instead of bubbles the surface appears to have coin-like indents.

11.6

IF ONLY THEY'D HAD KPT IN 1972 . . .

Timothy Drake's "Trippin'" (11.7) was created by
scanning in an old album cover and trying to bring
the image into the 90s while leaving the band far,
far behind.

11.7

11.8

❙ THINK I LOVE YOU

1. Drake started by separating the group from
their background and sticking them on their own
layer. This ensured that the group wouldn't end up
getting accidentally mangled while he concen-
trated on the background.

2. Working with only the background now, Drake
applied KPT Video Feedback using Video mode at
full strength, with no angle, and a glue setting of
Difference. "The Difference setting makes all the
difference in many of the KPT Tools," he says. "It's
the Glue option I use most after Normal."

3. Drake then created a special channel (11.8). In
this channel, he designed a black-to-white blend
at a slight angle. He then turned difference Mode
on again and applied KPT Twirl to the channel,
using about 65 percent Opacity.

4. Drake used that channel to select more Video
Feedback, this time with Normal Glue and a
large angle.

5. To modify the outside of the image, and not
the center, Drake created another selection channel out of a radial blend.

6. He used this channel with KPT Edge fx to produce edges that become more 3D as the image
fades out to its edges.

7. "At this point I was happy with the background, so I changed my focus to the foreground,
which was the band members," Drake explains.
"I wanted a certain effect, which KPT Convolver
was perfect for."

8. Drake massaged the band members in
Convolver until they matched his ideal look (both
Ted and Steve are still wondering how that look
could be "ideal"), then flattened the image into the
final piece.

THE SNAKE AND THE SPIDER

"The Rusty Snake" (11.9) fits nicely into this chapter because Victor Claudio began this work more as a water experiment than as an actual image. "Spidermon Too" is a related piece with some interesting textures as well.

RUSTING THE SNAKE

1. Claudio filled the background of a square canvas with the "LiquidityCity" preset in KPT Texture Explorer.

2. Claudio used Convolver to adjust the different parameters until he got the proper color and brightness balance and exactly the "right blue."

3. "I achieved a better water texture using Photoshop's ZigZag, Wave and Ripple filters," he says.

4. To offset the softness of the water effect, Claudio added a new layer with a "Pillowy Copper" Texture Explorer preset to a smaller square and set in the center of the document. He added noise for contrast.

5. Claudio made the edges of the central square uneven by using the Eraser tool and used the same tool to create the hole in the lower right.

6. The yellow screw head was made with another Texture, and then modified with Glass Lens normal.

7. Claudio drew the snake with the Lasso tool, and filled it with the preset texture "Sharp Scales."

"SPIDERMON TOO"

1. "Spidermon Too" (11.10) "almost drew itself," Claudio says. He produced the body of the spider by experimenting with the Elliptical Marquee tool and the KPT Glass Lens Normal filter.

2. The legs were drawn with the Lasso tool, while the Pencil tool was used to draw the hairs and spider web.

3. After make a few adjustments, Claudio used Bloodpine vertical, a texture from KPT Texture Explorer, to create the background.

11.9

11.10

LESTER YOCUM'S "GRANITE FIRE"

Lester Yocum created "Granite Fire" (11.11) with several different textures from KPT Texture Explorer. He used the same texture in each of the granite slabs, selecting the edges of each individually and lighting or darkening them with Photoshop's Levels controls. He created the background from a modified fire texture preset. The plastic-looking balls, which appear in stark contrast to the granite and fire, were designed in KPT Spheroid Designer with no texture whatsoever (and that is a texture by itself).

"METAROSE" BY JOSEPH LINASCHKE

"MetaRose" (11.12) by Joseph Linaschke is an example of a gorgeous application of both Convolver and KPT Video Feedback. The metallic look of the image and subtle drop shadow give the image the appearance of a photograph.

The metallic look was achieved with the Edges and saturation sliders in Convolver. The edges were increased and the saturation was decreased enough to achieve a smoothed, brushed metal appearance.

11.11

THE ART OF TEXTOSITY

Patterns and Textures can either subtly add interest to
an image or overwhelm the image, becoming more of
the focus than the objects within the images themselves. The result depends on several criteria, including the severity of the textures, the color intensity,
and the area affected with a particular texture.
Accomplished digital artists don't "know" what texture is right—they experiment until they achieve the
intended effect.

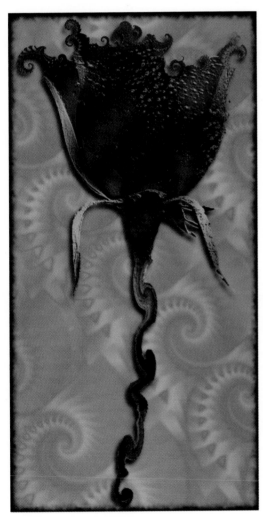

11.12

CHAPTER 12
TAKING KPT TO THE NEXT LEVEL

When Kai talks about KPT and the MetaTools mindset, taking an idea to "the next level" is one of the recurring themes. Rather than settle for the first image or technique that comes up, he says, you can achieve extraordinary results by adding only an extra step or two to make an image truly unique. Whether that extra step is an application of another filter, a final channel operation, or even using a completely different software package is for each of us to decide as we try to bring our own images to that "next level."

For each image in this chapter, the artist has combined techniques from several different sources: different MetaTools products, different tools within a single MetaTools product, or one or more MetaTools product used in conjunction with different graphics applications.

"TAMMY" BY BRUCE H. GLIDER

The first image we'll look at is Bruce H. Glider's "Tammy" (12.1). "Tammy" combines the best of several different Kai's Power Tools techniques with Photoshop's image-manipulation capabilities and a touch of RayDream Designer rendering. This image is built around a modified photograph of a woman's face. KPT Spheroid Designer spheres and KPT Vortex Tiling effects frame her, a RayDream Designer cube accents the lower-right corner, and KPT Gradient Designer and KPT Texture Explorer effects frame the entire image.

12.1

1. The woman's face has a uniquely blurred quality reminiscent of Japanese animation. To achieve this effect, Gilder first copied the face, then blurred the original image at 50 percent. He then pasted in the copy of the original image as a new layer using a Darken mode channel operation. Additional touch-up work was done on the face to remove unwanted elements and to further stylize the rings on her fingers.

2. He used an inner frame of black to separate the woman's face from the brightly colored background of pinks, yellows, and oranges. This frame was accented with two vortex effects in the lower-left and upper-right sectors. Unwanted portions of the vortex effects have been erased to reveal the underlying image and/or background.

3. Gilder then created the bar in the upper-right corner. He used KPT Spheroid Designer to create a single white sphere with red marbling. A dark, glossy red sphere was added to this initial white sphere to create a red and white button. This button was then copied and pasted onto the bar several times to create a column of red and white buttons.

4. To make the green bubbles in the upper right portion of the image, Gilder started with a default Texture Explorer texture. He gave the green bubbles of the texture a unique glow by using the technique he employed to stylize the woman's face (copying, blurring, pasting back with a Darken mode). Gilder then erased unwanted portions of the texture to reveal the underlying image as he did with the vortex effects.

5. He created the glowing green pattern on the left by repeatedly applying motion blurs and Gaussian weaves at a variety of settings.

6. The green cricket-thing at the bottom was painted in and then pulled out into its final shape by using Photoshop's Smudge tool.

7. The Minnie Mouse cube in the lower right was created in RayDream Designer, rotated to fit into this image, then saved as a TIFF file. Gilder then pasted the resulting TIFF into "Tammy."

8. Gilder designed the drop shadow by simply copying the cube, pasting it into a background layer, filling it with black, and blurring it somewhat. He added a smudge of pink to the top of the cube and pulled the image of Minnie out toward the cricket with Photoshop's Smudge tool.

9. Gilder created the background by using a combination of Texture Explorer and Gradient Designer effects. Custom gradients were created for both the yellow/pink/orange and the red sections. These gradients were then used to create custom textures that were layered on top of the original gradients with various channel operations to create the glowing edge effects.

"MEDITATION" BY SJOERD SMIT

This simple, yet striking, image by Sjoerd Smit begins with a KPT Texture Explorer texture. What makes "Meditation" (12.2) unique, though, is that rather than being a simple background element, the texture itself is used to frame additional effects. Smit then inserted several different perspectives of a Poser-created figure into various facets of the texture. He added two different views of a simple Bryce scene to two of the center facets. Finally, he stylized an image of the Poser figure (against a blue background) by using multiple applications of KPT Glass Lens and inserted the pieces of the resulting image into two more facets on the right. Nothing too fancy here, but the result is an image that is visually interesting and elegant in its simplicity.

"SANTA FE WITH SPHERE" BY ANDREW RODNEY

Another striking image, Andrew Rodney's "Santa Fe with Sphere" (12.3), combines two different pho-

12.2

tographs with Convolver, KPT Spheroid Designer and several of Photoshop's tools to create the overall impression of mystical turmoil in Santa Fe. In Rodney's words, "This image of a hotel in Santa Fe, New Mexico, was photographed on 35mm Fuji-Chrome and scanned onto Kodak PhotoCD. I replaced the sky with another image I shot that was also scanned on Kodak PhotoCD. I use Convolver to sharpen and correct tonality in many of my images because I prefer to do one set of corrections [convolutions] which produce[s] superior results. The spheres where created using KPT Spheroid Designer."

12.4

"BRIDGE OVER REFLECTION LAGOON" BY PHIL FREE

"Bridge Over Reflection Lagoon" (12.4) by Phil Free, one of Steve's favorites, is another great example of the kind of results that can be obtained by combining real images with imagined ones. To create this image, Free began with two photographs, added a Bryce background, and brought everything together with Convolver's color-correction capabilities. He explains how he created the image:

1. "One night after work, I decided to stretch some creative muscles and come up with something that had nothing to do with my work at hand—something just for fun," says Free. "I looked through some slides that I had taken earlier while at the Maine Photographic Workshops and found the jumping girl image (12.5) and the bridge image (12.6). The movements of her body and the gauze

12.5

12.3

12.6

she is holding suggested that they would fit nicely inside the curve of the bridge, so I went about placing her into the bridge photo.

2. "Well, it just didn't have enough zap, so I decided to let Bryce come up with a landscape that would bring all of the elements together. I came up with a good-looking landscape, added some reflecting spheres, and let it render a nice-size file overnight (12.7).

3. "The next night, I composited all of the images in Photoshop and found a new challenge for myself. You see, the beautiful blue sky behind the girl not only was reflected in the whites of her costume, but showed through the gauze. Of course, when placed against the golds and oranges of the rendered sky,

the jumper conflicted terribly with her surroundings. To get beyond this, I took the cloning tool, adjusted it for color only—about ten percent opacity—and brushed around the jumper image using the rendered background as the source. This replaced the blue hues with the more believable golds and oranges and even gave the illusion of the rendered sky showing through the gauze.

4. "For a final touch, I entered Convolver with the Bridge layer active and adjusted the saturation to 125 percent, the relief amount to 20 percent, sharpened it about 7 percent, in the tint control bumped the hue to 233 and the saturation another .4, and then finessed the color contrast by 2.7 for a little more pop. Being able to do all of this in one filter is pretty amazing to me, giving all that control in one place with some choices that you otherwise might not have even tried."

12.7

"LISA" BY JOSEPH LINASCHKE

"Lisa" (12.8), by Joseph Linaschke, which was designed by using four different plug-ins within the Kai's Power Tools set, nicely shows off the variety of effects that can be created within KPT itself.

1. Linaschke first scanned in an original charcoal drawing of the face itself at 300 dpi. This original scanned image is the basis for the three different "face" effects in the image.

2. He created the background coloration and "electric bolts" with multiple applications of the KPT Texture Explorer.

3. Linaschke made the back-most layer of faces by using KPT Planar Tiling, set to Perspective Tiling mode. This resulted in the repeated receding faces at the top of the image.

4. Below the Planar Tiling effect (in the image, but actually created on the next layer above it) is an application of the KPT Vortex Tiling filter.

5. The frontmost face with the greenish charcoal effects is the result of using KPT Gradient Designer with a thin white Gaussian glow behind it.

6. Finally, Linaschke converted the entire image to CMYK in Live Picture.

12.8

"GATEWAY" BY ATHENA KEKENES

Athena Kekenes, an artist/designer at MetaTools, created this "Gateway" image (12.9) with KPT Fractal Explorer 2.1, Photoshop channel operations, Convolver, KPT Texture Explorer, KPT Glass Lens and KPT Twirl. One interesting aspect of this image is that not only did Kekenes combine different plug-ins, she also took another one of her images (Inertial Nest) to the "next level" by using it as a foundation for this image. (And Inertial Nest was actually based on still another image, illustrating that recycling makes sense in the digital world as well.) We'll take a look at how Inertial Nest was originally created, then we'll see how Kekenes incorporated that image into Gateway.

12.9

1. Inertial Nest (12.10) shows how KPT Fractal Explorer's "Wrap image in place of gradient" option can be used. To create the purple background image, Kekenes ran Fractal Explorer once over an old image called "Exposure."

2. For the "leaves," she took an image of a chopped circle and fractalized it, using the same wrap image option.

3. Kekenes selected out the interesting portion and put it on its own layer for easy placement. She then duplicated it twice and tweaked the colors with Convolver.

4. Finally, she added subtle drop shadows between the layers to create the final Inertial Nest image.

5. To create "Gateway," Kekenes first designed the background texture by applying several applications of KPT Texture Explorer.

6. She then placed one Fractal leaf from the Inertial Nest image over the background texture.

7. Finally, she designed the circular objects with channel operations, KPT Glass Lens, and KPT Twirl filters.

12.10

12.11

"TIME POND" BY MICHAEL TOMPERT

"Time Pond" (12.11) by Michael Tompert is actually a springtime calendar that comments on the seemingly increasing speed with which time passes by as we get older. KPT's Gradient Designer and Texture Explorer, as well as Photoshop itself, were used extensively in the creation of this illustration—with a little help from Photoshop's vector-based sibling, Adobe Illustrator.

1. Tompert created the background image for "Time Pond" by laying a single flower stem onto the scanner bed and scanning it in. He then rotated this single stem extensively and duplicated it until it eventually disappeared (12.12). He used Adobe Illustrator to draw the precisely calculated masks for the progressively scaled and fading leaves.

2. Tompert then designed this radial gradient (12.13) using KPT Gradient designer as the basis for the following spiral mask.

12.12

12.13

3. He used this mask (12.14) to create the illusion of depth in the spiral. As you look down the spiral, the texture becomes darker and more out of focus.

4. This final mask (12.15), which was derived from the previous mask, was used to create the drop shadows in the spiral that not only darken as the spiral descends but become smaller, creating an even stronger sense of distance.

5. Tompert made extensive use of Texture Explorer and Spheroid Designer to create the calendar itself, as you can see from this detail shot (12.16).

6. Finally, he placed a frog on the leaves in the lower left portion of the image. KPT Texture Explorer, with its Procedural Apply mode, was a perfect tool for creating the "realistically surreal" skin of the frog (12.17).

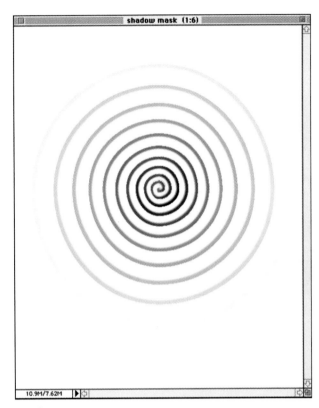

12.15

12.14

12.16

12.17

EASTERN SOFTWARE AD
BY DAVID GINK

Because MetaTools products encourage so much creative exploration, they sometimes get a bad rap for not being "production oriented." This ad for Eastern Software (12.18), created by David Gink, shows that just because the software is fun and easy, there's no reason it can't be used to create solid, business-oriented images. Gink's description of the way he created this ad does a great job of explaining how MetaTools products (Bryce in this case) fit into the process of taking an ad (or whatever) from original concept to finished comp.

1. "After the 'column' concept was chosen, I began by creating the floppy disk and column templates in Macromedia Freehand," says Gink. "Importing them into Infini-D, I extruded them and created 3D models [that] I set up in a simple scene without spending much time applying textures or placing lights. I then rendered the scene as a low-res pict image and output it to a laser printer. At this point, I shot a low-res photo of the meeting using office personnel (12.19) and a digital Connectix Quick-Cam Camera. Tracing the column scene, the meeting photo, and some QuarkXPress text onto marker paper, I created a traditional color comp.
2. "Once the client approved the comprehensive layout, I proceeded to 'finalize' the Infini-D scene, applying a custom marble texture to the columns, tweaking the models, and adding lights to create the shadow effects shown in the final image. After the first six columns were in their final position, I rendered it at 300 pixels per inch. This was output onto clear acetate and taken to the studio that was shooting the final photo of the meeting. This 'acetate template' enabled the scene to be shot at the proper angle.

12.18

3. "While waiting for the hi-res drum-scanned photo, I created the KPT Bryce background, squashing and stretching the terrain until the mountain peaks were very close to what the client had seen in my original comp.

4. "I used Macromedia Freehand to create the floppy disk labels, skewing them over the column scene placed onto the background layer. I also rendered a number of individual hi-res pillars in Infini-D that were to go up the mountainside and vanish over the top. Finally, I combined the columns, disk labels, mountains, and meeting scan in Adobe Photoshop to create the final 300 ppi artwork shown. QuarkXPress was used to create the final typeset document."

BEYOND THE NEXT LEVEL

These images—and many more like them—show how combining MetaTools products with other products (whether from MetaTools, Adobe, Fractal, or other software designers) can yield impressive results. The logical question, then, is what comes next? The answer may be combining some of the concepts embraced here with some of the innovations explored in Chapter 13, "KPT Can't Do That." Adding levels of detail and realism to multiple applications of different software packages can only yield progressively more impressive and effective results.

Of course, that's just one possible avenue to the "next level." Interform from KPT and Final Effects have opened up a brand new world of animation possibilities, and it is not hard to imagine a whole new level of "hey, check this out" that goes beyond cool KPT effects and Bryce renderings. Only time will tell.

> **NOTE**
>
> Gink created this image with Bryce 1.0. With Bryce 2's new Boolean capabilities and ability to import DXF files, he could have worked almost exclusively in Bryce 2.

12.19

CHAPTER 13
KPT CAN'T DO THAT!

O h yes it can. These days it seems as though every time we open a magazine or catalog, there's KPT artwork staring us in the face—a page curl here, a metallic gradient there, a Bryce landscape over there. As more and more artists make KPT products part of their digital toolbox, more and more KPT art is being produced (which is good); but more and more of that art is also starting to look awfully familiar (which isn't so good).

One of the factors that initially set the KPT line of products apart from the crowd was their ability to create never-before-seen effects relatively quickly and easily. That is why so many artists, designers, and illustrators buy and use the products every day. The problem, though, is in keeping your KPT artwork fresh and original, even after your 1,000th ad or presentation.

This chapter focuses on creating new looks using familiar tools such as Kai's Power Tools, Vector Effects, and Bryce. The following images and imaging techniques fall under two categories: "You Can't Do That with KPT" (creating "impossible" images) and "I Never Thought of Doing That with KPT" (creating images or image elements that are easier to do but are rarely seen).

"PINE TREE" BY SCOTT CROUSE

This image (13.1) of a suspiciously Christmasy pine tree was designed by Scott Crouse using Adobe Illustrator and Vector Effects. It is an excellent example of an "impossible" effect that is actually quite easy to create. The process used is outlined here for your edification.

13.1

1. Crouse began the piece by drawing a rough tree shape and filling it with a dark green color (13.2). This would provide a dark "interior" for the tree, creating the illusion of depth.

2. To create the branches, he first drew a tan stroked path for the center of the branch. Then he drew a light green stroked path for a needle at the top of the branch and a dark green stroked path (same color as the rough tree shape) for a needle at the bottom of the branch. Crouse drew these needles perpendicular to the branch and blended several steps to make the intermediate needles on the branch. The needles were then reflected across the center of the branch, and all the needles were shaped, duplicated, skewed, copied, and added to the branch. This produced a pine branch with a tan center and needles of different sizes and shapes that ranged in color from light green at the top, to the dark green of the rough tree shape at the bottom (13.3).

3. Crouse made several different-shaped branches this way and arranged them on the rough tree from top to bottom, with the lower branches overlapping the higher ones. Because the light color of the top of the branches gradually blended into the dark color of the background of the tree, the branches looked as though they were growing out of the dark tree shape (13.4).

13.2

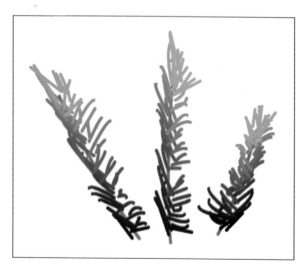

13.3

13.4

4. After arranging all the branches on the tree, Crouse selected them and applied the Vector Effects filter KPT Sketch. By moving the Amount slider slightly to the right, he gave the branches the soft look of a real Douglas Fir, rather than a mechanical, artificial look. Crouse was especially delighted with this terrific application of a very simple filter. "This filter saved me hours of time that would otherwise be spent individually editing the needles, trying to get a natural look. I know this because I drew two other trees a couple of days before my copy of Vector Effects arrived, and those drawings can't hold a light to this one." The key to maximizing the effectiveness of the KPT Sketch filter was to make sure that the needles all had at least three to four anchor points each so that the distortion applied by the filter would be noticeable.

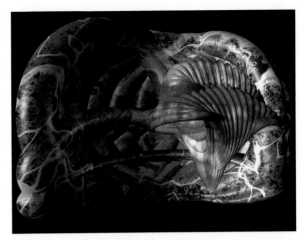

13.5

"MAGIC META" BY BILL ELLSWORTH

"Magic Meta" (13.5), one of many gorgeous images by Bill Ellsworth, falls under the category of "I Never Thought of Doing That with Bryce," rather than "Bryce Can't Do That." The image itself consists solely of toruses and lights, well within the grasp of anyone even moderately familiar with the software. What distinguishes Bill's work from everyone else's, though, is his ability to see simplicity as the key to beauty. Bill often uses unique applications of simple techniques and elements to create images that are astonishingly beautiful.

1. To start, Ellsworth created a simple torus with a nicely marbled texture (13.6). He then duplicated this torus many times, carefully rotating, repositioning, or otherwise modifying it to create the background element for the image.

2. Ellsworth then created a second torus with a slightly different texture for the "seashell" foreground element (13.7). This torus was also dupli-

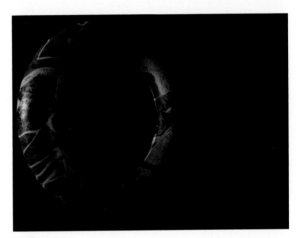

13.6

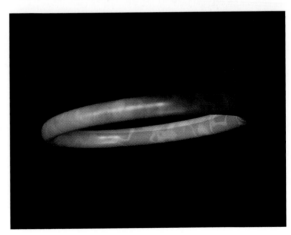

13.7

cated, rotated, and repositioned as needed to create the foreground element, giving us this intermediate image (13.8).

3. To really bring out the beauty of the two elements, Ellsworth added light to increase both the visibility and the dramatic effect of the background and foreground elements. He took special care to illuminate the "seashell" from the inside, giving us the finished image. The total object count for this image is a modest 62 (compared to some Bryce images that contain hundreds or even thousands of objects); and, as shown by the scene's wireframe (13.9), only toruses, a couple of spotlights, and one radial light were used.

"99.9% PURE BRYCE" BY GLENN RIEGEL

This amazing image (13.10), created by Glenn Riegel using Bryce, is a natural for this chapter because it introduces a new breed of images that several different artists are producing. The artists combine their unbelievable creativity and ingenuity with Bryce's astonishing rendering capabilities to create three-dimensional worlds and objects that have little (if anything) to do with Bryce's "real" function as a generator of natural and surreal landscapes. The key is patience, attention to detail, lots of time, and the effective use of grayscale height maps.

1. Riegel began by creating his grayscale height maps in Photoshop. Although he could create most of the image with Bryce's built-in terrains

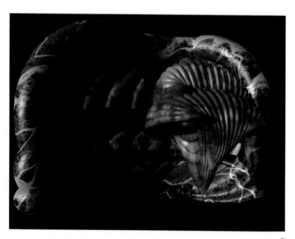

13.8

13.10

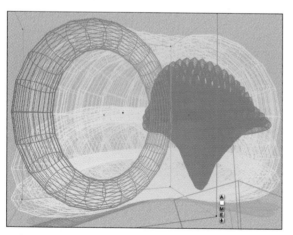

13.9

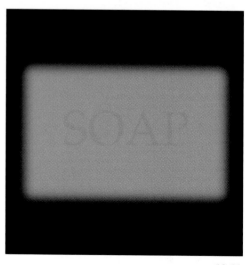

13.11

and materials, certain items (most notably the bar of soap) needed custom grayscale height maps. Riegel designed two height maps, one called Soap (13.11) for the bar of soap and another called Dimples (13.12) for both the floor and (in a modified form) the sponge.

2. After completing the necessary height maps in Photoshop, Riegel moved on to Bryce, where he used the height maps to create custom terrains for the bar of soap (13.13), the floor, and the sponge (13.14).

3. The bubbles are all simple spheres, but with a tremendously effective translucent, reflective material applied to them (13.15).

4. The water on both the floor and the bar of soap is simply additional terrain painstakingly shaped to interact with the bar of soap and the floor in a convincing fashion.

TWO MORE BRYCE MODELS

The key to Riegel's success with "99.9% Pure Bryce" is in the details. "USS Cordova" by Patrick J. Flaherty (13.16) and "Copper Gryphon" by Chris

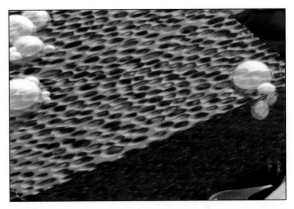
13.14

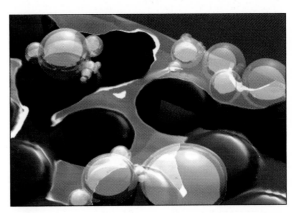
13.15

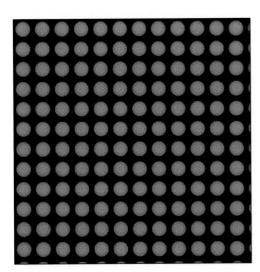
13.12

13.13

13.16

Casady (13.17) reflect the same attention to detail while creating two completely different images and image themes.

MISCELLANEOUS TECHNIQUES

Of course, many studio secrets don't fit neatly into standard categories, and we provide a collection of them for you here.

13.17

13.18

MULTIPLE PAGE CURLS (KAI'S POWER TOOLS)

A simple variation on a very popular theme, multiple page curls extend the illusion of a page curling up to reveal what's underneath. The image gives the appearance of several curled pages, as if you were flipping through a catalog or magazine. The technique is a fairly simple one, involving multiple applications of the page curl filter with a slightly altered selection for each application.

To create this image of a *Balloons!* magazine cover (13.18), we selected the lower right-hand corner of the image (using Photoshop's selection tool at a fixed dimension) and applied our first page curl at an intensity of 14. We then lowered the height of the selection by five pixels and reapplied our page curl, but this time with an intensity of 13. We continued this process of lowering the selection height by five and the curl intensity by one four more times, resulting in the multiple page curls.

13.19

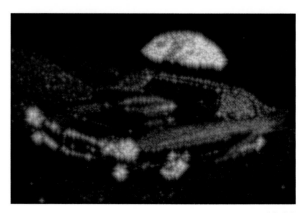

13.20

STARRY SKIES AND TEARY FAREWELLS (KAI'S POWER TOOLS)

With version 3, Kai's Power Tools introduced a couple of new variations on the Gaussian blur theme, namely Block and Diamond blurs. These two new blur variants are available in the options menu of the Gaussian f/x filter. The Gaussian Diamonds filter works most effectively when an image has single pixels (or small groups of pixels) with a higher degree of color contrast than the surrounding pixels. We can accomplish this effect by applying a very nice diamond blurring to the contrasting pixel(s), creating an effect similar to starry skies or lights seen through teary eyes.

We created these two images with the Diamond variation of the Gaussian f/x filter. For the first image (13.19), we made a new layer behind the desert landscape and used the Texture Explorer to fill it with a colorful texture. We then applied the Grime filter to the entire layer at a setting of approximately 75 percent intensity, covering a good portion of our texture. We then reapplied the Grime filter to cover even more of the texture. Because successive applications of the Grime filter would only cover pixels that have already been affected, we flipped the layer horizontally and reapplied the Grime layer twice, and then flipped it vertically and reapplied the grime layer twice. By this time, our texture was completely obscured, except for a scattering of isolated pixels here and there (perfect for the starry sky effect we want to create). We then applied the Gaussian f/x filter (Diamond variation) at an intensity of about 60 percent to create a night sky filled with gleaming stars in different colors. To achieve this surreal image, we masked out the original desert sky to reveal our "starry sky" behind it.

The second image was much easier to create. We simply added a little bit of noise to an existing image (remember: pixellation is good when using diamond blurs) and then applied a diamond blur to the entire image (13.20). This technique can be used to simulate a "teary farewell" effect (if applied judiciously) or simply to create a very cool-looking effect (if used with enthusiasm and complete disregard for your own personal safety).

REVERSE EXTRUSIONS (VECTOR EFFECTS)

Although designed to create extrusions by stretching your artwork away from you, Vector Effects' 3D Transform plug-in can be used to pull your artwork toward you. By entering negative values into the Extrusion field of the 3D Transform UI (as mentioned in the "Vector Effects" chapter), you can make your artwork look as though it were rising up off the page.

This image (13.21) of Ted's house in Cave Creek, Arizona was created using this "negative extrusion" technique. (Note to burglars: Most of the cool stuff is in either the first room by the front door or in the living room, their dog is really friendly, and the alarm code is. . . .) If you use the slider to control the extrusion, you will never be able to create this effect; the slider goes from 0 to 255 (positive numbers only), giving you varying amounts of "outward" extrusion. To pull your artwork toward you, you need to manually input negative extrusion values. You can accomplish this by Option-clicking on the Extrusion slider and entering a negative value.

13.21

DIGITAL SQUINTING (CONVOLVER)

Many Convolver users have heard the story of Convolver's being used as a digital image enhancer by the CIA (or FBI, Department of Defense, or local KMart security staff—well, maybe not the local KMart security staff—depending on who tells the story). In fact, a blurry car with an unreadable license plate is included with the software (13.22). (You'll need to look on the second install disk for the extra Convolver stuff.)

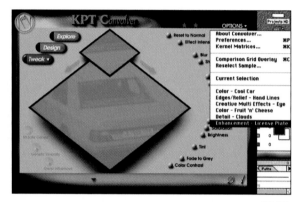

13.22

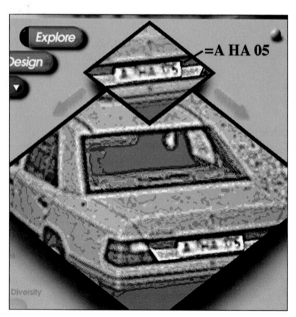

13.23

Many users have met with only limited success in trying to clarify the license plate number of the car. The key to success here is to use two of Convolver's three Tweak modes. Linear Convolution, the default mode, is often the only one used because few people think about the other two choices. While Difference Mask, the third mode, definitely won't help you here, Unsharp/Gaussian, the second mode, is the key to success. If you are working with an actual image, use the Linear Convolution tweaks to get it as clear as you can, then return to Convolver for more work with the Unsharp/Gaussian tweaks. Even if you are not working with an actual image, the Unsharp/Gaussian tweaks should pop the license plate right up (13.23). To do this, make sure that you are in the Unsharp/Gaussian Tweak mode, then simply drag the Unsharp control to the right to about 200, then drag the Effect Intensity to the right to about 25 percent. If you are working on an actual image that contains color, the Color Contrast control can also be helpful.

ARTEFFECT DESIGN STUDIO: THE KINGS OF "YOU CAN'T DO THAT!"

Although some impressive images and cool image techniques from a variety of artists appear in this chapter, when it comes to using MetaTools products to do the impossible, there are two reigning monarchs. Jackson Ting and Robert Bailey of ArtEffect Design Studio in Los Angeles have continually amazed the computer graphics world with images that simply shouldn't exist.

From "Big Rig" (the first Ting/Bailey image we presented in this book) to their latest efforts, their work amazes everyone who sees it. In the course of writing this book, we were fortunate enough to learn just how Jackson and Robert do what they do, and they have graciously allowed us to share their wisdom with you. We first look briefly at four of their earlier images, and then we dive deep (and we do mean deep) into "MetaStation," one of their more recent images (and the opening image in this chapter). So climb into your intellectual bathysphere and enjoy the ride!

"CARVED COAL"

The most surprising thing about "Carved Coal" (13.24) —at least to us—was that it wasn't created in Bryce. The entire image was created in Photoshop, using the Gradient Designer from Kai's Power Tools and Photoshop's built-in filters.

Jackson Ting explains: "The Shapeburst mode in Gradient Designer can easily be used to create realistic carved effects in Photoshop or [to] export to KPT Bryce for terrains and bump maps. For this image, we first made a selection from our company logo, then the Shapeburst mode in Gradient Designer was utilized to create a grayscale height map for Photoshop's lighting effects. The shapeburst was then blended with some images of rock to give it an organic texture. The height map was moved to a fourth channel, and an image of coal-like rock was loaded into the RGB channels. Photoshop's Lighting Effects filter was then applied, using the fourth channel to create the end result."

"CAMBRIAN PIPELINE"

At first glance, the "Cambrian Pipeline" image (13.25) doesn't seem very different from a lot of other Bryce images. The one aspect of "Cambrian Pipeline" that "can't be done" in Bryce, though, is the surf. How did they create the curling surf, and how did they create the realistic spray coming off the water?

Again, Ting explains: "One night we got a call that Herbie Hancock needed a Bryce illustration for an upcoming project. We got in touch with him and arranged a meeting that night. As it turns out, he needed a seascape image ASAP for a promotional video trailer. The time-frame was tight—we had 24 hours to come up with a complete illustration. That night we pulled a red eye and got the job out, minus the wave.

"We had been thinking about the wave ever since Ben Weiss had pulled a book out at Kai's entitled *Waves*—a book filled with photographs of pristine surf. He handed us the book and said, 'Try one of these. . . .' We took it as a challenge, and we built it up out of the image that we had done for Herbie.

"The wave was quite a challenge indeed. It required two separate C-shaped terrains and many meticulously placed small custom clouds to simulate foam and ocean spray. This image forced us to learn the Deep Texture Editor, and what a reward that has become."

13.24

13.25

"BIG RIG"

This Brycean "Big Rig" (13.26) has been widely seen and puzzled over ever since it first appeared on MetaTools' AOL Bryce forum. The single most common reaction has been, "They did this in Bryce? Those guys are crazy!" Crazy like a fox, it seems, because this image, and the excitement that it has generated, has secured ArtEffect's position at the very top of the Bryce mountain.

"Soon after we first got Bryce," says Ting, "there was a contest on the MetaTools AOL site. The contest was for 'The Best Desert Scene.' We went right to work; we began to create a sand dune image. We quickly found that creating grayscale height maps in Photoshop was a

13.26

13.27

very powerful way to make interesting terrains in Bryce. As the sand dune image neared completion, we added an asphalt road. This road needed something, perhaps a Big Rig? We did some tests using Illustrator to create some precise grayscale height maps, and we were pleased with the result. Soon the Big Rig took over our complete attention and we honed the technique of Illustrator-generated height maps. After the Rig was done, we decided to just plop it on a wet asphalt infinite plane; this really emphasized the truck."

"BLUES CLUB"

The extremely popular "Blues Club" image (13.27), and Ting's and Bailey's comments on it, reveal the real genius behind ArtEffect's success.

"The Fender Stratocaster was the first object we created," says Ting. "We used the same technique as we did for the 'Big Rig.' The detail on the Stratocaster is beyond overkill. We even put the phillips-head pattern on the screws. It's our observation that many of the 3D images out there have one thing in common, that's lack of details. Often things look too 'clean' and the viewer is not rewarded for taking time to really look into the image. We try to put as many details into each image as we possibly can; this seems to give it visual longevity. The detail is what keeps people interested after the initial impact has passed.

"After we created the Stratocaster, we needed an environment to frame the instrument. What better environment than a small 'Blues Club?' So we set out to create a scene with that small club feel."

THE CREATION OF "METASTATION"

In this section, ArtEffect Design Studio principals Jackson Ting and Robert Bailey describe in their own words the creation of "MetaStation."

The "MetaStation" image (13.28) was commissioned by MetaTools, who wanted a circa 1949 service station in Bryce. We began the project by making a photographic field trip to many of the older service stations around our area so we could really get a feel for the environment we were about to re-create. One of the stations even had a '39 Chevy on the lift! We also obtained some books that documented many vintage service stations. With references in hand, we set out to design the scene.

To get a really good idea of the spatial relationships with which we would be working, we first created the architecture. After setting up the camera angle, we used primitives to block out rough placement of the scene's elements. This planning helps greatly in latter stages of development. As complexity builds, planning becomes the key to success as it helps minimize costly mistakes.

We analyzed the objects and used Boolean operations as often as possible. Boolean objects created with primitives render both faster and cleaner, and eliminate the need for worrying about imported meshes (DXF files, and so on). We can also quickly edit the Booleans to make subtle adjustments easily in Bryce's solo mode. In some cases, it was much easier to create some of the complex 3D forms in a modeling program and then import them into Bryce.

When creating a mesh in a third-party application for import into Bryce 2, we always look at the object's silhouette to determine the required mesh density. If your silhouette looks polygonal (on curved surfaces), you need to increase density. Bryce does an excellent job of smoothing imported objects, but you need to use the proper mesh density. If it is too low, it will show on the edges of the objects.

Most of the textures were created from scratch in Bryce's powerful Deep Texture (or Materials) Editor. We obtained a "settled dust" effect quite easily with the slope filters. We set them to apply a dusty or rusty texture to the horizontal surfaces. This resulted in a natural dirtiness that you would expect in a service station. The edges of the horizontal surface would bleed the texture down the side, creating a realistic rust stain. Because many of the other apply modes function strangely with the imported nonnative meshes, we used world space or object space on most of the 3D imports.

For some of the decals on the objects, we used the new Alpha-Blend mode (Control-click on the "C" component bead for diffuse color and other effects) in the Materials Composer. This mode is great for combining text with Bryce 3D materials, the "C" component becomes an alpha channel that controls blending between "A" and "B."

This project was the most complex that we have ever done with Bryce, and the new features in Bryce 2 made this level of complexity much easier to deal with. There are more than 1,400 objects in this scene, including all the primitives that make up the Boolean objects.

13.28

13.29

13.30

CREATING THE TOOL CART

All objects in this portion of the "MetaStation" image (13.29) were generated within Bryce 2, using Boolean functions and primitives. The only elements imported were the decals for the oil and gas cans. As you can see, Boolean functions are a powerful way to create complex models. If the same models were imported mesh, they would consume far more memory and dramatically increase the project's file size. This image clearly shows the Boolean modeling power within Bryce 2.

The simplest of objects is the oil can, which consists of a cylinder, two toruses, a 2D horizontal disk and a pict decal. We applied the decal to the cylinder with object front mapping. You must take some care when creating the decals with this technique. If the decal is narrower or wider than your object, horizontal distortion will result. This is due to the fact that with object front mapping, Bryce will scale your image to fit the width of the object, edge to edge. An easy way to assure proper dimensions of your decal is to simply take a front-view screen shot of your object, load it into Photoshop and use it as a template.

Another technique that works nicely is demonstrated on the red gasoline can. Look carefully and you will see that this decal actually lets the underlying texture show through; the gasoline decal is, in fact, only an alpha channel—no color information.

For the gas can (13.30) decal, we started out in the Materials Composer with the rusty red texture in component "A" and created a variation in which we changed the red color to white and made this the "B" component. In Photoshop, we created a weathered grayscale text mask (alpha channel) and loaded it into Bryce as the "C" component. If you are using this technique, make sure to load the mask into the second (alpha) window of the pict library, not the first (color) window. The mapping mode for the "C" component is object front. Control-clicking on the "C" component for diffuse color will activate a bead in "A," "B," and "C." This is the alpha blend mode. Now "A" and "B" are blended based on the grayscale values of "C." What you get is a red texture with the white texture poking through where you have the text in your mask.

What's nice about this method is the fact that you can change the colors around all you want in Bryce, and you don't have to go back to Photoshop. If your text comes out the reverse of what you wanted, simply invert the alpha channel in the pict library.

The screwdrivers and wrenches are the result of various Boolean functions; the screwdrivers, in particular, make use of the Intersection Boolean function. This function will discard any material outside the object that has Intersect selected. If you create the basic form of the screwdriver (a flathead in this case), you can easily trim the tip to a nice taper by using a stretched pyramid for intersection. For Phillips, you need to make the Phillips head pattern and trim it down with a stretched cone. It takes a bit of practice, but intersection is a very powerful function that should not be underestimated.

CREATING THE WELDING TORCH

This model (13.31) is a hybrid, demonstrating how primitive-based objects can seamlessly blend with imported geometry. Most of this model is Boolean modeling, but the blue dolly frame and the hoses are imported geometry.

When modeling with primitives, we start in a fresh file and build our object in world center. This makes it easy because all the primitives will pop up in the same place. Another handy item is the swap tool in the upper right corner of the edit palette. If you have moved a primitive from world center, and you want to add another primitive into the exact same spot for alignment, simply copy and paste your selected primitive and then change it to another form with the swap tool. Now use the nudge keys or Control/ Option/ Command keys to constrain your primitive's movement to the desired axis. If 90 degree rotation is necessary, use the Shift key to constrain while rotating.

The tanks, valves, tires, and gas nozzle assembly were all generated with primitives and Boolean functions. Decals were applied to vertical disks for the psi gauges.

If modeling with primitives, we usually use world space mapping when applying textures. This creates a texture that will flow from one primitive to the next and gives the impression that they are one object. Parametric or other modes usually create a seam where the textures do not line up from primitive to primitive.

The imported hoses were created last because their construction requires precision. If any of the curves for the hoses were off by even a fraction, the hoses would not align properly. The key is to finish all elements of your model except the hoses and then take screen snapshots of the wireframe from top, front, and right. It is easier if you select the objects to which the hoses attach so they are highlighted in the wireframe. Now you can use these snapshots as templates in your 3D modeling application. We have employed this technique many times, and it really makes it simple to create precision objects in other modelers that mesh right into your Bryce model.

WHAT CAN'T KPT DO?

If this chapter has shown us anything, it's that what's possible with KPT is limited only by the imagination and ingenuity of the artists who use it. And if Jackson Ting and Robert Bailey are any indication, that won't be a limiting factor at all.

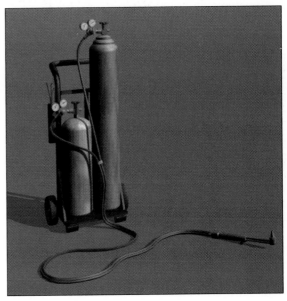

13.31

CHAPTER 14
SPECIAL EFFECTS SHOWCASE

Unlike the rest of this book, the goal of this chapter is to provide you with an almost exclusively visual feast. Here we present you with a gallery of some of the most beautiful, interesting, or technically impressive artwork being created with MetaTools products. For the most part, the artwork shown in this chapter does not appear elsewhere in the book. A lot of the art didn't fit clearly into any specific topic, but we couldn't bear not to share it, so we've placed it here. Some of the images *do* appear elsewhere, but we wanted you to be able to see a few of these images at a larger size to fully appreciate their detail.

In this chapter you will see artwork utilizing all of the MetaTools image-generation or image-manipulation products. Such esteemed digital artists as Bill Ellsworth, Greg Carter, and Jackson Ting and Robert Bailey are represented here, as well as numerous lesser-known but extremely talented individuals.

But enough introduction—time for the art. Sit back, relax, and enjoy the show.

#5
This image by Brian Strauss combines both KPT 2.1 and KPT 3.0 effects. The Fractal Explorer from KPT 2.1 provides the "dark lightning," while Planar Tiling, Glass Lens and other KPT 3.0 effects do the rest.

ELECTRIC POWWOW
Our chapter opening image, by Michael Tompert, began as a photograph taken by his wife Claudia Huber Tompert. Michael then used Kai's Power Tools, as well as Photoshop's built-in capabilities, to apply a glowing "electric" aura to the image edges, giving this image its unique look.

179

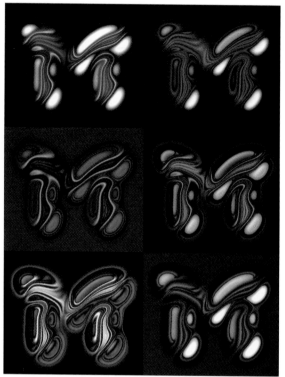

38TH ANNUAL GRAMMY AWARDS
The work of C. David Piña is probably the most visible of all artwork done with MetaTools products. This image and many others have appeared on national television. David and his wife, Shelley, have done outstanding work on the Academy and Tony Award shows as well, and are probably the best in the business when it comes to metallic lettering effects. © NARAS, courtesy of Cossette Productions, Inc.

ALIEN M'S
This is a great example of what brought Athena Kekenes to MetaTools' attention. After showing Kai her images (several of which are included in this book), Kai brought Athena onboard as an artist/designer at MetaTools, where she now works on user interface development with Kai and Phil.

BRIDGE BETWEEN
One of several of Bill Ellsworth's images appearing in this book, this is a great example of the flowing, sleek nature of Bill's work. Much of Bill's work is Bryce-based, although KPT effects are generally used to complete the image.

ART OF DREAMING
Bill Ellsworth's artistic dream is actually a collage of four different Ellsworth images. One of the features that makes "Art of Dreaming" so compelling is its alternating slices of texture-heavy and lighting effect images.

BJORKLUND 2
This the simplest of Mark Smith's images in this book, which is one reason that we like it. Mark's work is exclusively Bryce-generated, but rises above a lot of Bryce-only imagery in its juxtaposition of stark objects with rich colors and textures.

ATLANTIS LOST
Chris Casady, the man responsible for this aquatic discovery, is one of the premiere Bryce artists out there. His work is featured in this book, as well as on the Bryce 2 box and in MetaTools' full-page ads for Bryce 2. This image shows Chris's mastery of Bryce's atmospheric effects, enabling him to create a convincing underwater scene with (essentially) colored smog.

BLUES CLUB

This image by the wizards at ArtEffect Design Studio (Jackson Ting and Robert Bailey) also appears in the "KPT Can't Do That" chapter. We think that it's such an impressive image, though, that we wanted you to get a better look at it. This image is a shining example of some of the unbelievable results that can be achieved with patience, attention to detail, and lots of time.

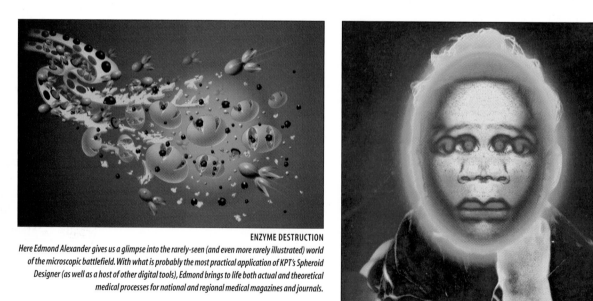

ENZYME DESTRUCTION

Here Edmond Alexander gives us a glimpse into the rarely-seen (and even more rarely illustrated) world of the microscopic battlefield. With what is probably the most practical application of KPT's Spheroid Designer (as well as a host of other digital tools), Edmond brings to life both actual and theoretical medical processes for national and regional medical magazines and journals.

BABY BOO—WIERD

This image, by Larry Auerbach, is one that definitely lives up to its name. Larry's other creations are equally disturbing, and show his affinity for using Bryce as a portraiture tool.

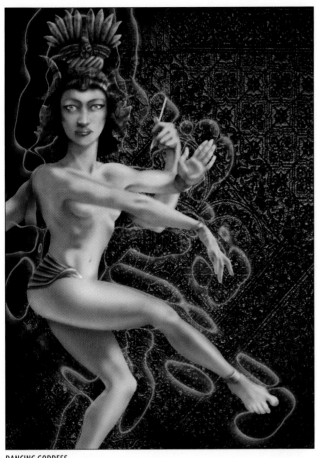

DANCING GODDESS

Todd DeMelle's goddess is an excellent example of image enhancement with Kai's Power Tools. Unlike many of the other artists represented in this book, Todd is an illustrator first, and a digital artist second. Many of his images, while impressive enough on their own, are enhanced with subtle applications of Texture Explorer or Gradient Designer effects.

CYBORG REFLECTING POOL 2

Here's an amazing image from an equally amazing artist. Greg Carter's images are always disturbing, technically impressive, and amazingly detailed. Greg's art has been described as "Equal parts compelling gruesomeness and exquisite detail. Haunting and thought-provoking." We couldn't agree more.

RING SPACEWORLD OUT

No one makes Bryce shine like Eric Wenger, and "Ring SpaceWorld Out" is an exceptional example of this. Anyone else would have made the world actually on the world (the platen) and used the torus as mere decoration. Only Eric could put a convincing world inside a simple primitive shape and make it not only believable, but beautiful as well.

CHECKERS VIRUS

Edmond Alexander makes his living creating detailed illustrations of microscopic medical phenomena, and one look at this example explains why. A traditional artist for virtually all of his career, when Edmond discovered that computers (and Kai's Power Tools) could take him far beyond his airbrushes he never looked back.

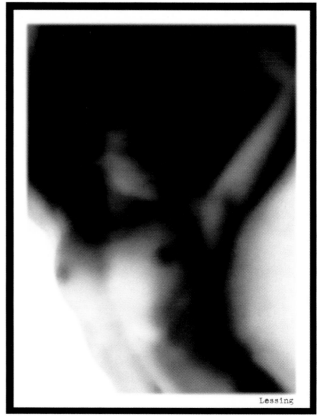

MEXICO #1

This evocative image by Pieter Lessing is an example of a splendidly "convolved" image. Here the combination of neutral colors, deep shadows and earthy texture emphasize the essence of the nude form by trading details for mood, the visual for the visceral. Who knew that Convolver could do all that?

MOVIE SET

The great thing about Chris Casady's "Movie Set" is that it combines the ordinary with the extraordinary. A typical use for Bryce would be to create a rocky canyon to use as a backdrop for other "action." Chris takes this unremarkable premise and adds all of the movie accouterments that let us see the "set" for what it is.

ORBITAL

With this image, Pieter Lessing shows off Bryce's reflective capabilities as well as any image we've seen. The combination of shapes and reflective surfaces works nicely here, and the vertical imperfections on the cube add visual interest and illustrate how one simple alteration can transform a simple primitive object.

LIVING HANDS

One of the rare Convolver-centric images by ArtEffect Design Studio, this image actually started out as a line drawing. Intrigued by the idea, Jackson Ting and Robert Bailey took the necessary photographs, composited them together, then used Convolver for all of the color and texture manipulations necessary for this image.

INDUSTRY—PAIN OF HARRY CREWS

This is another example of Greg Carter's unique artistic perspective and virtuosity. This image makes excellent use of KPT's Texture Explorer and Spheroid Designer, as well as Photoshop's lighting effects.

SHINY TURKEY 2

Mark Smith's image here is a variation on his "Shiny Turkey," which appears in the Bryce chapter. This image, besides looking great, really shows off Bryce 2's Replicate command, which is invaluable when creating objects based on a single primitive or terrain, such as the "feathers" of this turkey.

METAVIRTUAL COCKPIT

This interplanetary vision by ArtEffect Design Studio was commissioned by MetaTools for one of their Bryce 2 ads. Jackson Ting and Robert Bailey created the image entirely in Bryce. One of the especially impressive aspects of this image is the reflection of the cockpit's interior in the glass of the viewing bubble.

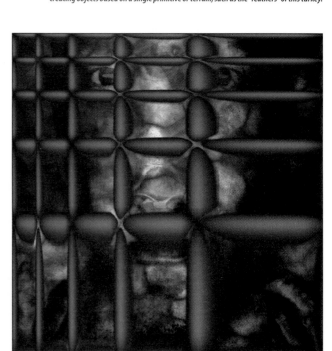

PRISONER

Larry Auerbach's haunting image of despair combines a clever use of gradient "bars" with a combination of colors and textures that is disturbingly reminiscent of dried blood and brings to mind either the guilt of the prisoner and the suffering of society (as victims/jailers) or the other way around.

MARTIAN DESERT

This spacescape by ArtEffect Design Studio was created as part of another image (see "MetaVirtual Cockpit" above), but it looks so good on its own that we wanted you to be able to appreciate it as a piece of art in its own right.

TRIBUTE

When Chris Casady purchased a home in the hills above Hollywood, he had no idea that the garage of the house contained a collection of actual Batchelder tiles (Ernie Batchelder was a master tile designer and artist from the turn of the century). This discovery inspired Chris' fascination with tiles and this Brycean tribute.

THE PHONE PRANKSTERS

One of three Greg Carter images in this chapter (and four in the book—see the "Power Photos" chapter opener), this zinger shows yet another glimpse into the sometimes-scary-but-always-fascinating creative psyche of Greg Carter. Greg's ability to create such deep, rich tableaus using only a computer and his imagination is undeniably impressive, as is his mastery of his tools, in this case primarily Kai's Power Tools (with a little help from Photoshop). This image particularly shows off the great textures that can be created with the right tools.

SPHEROPOLIS

Sitting halfway between the stark beauty of Mark Smith's work and the sensual complexity of Bill Ellsworth's, "Spheropolis" by Joseph Linaschke has a texture and a smoothness that makes you want to reach out and touch it. Like Athena Kekenes, Joseph Linaschke is another artist who's talent and technical expertise have engendered invitations to join the MetaTools team.

DEPP

Pieter Lessing's portrait is a nice example of the results that can be achieved by exploring the "less is more" end of the MetaTools spectrum. Created primarily with Convolver, "Depp" is the result of manipulating a photo of film star Johnny Depp taken by Pieter. As a photographer, Pieter relies heavily on Convolver for production tasks, as well as using it as a creative tool.

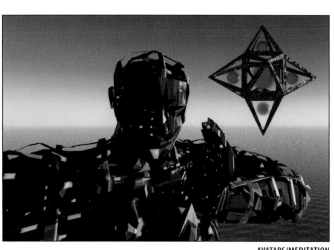

AVATARS/MEDITATION

One of two Avatar images in this chapter, this first one by Henry Lim cleverly combines a Poser figure (possible with Bryce 2) with Bryce 2's Boolean object capabilities to create this thought-provoking image, vaguely reminiscent of Rodan's "The Thinker" or "The Kiss" sculptures.

FALL

A clever idea and an excellent execution of it brings us "Fall," by Todd DeMelle. As with Todd's other images, "Fall" combines outstanding illustration skills with subtle Kai's Power Tools image enhancement.

THINGS 2

Our favorite of Mark Smith's images, "Things 2" really shows off what Bryce can do. The reflective globes and water, the richly colored and textured materials, and the crystal clear rendered image speaks volumes for this amazing software package (and Mark's skill at getting the most out of it).

SCHLOSS FLUSSBOGEN EVE
Another Bryce-only image, this one by Glenn Riegel combines some of the 3D modeling elements similar to those seen in the works of Chris Casady or ArtEffect Design Studio with probably the best stone texture we've ever seen. The background is, of course, another Bryce image.

AVATARS/WORSHIP
Henry Lim's creation combines three of Bryce 2's new features to create a compelling representation of an acolyte worshipping in a temple. The Poser-modeled acolyte is courtesy of Bryce 2's DXF-import capabilities, the globe is made possible with Bryce 2's Boolean rendering capabilities and the glowing lights are made with the new radial light primitives.

GFX BOARD
Here Andrew M. Faw provides a good example of a commercial application of what is all-too-commonly seen as a creative toy. Andrew created this ad for a circuit board by cleverly combining effects created with the Gradient Designer and Texture Explorer from Kai's Power Tools with the image of the circuit board and other graphic elements.

SANTA BARBARA MISSION
Another amazing Bryce image by Chris Casady, this one reflects Chris' fascination with tiles (his AOL name is TileNut),
a fascination that shows itself in many of Chris' images. In addition to the tiled roof and stone walls, Chris has also
done a great job here of creating convincing grassy outcroppings (not an easy task in Bryce).

SUMMER RENDERING
Scott Tucker's summertime distraction is a Brycean version of Jimmy Buffett, Beverly Hills style.
The entire image was created in Bryce, and the translucent textures and pale colors keep
"Summer Rendering" as "refreshing" as a picture can be.

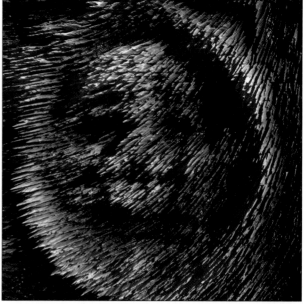

FROST KING
The clever use of materials, terrain effects, and shadows brings this simple portrait of a mythical
"Frost King" (by Larry Auerbach) to life. Like his other images, Larry's "Frost King" builds on Bryce's
ability to use any grayscale image as a height map for a custom terrain.

ANSEL

Scott Tucker's "Ansel" is such a great idea that we wonder why we (or no one else) ever thought of it. Bryce is the perfect tool for creating landscapes, Ansel Adams was arguably the premiere photographer of landscapes, and black and white is always only a menu command away in Photoshop. But we didn't think of it, and Scott did, and all we can say is that he did a great job of bringing the spirit of Ansel Adams to the digital world.

REFLECTIONS

George Hazelwood's image, with its reflecting globes, carpet of water, and backdrop of mountains is the quintessential Bryce image. For all of you who have ever dropped a globe over water and some mountains and wondered what went wrong, this is what it's supposed to look like.

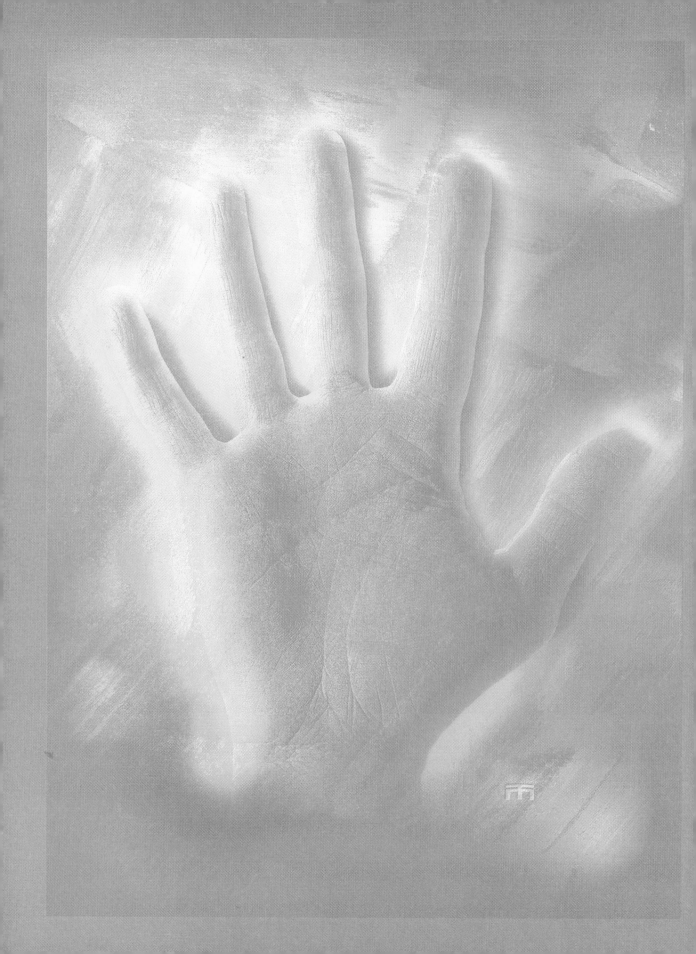

AFTERWORD

You'll find plenty of other software packages out there that are all about the pragmatic goal to get some job done and go home. KPT is not that. It's about being home.

KAI KRAUSE

Every time I read something written about me it "fills me with inertia," to quote the movie *Bedazzled*. It's already goofy enough to have one's thoughts squelched into language, having to live with the few possibilities we have to "coalesce them from vapor," but it's really odd to have the language be quoted, edited, and cut to fit someone's story, particularly in "the quick article due the next afternoon." So it's a relief to see someone take time, have the space, possess the attitude to get it right, include the background, and weave a story with real characters and not mere caricatures. Hooray! I love it, a tome dedicated to all the bits 'n' pieces behind the story. Man, I wish this book existed three years ago, when all the ingredients within were mere wishful thinking on our part.

Put yourself in the shoes of the first round of investors, holy men that they were, to be sinking in what can only be technically described as "serious dough" in those first days of '92. We were but a handful of people under the HSC banner, and I had freshly designed a lovely little video editor to be marketed as Sony VideoWare and built into every camcorder on our small blue planet. Alas, it was not to be. And as we met again a few months later we greeted them not with the first sales numbers of VideoWare but with a lovely round of "Hey, guess what? We wrote Power Tools! Cool . . . !" Well, let the record show that these wise men named Sam and Howard looked me in the eye and trusted me to do the right thing (or at least that's how one likes to remember such times in the context of revisionist historical accounts . . . no seriously, these guys were great). At that stage the idea that we would have ten products out, repeatedly double our revenues annually, move to Santa Barbara, go public on NASDAQ, pay all debts, and put serious capital behind us, employ well over 100 people in buildings locally and in Japan, England, Germany, Ireland . . . and all the other things that now describe our situation were mere pipe dreams, at least to all others at whom we aimed our dream pipes. To *us* it was all clearly in front of us (spiteating grin . . .). We saw this book way back then. Kind of . . .

Well, seriously . . .

Many elements in this story were hard to divine ahead of themselves and much would have been absolute hubris to predict. When we first set out with the Gradient Designer it was apparent that it could do more than interpolate two colors. That it could make neat gold effects and be used in the Academy Awards on TV as golden fonts was *not* predictable. When we made the first Texture Explorer, we felt that it clearly harbored many interesting cutting-edge creations. Going through the bins of Tower Records and finding all the hundreds of CD covers incorporating odds and ends of KPT was *not* foreseeable. At first, that 1960s psychedelia kind of look took over, even if I myself always thought of it more as a 2060s new-edge kind of thing.

A book such as this (and that's the red line that flows throughout this little meandering soliloquy) is a lovely reminder for me that all of the toys and tools we have concocted over the years are not merely idle on shelves but have touched a lot of lives all over the world. I revel in all the stories of the human side: the professors in Moscow huddling in front of a lone Quadra, the guys on the Borneo oil rig noodling in KPT, the Los Angeles airport immigration officer grilling me on Bryce animation, the lawyer-by-day changing to KPT-monster-at-night stories of professional metamorphosis and career change. Lots of young kids find play value in creativity—toddlers getting comfy with a mouse, grandmas introduced to the not-so-evil-technology angle when getting goo'ed by their grandsons, teachers using Bryce to coax unruly high school seniors into math-is-relevant revelations. These are good things that warm the cockles of our hearts.

I like that this book shows that aspect, brings in the people behind the scenes, shows some of the faces, tells the stories, gives concrete examples of imagery that is no mere toy: it's not psychobabble, it's not pixelsoup, it's not fake, it's not simple pushbutton auto-art. True and real beauty is being created by true and real humans being. MetaTools is not some faceless corporate holding tank, it's not syphoning off charges on some kind of product "stuff" being shipped hither and yonder, it's not a shelfboxes-to-revenue conversion utility. We started this adventure to make a dent and have always called ourselves "The Dentists" for that very reason. The slogan underneath the pirate flag was "lets move the planet an inch to the left."

The pages here reflect that. You can sense that this is not a history of three accountants and their nine lawyers having a field-day in some marketing niche. It's a dream of impossible results being whittled into reality by a cast of unlikely-yet-likable characters. In a way these things even have to be said by someone other than us. I would feel a pigheaded Goodyear-Ego syndrome looming if I had to dissect this myself. I have some of my own thoughts that will some day come out in my own writing. Working Title is often something like *Life 2.0—Sometimes I Want to Reboot Planet Earth*, and that might happen sooner than later. For the moment, though, I think this book is the most comprehensive insight into our little bits-of-beauty factory that I know of. And anyone spending even an hour with this magic is bound to gain a better insight into the process and appreciation of the possibilities that our tools afford.

Ultimately, nothing quite matches full immersion into the staring-at-the-phosphor state (remember my old line, "sleep is a highly overrated concept"?). You can take no shortcut to knowledge, and nothing replaces the sheer experience of logging frequent-filter miles. In that sense, the reader is well advised to not look for panacea quickie answers on how to remove that scar on the bridal photograph or how to goo Aunt Emma to look more like Uncle Bob. This book should leave one thing hanging there (wow, midspace-projection . . . MSP, the nirvana holy grail) in front of the reader's pixellated eyes: this stuff is all about the *process* of exploration and creativity, it's *not* about timely production schedules and efficient task executions. . . . You'll find plenty of other software packages out there that are all about the pragmatic goal to get some job done and go home. KPT is *not* that. It's about being home. With KPT you want to get a job done on your assessment of what's all possible and what *you* are able to be The Creator of.

When you thumb through this book and you see the pictures and examples of an accomplished KPTologist or MetaToolesse, remember that his or her *first* set of images on that first 286/Centris vx were three yellow triangles with ugly edges. They were four pink ovals with ugly edges. Get them to admit it! They all conveniently forget that they, too, were newbies once and went through phases of utter nonsense before they got good and got goo'ed. When I receive mail with one of the inevitable 12 glass balls on a Mandelbrot, page-curled example image, I do *not* cry out over "the sad state of art in our society today." What I see is a result of a millisecond where something ran down this person's spine and screamed to the heavens, "I DID THAT. IT IS GOOD. I AM COOL. HEY BOB, CHECK THIS OUT, DOOD," and I smile.

A book such as this can then follow that line of thought and go to the next stage: life after page curls, and life on Io, where fractals are forbidden. And there is life on Zontar where glass balls are considered hardcore obscene. Seriously, anyone casually dabbling in *one* of the KPT tools simply cannot divine by such once-in-a-while exposure that such a vast potential landscape of ideaspaces exists that not only *they* have not thought of, but possibly *no one* has yet discovered (my proverbial "virgin snow" concept). This book hasn't tried to pave the road to such realms, but it has pointed the way and in general set up the triangulation hinting that such spaces exist. In other words, as I always say: we have not seen *anything* yet.

Let these pages be your guide to the fact that even just this one set of tools can yield that hardest-of-all attainment: true newness. . . . To come up with images that "have something" is already a good first step. To come up with pictures that incorporate something "no one has ever seen" before is very very hard to do—and is getting ever harder. I am very proud to say we have seen many pictures that are the incarnation of a whole new look, one that *has* never been seen before. It may be a little loud in the rave flyers and on the Dance CD compilations that seem to be entirely KPT-centric, but it's just as lovely for me to see pristine subtle work now including a whole new vocabulary of extruded designs, negative spaces, layered and shadowed with soft glows and textures, organic shapes. . . . Much of what this book showcases is only a *hint* of what the art can look like in the full glory of a 48-inch Iris print or in animated motion.

I surely would not feel comfortable to have the work so far be the total summation of achievement or the end-all of "my style." I think I have not done my best work yet, by far . . . much more looms on the horizon for me personally and MetaTools as a company.

As alluded to earlier, this book would have been a godsend to have a few years earlier just to prove that these things *are* worth doing. A few years from now, who knows, probably our kids will find this book and gaze nostalgically at the innocent little pixel dabblings we used to do back in the '90s . . . Remember? The *good old days*?

I guess they will also be able to double-click on the paper then.

Kai Krause
Senior Science and Design Officer
MetaTools, Inc.

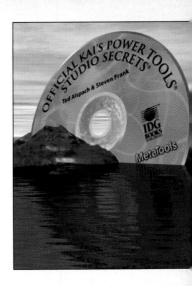

APPENDIX
USING THE CD-ROM

The Mac-Windows CD-ROM included with this book is packed to the gills with all sorts of valuable software and MetaTools' product-related goodies, including:

■ Kai's exclusive personal preset collection for Texture Explorer and Interform on the Mac (available nowhere else!)
■ A fascinating QuickTime interview with Kai Krause (another exclusive!)
■ A searchable Acrobat version of Kai's extensive interview transcript
■ Megabytes of exclusive QuickTime *Studio SECRETS* tutorials
■ Bryce images and animations from Kai and company (Mac)
■ A special collection of high-res Power Photos
■ Cool Final Effects sample movies
■ Stunning images and movie clips created with Kai's Power Tools and other MetaTools products, *plus* backgrounds, textures, and bump maps
■ Demos of the MetaTools product line, including Kai's Power Tools 3 and Convolver for Mac and Windows, as well as Mac demos for Bryce 2, Vector Effects, and Final Effects.
■ Image galleries, useful utilities, and more!

Macintosh users can access all software from the Finder. Windows users should use Windows Explorer, My Computer, or File Manager.

MACINTOSH SYSTEM REQUIREMENTS

To use all of the files and demo all products, you'll need a 68040 or PowerPC Macintosh with a math coprocessor running MacOS 7.1 or above, a CD-ROM drive, at least 8MB of RAM, and a color display. Some software on the CD-ROM requires QuickTime 2.0 or above, or plug-in-compatible applications such as Adobe Photoshop, Fractal Designs Painter, Adobe Illustrator, and Macromedia FreeHand.

WINDOWS SYSTEM REQUIREMENTS

Windows users require a 486 or Pentium PC running Windows 3.1, Windows 95 or Windows NT, CD-ROM drive, at least 8MB of RAM and a VGA color display. Some software on the CD-ROM requires QuickTime for Windows 2.0 or above, or plug-in-compatible applications such as Adobe Photoshop, Fractal Designs Painter, Adobe Illustrator, and Macromedia FreeHand.

USING THE QUICKTIME MOVIES

The CD-ROM contains numerous sample movies (found in the Demos folder), as well as several QuickTime Movie tutorials covering various topics from basic to advanced areas on most of the products (found in the QTMovies folder). Because several MetaTools products are not available for the Windows platform, some may not be useful for Windows users.

PLAYING THE QUICKTIME TUTORIALS ON THE MACINTOSH

To play the CD-ROM Tutorials on a Macintosh, you must have:

- QuickTime 2.0 or later
- 5MB (more is better) of application RAM
- A color 13-inch (640 × 480) or larger monitor
- At least a 68040 processor (PowerPC is preferable)

To play the CD-ROM Tutorials, drag the file "KPT SS Tutorial Program" located in the QT Movies folder (in the main window of the KPT SS CD-ROM drive) to your hard drive, and double-click on it.

In the Tutorial Program, choose a movie from the product-based menus along the top of the screen. Some movies are short, while others are quite detailed. Don't let the name of the movie throw you; often you'll find useful information in the movie that may not be related to its title.

To Quit the Tutorial, select Quit from the File menu.

If you jump between the Tutorial program and any other application, click once on the main screen to restore the menus.

QuickTime and related files for Macintosh users can be found in the QuickTime & Helpers folder.

PLAYING THE QUICKTIME TUTORIALS ON WINDOWS PCS

To play the CD-ROM QuickTime movies under Windows, open the movies from within any Quick-Time movie player.

KAI'S PRESETS AND MORE

Kai Krause has provided some of his own personal presets for use on the Macintosh, located within the Kai's Power Tools product folder. We've also included for your enjoyment numerous additional Macintosh presets, Goovies (Kai's Power Goo movies) and source files (including Bryce Source files and bump maps). To use presets, import them from within the MetaTools product. Bryce source files can be opened with Bryce and Bryce 2.0. Goovies can only be viewed within Kai's Power Goo.

All presets and source files are provided for your use only and are copyrighted by the respective creators of those files. Please do not distribute, give away, or sell any of these or any other files on the CD-ROM.

IMAGES

Several images from the book have been provided for you on the CD-ROM for you to inspect in their native formats. In addition, several KPT product folders contain galleries and sample movies for your enjoyment.

PRODUCT DEMOS

In addition to the tutorials, which show off quite a few product features, limited versions of the products are located in the Demos folder. Most of the products (with the exception of Power Photos) are crippled in some way (usually save-disabled), but they are functional enough to give you the flavor of the product. If you wish to purchase a product you're demoing, call MetaTools sales at (805) 566-6200. MetaTools will *not* provide support for either the CD-ROM that comes with *Official Kai's Power Tools Studio SECRETS* or any product demo.

FONTS

For Macintosh users, two popular fonts have been included in the Fonts folder. Follow the instructions on the ReadMe files for installation and use.

TROUBLESHOOTING

If you have trouble running the QuickTime tutorials, do the following (in order of most effective to scraping the bottom):

■ Give more memory to the "KPT SS Tutorial Program" (the more the better) and leave about 200K for your system if possible.

■ Install QuickTime 2.1 (found in the QuickTime and Helpers folder). This should solve 99 percent of problems.

■ Quit any other applications.

■ Turn off all system extensions but QuickTime and any needed CD-ROM files.

If you still have problems:

■ Play the movies individually with the QuickTime movie player in the QuickTime and Helpers folder.

There are no incompatibilities with RAMDoubler, though don't allocate more than your physical RAM to the "KPT SS Tutorial Program" file.

ARTIST INDEX

This book would not have been possible without the generous contributions of the many artists who have spent hundreds or even thousands of hours exploring the depth and breadth of Kai's Power Tools, Bryce, Convolver, Vector Effect, Power Photos, and Final Effects. The following pages list all the artists who contributed to this book, and wherever possible we have included photos of the artists and contact information. If the work of any of these talented individuals particularly impresses you, we strongly encourage you to contact them directly and share your admiration with them. As most of these people make their living with their art, we also encourage you to support their work by contacting them for your (or your company's) photographic, illustration, or graphic design needs.

EDMOND ALEXANDER
Phone: 904/231-4112

Edmond Alexander is a partner in Alexander & Turner, a medical illustration studio located in Grayton Beach, Florida. Edmond and his partner Cynthia Turner provide medical illustrations for medical advertising agencies, pharmaceutical companies, and medical publishers.

FEATURED IMAGES: Inflammatory Response (Chapter 11), Enzyme Destruction, Checkers Virus (Part 1 and 2 Openers, Chapter 14)

JENNIFER ALSPACH
E-mail: JenAlspach@aol.com

The "artist formerly known as Jennifer Alspach" has coauthored the best-selling *Illustrator Filter Finesse* and *Microsoft Bob.* Her artwork has appeared in a number of books, ranging from the *Macworld Illustrator Bible* and *The Illustrator Wow Book* to childrens' books and mind-bending chemistry texts. When she's not mucking about with Adobe Illustrator for outrageous freelance rates, Jennifer teaches a variety of different applications for Computer Support Professionals in Cave Creek, Arizona.

FEATURED IMAGES: Crystal Castle (Chapter 2), Bézier business card (Chapter 5)

TED ALSPACH

Ted Alspach, author of several books on computer-based drawing and graphics applications, provided several pieces of artwork for *Official Kai's Power Tools Studio SECRETS.* When Ted isn't creating artwork for books he writes just to get his name listed in the Artist Index, he's still in front of his computer, trying to figure out what this "life" thing is . . . all his friends say he should get one, but Ted is unsure if there's a Mac-compatible version available.

ARTEFFECT DESIGN STUDIO
Phone: 818/996-8391
E-mail: tingj@aol.com, afxrobert@aol.com

Jackson Ting and Robert Bailey became friends in high school while involved in the Vocational Industrial Clubs of America (VICA). They both shared an avid interest in architectural design and worked closely together, attending regional, state, and national events. In 1993 Jackson and Robert again began working together at a motion picture advertising studio, but soon decided to leave behind the restrictive confines imposed upon them and start their own company, ArtEffect Design Studio. Robert and Jackson's work has appeared in multiple publications including *Macworld, MacWeek, Publish, 3D Design, The KPT Bryce Book,* and *Kai's Magic Toolbox.* Clients include Herbie Hancock, the Steve Miller Band, blues musician Sy Klopps, XYPRO Technology Corporation, and MetaTools, Inc.

FEATURED IMAGES: Big Rig (Chapter 3, Chapter 13), MetaStation (Chapter 13 Opener), Carved Coal, Cambrian Pipeline (Chapter 13), Blues Club (Chapter 13, Chapter 14), Living Hands, MetaVirtual Cockpit, Martian Desert (Chapter 14)

LARRY AUERBACH
E-mail: laarree@interport.net

Larry Auerbach is a New York digital artist whose work leans heavily toward experimental portraiture. He uses Bryce for most of his work, most of which you can find on his Web site. Larry typically has many threads of experimentation in his work, some of which have led him to create images that he (or anyone else for that matter) never envisioned.

FEATURED IMAGES: Baby Boo—Wierd, Prisoner, Frost King (Chapter 14)

GREG CARTER

Phone: 919/676-0238

E-mail: gregc@nando.net

Greg Carter's computer "painting" exists outside the mainstream of computer imaging because, he says, "my images retain the obvious mark of their creator rather than the mark of the software." Greg works for Eyebeam, a Color Postscript Service Bureau in Research Triangle Park, North Carolina. When not digitally manipulating client product shots or otherwise fixing their files, Greg can be found either on the soccer fields of Raleigh with his children Sonja and Beckett, or wandering the thrift shops with his wife Grace, searching for previously owned treasures that he didn't know he needed until he saw them.

FEATURED IMAGES: Invasion (Chapter 1), City of Angels (Chapter 7 Opener), Cyborg Reflecting Pool 2, Industry—Pain of Harry Crews, The Phone Pranksters (Chapter 14)

CHRIS CASADY

E-mail: TileNut@aol.com

Chris Casady lives and works in the hills above Hollywood, California. He is one of the premiere Bryce artists in the business, having created images that have been widely hailed for their innovation and technical expertise. His images appear on the Bryce 2 box and manual cover, and MetaTools built its initial ad campaign for Bryce 2 around his "Sedona Strikes" image.

FEATURED IMAGES: Movie Set (Chapter 3, Chapter 14), Sedona Strikes (Chapter 3 Opener), Atlantis Lost (Chapter 3, Chapter 14), Copper Gryphon (Chapter 13), Tribute, Santa Barbara Mission (Chapter 14)

DOUGLAS CHEZEM

Phone: 703/591-5424

E-mail: DugR@aol.com

Doug Chezem started out as an airbrush illustrator and has been a commercial artist since 1974. He made the transition from airbrush to electronic media in 1985 and now specializes in digital painting for the corporate, high-tech, and "new media" markets. Doug has lectured on electronic art at George Washington University, the Corcoran School of Art, and for the Washington, DC Art Director's Club. Doug's background includes advertising, graphics, and exhibit design, but his first love is science fiction art. Doug's work is a mix of traditional and digital methods, using Power Macintosh computers.

FEATURED IMAGE: Power Tools (Chapter 1)

VICTOR CLAUDIO

Phone: 813/891-6188

E-mail: Madcirq@aol.com

Victor Claudio is a Pratt Institute graduate; worked as art director for Norman, Craig & Kummel; was graphic creative director for Grey Advertising in Puerto Rico; and is presently senior art director for AAA Auto Club South's marketing department in Tampa, Florida. He has been illustrating on the Mac since 1988. His painting background strongly influences his illustrations, which incorporate a wide range of techniques.

FEATURED IMAGES: Rusty Snake, Spidermon Too (Chapter 11)

PHIL CLEVENGER

E-mail: KPT Phil@aol.com

Phil Clevenger is the person at MetaTools who is responsible for implementing all of Kai's interface designs. In the two and a half minutes per day that he has free, he plays his guitar or creates impressive art. You can find more information about Phil in the "Once Upon a MetaTime" chapter (Chapter 1).

FEATURED IMAGE: Necrofelinia (Chapter 3)

SCOTT CROUSE

E-mail: ScotMan421@aol.com

One of the few artists featured in this book to work primarily in the vector world, Scott's innovative approach keeps his work fresh and gives it a much more natural look than that of most vector-based artwork. In addition to Adobe Illustrator and Vector Effects, Scott uses a wide variety of digital tools, but has never lost his touch with the traditional tools of the trade (that is, good old pen and ink). He lives in Winter Haven, Florida with his wife.

FEATURED IMAGE: Pine Tree (Chapter 13)

TODD DEMELLE

Phone: 617/254-9384

E-mail: Ejwize@aol.com

Todd DeMelle is a freelance illustrator living in Boston. He received his M.F.A. in illustration from the Savannah College of Art and Design. His work involves a careful integration of traditional rendering techniques with digital technology. The themes in Todd's images draw largely upon the rich literary and mythological traditions of cultures all over the world. Todd's work has appeared in a variety of printed and digital forms including books, magazines, computer games, interactive multimedia, Web sites, and more. If you'd like to see an online portfolio of his work, you can find his Web site at http://users.aol.com/ejwize/.

FEATURED IMAGES: House of Asterion (Chapter 10 Opener), Dancing Goddess, Fall (Chapter 14)

TIM DRAKE

E-mail: bw@waynetech.com

Timothy Drake is one of the new generation of KPT artists, having used the product since high school. Several national publications have already featured his work, including *Spry, Unlimited Graphics,* and *Gotham After Dark*. Since graduating summa cum laude in 1994, he's lived in one of the largest cities in the country, trying nobly to continue his life as an artist despite having an overactive nightlife that threatens to steal the zest from his waking hours during the daytime.

FEATURED IMAGE: Trippin' (Chapter 11)

BILL ELLSWORTH

E-mail: Loa9@aol.com

Bill Ellsworth discovered computers as a means for creating art when he began to notice that the artwork in computer magazines interested him as much as the artwork in traditional art magazines. He quickly got himself a Macintosh computer, as much RAM as he could afford, and has been a Photoshop and KPT user ever since. "The main thing I tell people about using the computer to create art is how simple and powerful the tools are. Adobe Photoshop, Kai's Power Tools, and KPT Bryce are deep and sophisticated programs, but their clear and intuitive interfaces enabled me to create exciting work right from the beginning."

FEATURED IMAGES: Art of Dreaming (Chapter 1, Chapter 14), Ten Dragons Draggin' (Chapter 2), Magic Meta (Chapter 3, Chapter 13), 96-2-9, 96-2-19, 96-2-25 (Chapter 11)

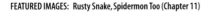

ANDREW M. FAW
Phone: 212/633-9063
E-mail: afaw@crl.com

Andrew Faw, recently relocated to New York City from Denver, notes about the change of scenery: "The view of the monitor is the same in NYC, but Kai's Power Tools makes it look better!" Andrew has been a big fan of Kai's Power Tools since they were first released, and hopes the *Official Kai's Power Tools Studio SECRETS* book doesn't dispel the illusion clients may have that "we slave for hours creating incredible images for them pixel by pixel." He believes the key is using these tools to enhance ideas without overwhelming the image. Andrew has done an extensive amount of ad design, illustration, and packaging for software companies, as well as product design for Disney and Warner Bros. licensees.

FEATURED IMAGE: GFX Board (Chapter 14)

PATRICK FLAHERTY
E-mail: FatherOne@aol.com

An accomplished architectural designer and 3D graphic illustrator, Patrick Flaherty admits that he still (as of this writing) hasn't had a chance to even look at Bryce 2 yet. It seems that his proficiency with the original Bryce has kept him in high enough demands with his clients that he simply hasn't had time to check it out. Patrick uses Bryce more as a 3D modeler and for placing Pict images into scenes than as a simple "landscape generator." He lives in Wilmette, Illinois.

FEATURED IMAGE: USS Cordova (Chapter 13)

STEVEN FRANK
E-mail: MicroQuill@aol.com

After almost a year and a half of writing about MetaTools products, Steve is finally enjoying actually *using* the stuff! In addition to co-authoring this book, Steve created the example images for the Bryce presets pages and contributed to a few of the chapter opening images. More than anything, this entry is just an excuse for Steve to get his picture in the book. While he is just starting to spread his artistic wings, Steve promises great things for the book's next edition.

PHIL FREE
Phone: 205/250-1494
E-mail: PhilFree@aol.com

"I am a corporate photographer for Alabama Power, an electric utility, which, believe it or not, gives me a great degree of creative freedom. No stodgy, backwards place to work, Alabama Power has outfitted my fellow coworkers and I with some great technology and allows us to use it to its fullest extent. Most of my images are digitally enhanced, with Photoshop being the software I live in from day to day. I use Bryce to photograph landscapes that don't exist. I use Kai's Power Tools and Convolver seemlessly with Photoshop for effects that I could not even have dreamt of before they existed."

FEATURED IMAGE: Bridge Over Reflection Lagoon (Chapter 12)

DAVID GINK
Phone: 414/456-9733
E-mail: DaveGink@aol.com

Dave Gink is an illustrator/designer working out of the Milwaukee, Wisconsin area. Primarily a self-taught artist, Dave combines traditional design and illustration with modern computer graphics. He produced his featured piece for Eastern Software, a client of the Brookfield, Wisconsin advertising agency Seroka & Associates, where Dave is employed as senior computer artist. He also enjoys a successful freelance career, his work having been used by clients such as Harley-Davidson, Miller brewing, and the Walt Disney company. When not in front of a monitor, Dave enjoys science fiction, Wisconsin's lakes and forests, and listening to music performed by live bands.

FEATURED IMAGE: Eastern Software ad (Chapter 12)

BRUCE H. GLIDER
E-mail: Glider54@aol.com

An avid photographer as well as digital artist, Bruce is one of the best we've seen when it comes to combining real images and imagined effects. In addition to the MetaTools line of products and the prerequisite proficiencies with Photoshop, Bruce is also quite adept at RayDream Designer and other 3D modeling applications. He finds that sometimes combining 3D images with photos can give his work a unique quality that would be impossible to create using a straight pixel-manipulation approach.

FEATURED IMAGE: Tammy (Chapter 12)

GEORGE HAZELWOOD
Phone: 303/683-8096
E-mail: GeorgeH521@aol.com

George Hazelwood owns GH Designs, a Denver-based design firm specializing in digital imagery and multimedia projects. He has used the Macintosh since its beginnings to create, illuminate, and teach. He holds three degrees from colleges and universities in business, advertising, and computer graphics. He has contributed images to the Kai's Power Tools 3.0 CD and helps in the test development of various companies' software tools as well as graphic and multimedia design. George is a regular contributor on AOL's graphic forums as well. He lives on the outskirts of Denver with his wife and daughter.

FEATURED IMAGE: Reflections (Chapter 3, Chapter 14)

PAMELA HOBBS
E-mail: xray4u@aol.com

British illustrator Pamela Hobbs has been living and working in London, Manhattan, and Tokyo, and has now relocated to San Francisco. She has been on the faculty of computer graphics departments at The School of Visual Arts, The New School For Social Research (Affiliate Parsons School of Design), and the California College of Arts & Crafts, where she currently teaches a computer class in design and new media. Her artwork has been widely exhibited and featured in publications including *Verbum, How, Step by Step Graphics, American Illustration,* and *Mac Life Tokyo.*

FEATURED IMAGE: *Business Week* cover (Chapter 2)

JOE JONES
Phone: 303/377-7745
E-mail: DuJaVe@aol.com

Joe Jones has been a professional graphic artist in the Denver area since 1983, eight of those years as vice president and art director of his own production screen printing shop, Cotton Grafix. There Joe had his multicolor, hand-separated preprint work sold at the retail level over the entire Mountain region of the United States. He has created artwork for almost every conceivable application and requirement. Joe's other passions include his wife Carmen, and his two beautiful daughters, Layla and Cyanne.

FEATURED IMAGE: Art Works logo (Chapter 10)

ATHENA KEKENES
E-mail: KPT Athena@aol.com

Athena Kekenes is a digital artist specializing in Photoshop and Photoshop channel wizardry, which was probably the primary reason that Kai hired her to join the MetaTools team. Athena currently works as an Artist/Interface Designer for MetaTools. One look at her artwork and the "kindred spirit" with Kai's interfaces is immediately apparent. Athena lives in the Santa Barbara area.

FEATURED IMAGES: Nostalgia Device (Chapter 7), Inertial Nest, Gateway (Chapter 12)

KURT KRAMES
Phone: 415/655-3164
E-mail: kkrames@idgbooks.com

Kurt Krames is a graphics specialist at IDG Books Worldwide, Inc. in Foster City, California. He has a degree in applied art and design, and has been doing illustrations ever since he could hold a pen. He created his computer-generated work in this book using Kai's Power Tools and Bryce. It was the first time he had used either program. Special thanks to Stephen Noetzel and Katy German for technical advice and artistic counsel.

FEATURED IMAGE: Creation (Appendix Opener)

KAI KRAUSE

A bio of Kai would be totally redundant here, because quite a bit of Chapter 1 ("Once Upon a MetaTime") is about him. Check it out!

FEATURED IMAGE: Absolut Kai (Chapter 2)

CRAIG LAWSON
E-mail: Outpost31@aol.com

Craig Lawson is a digital artist specializing in motion graphics, animation, and video editing. After recieving a digital video certificate from the American Film Institute, Craig began his own company, Digital Alchemy. Clients have included MetaTools, Toad the Wet Sprocket, and the Santa Barbara Museum of Art.

FEATURED IMAGES: Various effect samples (Chapter 6 Opener)

PIETER LESSING
Phone: 310/390-5767
E-mail: Lessing@aol.com

Pieter Lessing is a Los Angeles-based photographer and digital artist who specializes in photographing personalities in the entertainment industry (film, television, and music). His photographs of celebrity personalities have been published in *Time* magazine, *Vogue, Cosmopolitan, US, Entertainment Weekly, Axcess,* and other domestic and international publications. He also did the photography for Kai's Power Goo image library. He's involved himself with digital imaging ever since buying his first Mac in 1985. He was also fortunate enough to have been one of the first alpha testers for the initial Bryce 1.0.

FEATURED IMAGES: Visage (Chapter 1, Chapter 3), Orbital (Chapter 3, Chapter 14), Grease Collage (Chapter 4 Opener), Mexico #1, Depp (Chapter 14)

HENRY LIM
Phone: 415/274-8625
E-mail: LimPhoto@aol.com

Henry Lim currently heads up the Digital Imaging section of the Computer Art department at the Academy of Art College in San Francisco. He also produces computer animations and digital images for corporate and editorial clients. Henry comes from a background in commercial photography. His first published images appeared in 1979. Henry has two college degrees in photography, one in the sciences, and one in fine art. "I love it," he says, "when Silicon Graphics dudes drool all over my Brycescapes."

FEATURED IMAGES: Stone Age Coffee Cup, Earth Avatar (Chapter 3), Avatars/Meditation, Avatars/Worship (Chapter 14)

JOSEPH A. LINASCHKE
E-mail: KPT Joseph@aol.com

Joseph Linaschke graduated from Cal Poly, San Luis Obispo's Art & Design/Photography program. He began his life in the arts in the early '80s when he was about ten years old and got his first camera. "I started in photography, and until my first year of college thought that that was what I was going to do forever," Joseph acknowledges. "But then (1991) the Macintosh was just beginning to become a viable graphics tool. Starting with a Mac IIsi, 5MB RAM, and a pirated copy of Photoshop 1.0, I started to play. Less than five years later I'm on a PowerMac with 88MB RAM, and getting paid to play! I am now an independent photoimager, combining my photography and computer graphics, climbing up in the world with my fiancée Samantha by my side."

FEATURED IMAGES: MetaRose (Chapter 1, Chapter 11), Lisa (Chapter 2, Chapter 12), Spheropolis (Chapter 14)

BILL NIFFENEGGER
Phone: 505/682-2776
E-mail: AFCBill@aol.com

Bill is one of the undisputed Grand Masters of digital imaging. His images have appeared worldwide in books and magazines, and his clients include many Fortune 500 companies, as well as MetaTools (for whom he designs every product box and manual cover). He is in demand internationally as a speaker, educator, and designer. Bill lives and works in Cloudcroft, New Mexico with his wife, B.J., and son, Hunter.

FEATURED IMAGE: Vase with Wildflowers (Chapter 5)

TRAVIS O'HEARN
E-mail: Catch@pdk.com

Travis O'Hearn, nationally reknowned artist of several fine arts pieces, including the popular print "My World's Photo-Op Bible" (which you can find in most "framing" stores that offer art prints), has had artwork appear in over 25 national publications. He's a contributing artist to several magazines and also writes for a few others. He received the Jonathon Frankin Best Computer Art Award in 1993 and won a prestigious Computer Art Association Award twice, in 1994 and 1996. Travis O'Hearn lives to create artwork on his Macintosh 8100/80. He has no other life at all at this time.

FEATURED IMAGE: Type Magic (Chapter 9 Opener)

CHARLEY PARKER
E-mail: cparker@netaxs.com

Charley Parker is a Philadelphia area cartoonist, illustrator, and Web page designer. *Argon Zark!*, his virtual, online "comic book" has garnered a number of Internet awards. Charley uses Kai's Power Tools throughout *Argon Zark!* and occasionally thows in a touch of Bryce as well. You can peruse the virtual comic itself at http://www.zark.com or http://www.netaxs.com/`cparker. Charley credits KPT and Bryce as the main reason that he doesn't play computer games.

FEATURED IMAGES: *Argon Zark!* panels (Chapter 10)

C. DAVID PIÑA
Phone: 818/972-9239

Award-winning designer C. David Piña's main titles and computer graphics for television are seen by billions of viewers around the world. Among his credits for animated graphics are the Grammy Awards, the Academy Awards, the Tony Awards, America's Funniest People, Miss America, the Presidential Inaugural, the Country Music Awards, the American Music Awards, and many others. His commercial work is seen on all three networks as well as on several cable channels. Additionally, David's art is exhibited in fine art galleries, and included in several private collections. He also teaches 3D computer animation at a private school, Mind Over Technology in Culver City, California.

FEATURED IMAGE: 38th Annual Grammy Awards (Chapter 14)

GLENN RIEGEL
E-mail: Glimage@aol.com

Glenn Riegel has been in the commercial photography business for 15 years. During his tenure with two advertising studios in the Reading, Pennsylvania area, he handled just about everything from semiconductors to Mac trucks. Part of the time he spent managing an in-house photo lab. His second career has been teaching. For the past seven years he has taught commercial photoimaging and DTP to 10–12th grade students at the Berks Career and Technology Center, Leesport, Pennsylvania. Glenn currently uses KPT 3.0, Convolver, and After Effects. Bryce is a major addiction (according to his wife). He has images placed on the Terraformers Guild Web site: http://www.emr.ca/~hbrand/brycegal.riegel.html. In addition, his work has appeared on the MetaTools AOL area under the Bryce folders, and the new Bryce 2 CD shipped with some of Glenn's images on it as well.

FEATURED IMAGES: 99.9% Pure Bryce (Chapter 13), Schloss Flussbogen Eve (Chapter 14)

STEPHANIE ROBEY
Phone: 310/265-1313

Stephanie Robey is one of the principals of PhotoSpin, the company that produces the vast majority of Power Photos for MetaTools. You can find more information about Stephanie and PhotoSpin in the "Power Photos" chapter (Chapter 7).

FEATURED IMAGES: Row-Bee, Butterfly and Paint (Chapter 7)

ANDREW RODNEY
E-mail: Andrew4059@aol.com

In early 1990 after graduating with honors from the Art Center College of Design in Pasadena, California, Andrew Rodney purchased his first color Macintosh system in order to run a new and revolutionary product called Adobe Photoshop. He spent considerable time learning and mastering Photoshop and digital imaging. Soon, other photographers were coming to Andrew for instruction. Andrew began lecturing and continues to do so around the country. He has contributed to *Publish* magazine, *Computer Artist, The Official Photoshop Handbook,* and many other publications.

FEATURED IMAGE: Santa Fe with Sphere (Chapter 12)

SJOERD SMIT
E-mail: Swan56652@aol.com

Sjoerd Smit is a graphic designer and illustrator living and working in the Cincinatti, Ohio area. His work makes heavy use of Bryce, although his digital toolbox also includes Kai's Power Tools and many other products (from MetaTools as well as other companies).

FEATURED IMAGE: Meditation (Chapter 12)

MARK SMITH
E-mail: DramaSmith@aol.com

Mark Smith has been a professional digital artist and animator for the past 11 years. Computer-generated images have interested him since "pixels were monochrome and postage-stamp size." After attending Penn State and purchasing one of the first Amigas in the country, he began writing graphics software reviews for many early *Amiga* magazine issues. Mark is currently the digital FX supervisor at Digital Drama in Newark, New Jersey, whose client list includes Showtime, Trimark Pictures, and MCA Universal. He spends his free time as an accomplished Chef Garde Manger and ice sculptor. He would give it all up, though, for his wife Nella and their children: Franco, Kathy, and Marco.

FEATURED IMAGES: Shiny Turkey (Chapter 3), Bjorklund 2, Shiny Turkey 2, Things 2 (Chapter 14)

BRIAN STRAUSS
E-mail: Dr.Zox@aol.com

Brian Strauss (aka Dr. Zox) has been producing imagery with Macintosh computers since the mid 1980s. Early efforts in MacPaint, Full Paint, Digital Darkroom, and Pixelpaint have evolved into today's algorithmic Photoshop techniques. "MetaTools products are a constant companion of mine on my digital journeys," Brian reports. "I first discovered Kai's Power Tips on a BBS. I copied the files and carried them with me on my travels, teaching at graphic design shops. KPT became jumping-off points for countless new exporations. Gold type ripples, fuzzy faxes sharpen, and magic happens."

FEATURED IMAGES: Old Dog (Chapter 10), #5 (Chapter 14)

DARIN SULLIVAN
E-mail: KPT Darin@aol.com

Darin is a digital artist working at MetaTools as a graphic designer. Prior to working for MetaTools, Darin had his own design studio where his clients included the National Park Service, the American Institute of Architects, and Merrill-Lynch. Darin lives in Santa Barbara with his wife, LaRea, his son, Kelson, and his daughter, Caitlin.

FEATURED IMAGE: VEX Diner (Chapter 5 Opener)

SULLIVAN & BROWNELL, INC.
Phone: 802/728-3300
E-mail: SB@quest-net.com

Sullivan & Brownell, Inc. is a full-service advertising, marketing, and design company located in the Green Mountains of Vermont. The company serves a diverse mix of clients and industries ranging from high technology to consumer products and from recreation to financial services. Sullivan & Brownell has received industry recognition for its design of collateral materials for high technology and recreational products and packaging for the food and beverage industry.

FEATURED IMAGE: VisuLink cover (Chapter 2)

MICHEL TCHEREVKOFF
Phone: 212/229-1733

Michel Tcherevkoff was born in Paris to Russian parents. After graduating from law school, Michel came to the United States where a series of unrelated circumstances took him to photography. Today Michel is recognized as one of the world's preeminent conceptual photographers and is internationally known for his unique ability to create visual metaphors for clients ranging from Canon and Kodak to Federal Express, Bell Laboratories, General Motors, and *Omni* magazine. Michel has received numerous awards for creative advertising and editorial imagery, and has been exhibited internationally. He lives in New York City's photo district with his wife, son, daughter, and his Dalmatian, Tache.

FEATURED IMAGE: *Popular Mechanics* cover (Chapter 2)

RAY TERRILL
E-mail: ray@lightsource.com

Ray Terrill creates electronic artwork for Bauer and Bauer Advertising. His freelance clients include Southland Broadcasting Company, Ray-D-One, Southern Fiduciary, and Mountain Department Stores.

FEATURED IMAGE: S's (Chapter 9)

MICHAEL AND CLAUDIA HUBER TOMPERT
E-mail: michael@tompert.com

Michael Tompert, a graphic designer in Palo Alto, California, began his career in the graphic arts with a typesetter's apprenticeship at the age of 17 in Stuttgart, Germany. At 20, he headed for the Silicon Valley where he had his first encounter with a Macintosh 128K in 1984. As with many other typesetters back then, he eyed the Mac with suspicion. In 1989, however, he started learning Quark on a CX, got ahold of an evaluation copy of Photoshop 1.0, and was hooked. Around the time Adobe introduced version 2.0, he started studying graphic design in San Francisco. Waiting for 4.0 and finally having graduated, he keeps busy doing Photoshop imagery in 3.0 in his design studio, which he shares with his wife Claudia, also a designer from Germany. Any time away from the computer they enjoy with their three-year-old daughter Alina.

FEATURED IMAGES: Electric Powwow (Chapter 1, Chapter 14 Opener), Hand Painting (Chapter 11 Opener), Time Pond (Chapter 12 Opener)

DONNA TROY
E-mail: dtroy@darkstars.earth.org

Donna Troy's daughter sums up her mother's work best: "Mommy does fun toys all day." Donna has created outstanding artwork for several years for major ad agencies, and recently went solo in order to focus more on fine artwork. KPT has been a major influence in her design work in recent years.

FEATURED IMAGES: Night Butterflies (Chapter 7), AMUG logo (Chapter 9)

SCOTT TUCKER
Phone: 303/666 -3395
E-mail: Tuckersaur@aol.com

"This past year and a half has been a wild ride and I owe a lot to the cool products coming out of MetaTools—especially KPT Bryce," Scott recounts. "Bryce was the first 3D program I ever tried, and its ease of use encouraged me to explore its deeper controls. Bryce opened me up to a whole new world of 3D graphics—an entirely new way to create art. By day I am a mainframe systems engineer, but when night comes I am busy creating images and working on freelance graphics projects. I wouldn't have it any other way."

FEATURED IMAGES: Ansel, Summer Rendering (Chapter 14)

LEE VARIS
Phone: 213/937-3793
E-mail: LeeVaris@aol.com

Lee Varis, the owner and founder of Varis PhotoMedia, is a photo-illustrator working in Hollywood. He has been involved in commercial photography for the last 20 years. He started working with computer imaging about seven years ago after being introduced to the Quantel Paintbox system. Lee currently works with digital as well as conventional photography in conjunction with computer graphics to create images for use in entertainment industry print advertising. His work has been featured on movie posters, video box covers, CD covers, and numerous brochures and catalogs. He often combines his photographs with digital painting and effects or with additional photo elements to create digital images that transcend the original source materials.

FEATURED IMAGE: Stairway to Heaven (Chapter 2 Opener)

ERIC WENGER
Eric Wenger is the designer and lead developer of the original Bryce software. While much of the programming for Bryce 2 took place at MetaTools, Eric's core code was still responsible for much of the functionality within Bryce 2. His deep understanding of what the software is capable of, combined with the love of natural beauty that first inspired him to create Bryce, makes Eric the world's preeminent expert on Bryce. This expertise and passion make Eric's landscapes second to none.

FEATURED IMAGES: Winter Landscape (Chapter 3), Xanades Fjord (Chapter 3), Ring SpaceWorld Out (Chapter 14)

LESTER YOCUM
Phone: 301/688-7393
E-mail: LYocum@aol.com

With over 15 years of traditional and digital illustration and design experience, Lester's credits range from posters, books, and signage displayed worldwide to Web pages. His latest illustrations appear in the color sections of the *Macworld Illustrator 6 Bible*, Sharyn Venit's *Illustrator 6 MasterWorks*, and on Sharon Steuer's *Illustrator 6 Wow! Book* CD. Lester got hooked on KPT products the first time he loaded a KPT 1.0 Photoshop filter. Many of the images he now markets are created almost entirely with KPT effects.

FEATURED IMAGES: Party Time (Chapter 2), Granite Fire (Chapter 11)

INDEX

B

D

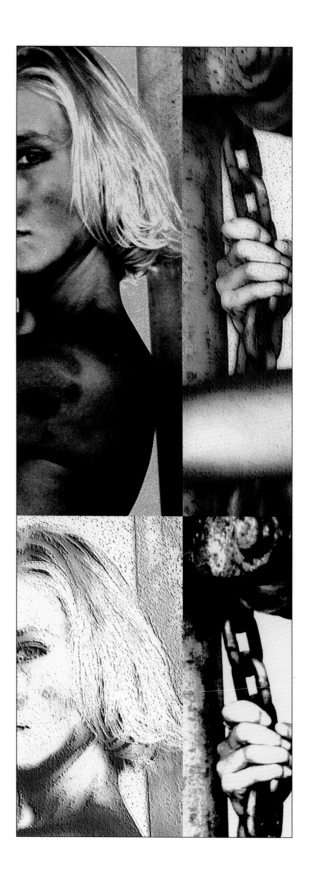

E

F

G

N

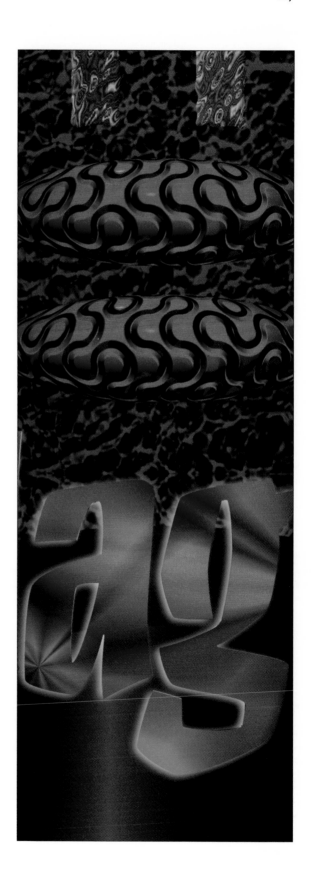

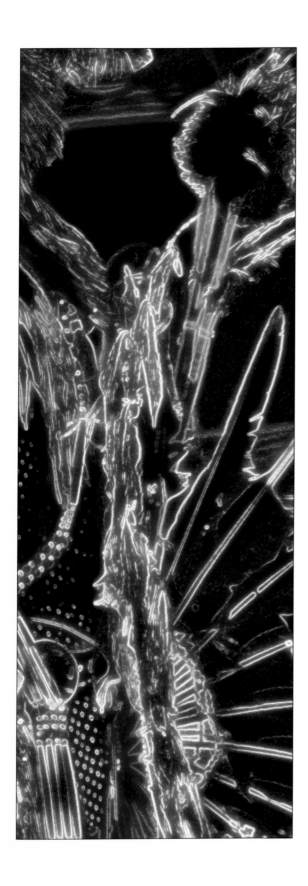

ABOUT THE AUTHORS

Ted Alspach is the author of several books, including the best-selling *Illustrator Filter Finesse, Macworld Illustrator 6 Bible, 2nd Edition, The Complete Idiot's Guide to Photoshop, The Complete Idiot's Guide to QuarkXPress,* and *Internet E-mail Quick Tour.* Considered one of the leading experts on computer graphics, Ted has given hundreds of seminars in the areas of graphic design and illustration. In addition, Ted is a forum consultant on America Online, where disguised as AFC Touls he cohosts the Adobe Illustrator special interest group.

Joined by his four unruly and quite furry sidekicks, Ted runs Bézier, a graphics and desktop publishing training company located somewhere in the untamed desert of Arizona. He occasionally writes for various magazines, including *Adobe Magazine* and *Mac Addict.* Ted has also edited several other books, including *The Macintosh Bible* and the *Mac Internet Quick Tour, 2nd Edition.*

Steven Frank is an independent computer consultant/trainer/author specializing in educational and technical writing, contributing to *The Macintosh Bible, 7th Edition* as well as numerous industry periodicals. Steve's position as Manager of Technical Documentation for MetaTools allowed him insider access to the development of the products covered in this book.

Prior to his stint at MetaTools, Steve developed training curricula for a wide variety of national clients, including McDonnell-Douglas, Bank of America, and Toshiba. In addition to his writing, Steve is an accomplished game designer, and has created several well-received games including *Quest!* and *Sword for Hire.*

COLOPHON

This book was produced electronically in Foster City, California. Microsoft Word Version 6.0 was used for word processing; design and layout was produced with QuarkXPress 3.32 on a Power Macintosh 8500/120. The type face families used are Myriad Multiple Master, Minion Multiple Master, and Trajan.

Acquisitions Editor: Michael Roney
Managing Editor: Terry Somerson
Development Editor: Michael Roney
Copy Editors: Jayne Jacobson, Michael D. Welch
Editorial Assistant: Sharon Eames
Technical Reviewer: Jim Tierney
Production Director: Andrew Walker
Supervisor of Page Layout: Craig A. Harrison
Production Associate: Chris Pimentel
Project Coordinator: Phyllis Beaty, Ben Schroeter
Production Staff: Diann Abbott, Mario F. Amador, Laura Carpenter, Renée Dunn, Ritchie Durdin, Kurt Krames, Stephen Noetzel, Andreas F. Schueller, Elsie Yim
Proofreaders: Christine Langin-Faris, Mary C. Oby
Indexer: Elizabeth Cunningham
Book Design: Margery Cantor
Cover Design: Damore Johann Design
Cover Art: Bill Niffenegger

IDG BOOKS WORLDWIDE, INC.
END-USER LICENSE AGREEMENT

<u>Read This</u>. **You should carefully read these terms and conditions before opening the software packet(s) included with this book ("Book"). This is a license agreement ("Agreement") between you and IDG Books Worldwide, Inc. ("IDGB"). By opening the accompanying software packet(s), you acknowledge that you have read and accept the following terms and conditions. If you do not agree and do not want to be bound by such terms and conditions, promptly return the Book and the unopened software packet(s) to the place you obtained them for a full refund.**

1. <u>License Grant</u>. IDGB grants to you (either an individual or entity) a nonexclusive license to use one copy of the enclosed software program(s) (collectively, the "Software") solely for your own personal or business purposes on a single computer (whether a standard computer or a workstation component of a multiuser network). The Software is in use on a computer when it is loaded into temporary memory (i.e., RAM) or installed into permanent memory (e.g., hard disk, CD-ROM, or other storage device). IDGB reserves all rights not expressly granted herein.

2. <u>Ownership</u>. IDGB is the owner of all right, title, and interest, including copyright, in and to the compilation of the Software recorded on the disk(s)/CD-ROM. Copyright to the individual programs on the disk(s)/CD-ROM is owned by the author or other authorized copyright owner of each program. Ownership of the Software and all proprietary rights relating thereto remain with IDGB and its licensors.

3. <u>Restrictions on Use and Transfer</u>.

(a) You may only (i) make one copy of the Software for backup or archival purposes, or (ii) transfer the Software to a single hard disk, provided that you keep the original for backup or archival purposes. You may not (i) rent or lease the Software, (ii) copy or reproduce the Software through a LAN or other network system or through any computer subscriber system or bulletin-board system, or (iii) modify, adapt, or create derivative works based on the Software.

(b) You may not reverse engineer, decompile, or disassemble the Software. You may transfer the Software and user documentation on a permanent basis, provided that the transferee agrees to accept the terms and conditions of this Agreement and you retain no copies. If the Software is an update or has been updated, any transfer must include the most recent update and all prior versions.

4. Restrictions on Use of Individual Programs. You must follow the individual requirements and restrictions detailed for each individual program in the "Using the CD-ROM" appendix of this Book. These limitations are contained in the individual license agreements recorded on the disk(s)/CD-ROM. These restrictions may include a requirement that after using the program for the period of time specified in its text, the user must pay a registration fee or discontinue use. By opening the Software packet(s), you will be agreeing to abide by the licenses and restrictions for these individual programs. None of the material on this disk(s) or listed in this Book may ever be distributed, in original or modified form, for commercial purposes.

5. Limited Warranty.

(a) IDGB warrants that the Software and disk(s)/CD-ROM are free from defects in materials and workmanship under normal use for a period of sixty (60) days from the date of purchase of this Book. If IDGB receives notification within the warranty period of defects in materials or workmanship, IDGB will replace the defective disk(s)/CD-ROM.

(b) IDGB AND THE AUTHORS OF THE BOOK DISCLAIM ALL OTHER WARRANTIES, EXPRESS OR IMPLIED, INCLUDING WITHOUT LIMITATION IMPLIED WARRANTIES OF MERCHANTABILITY AND FITNESS FOR A PARTICULAR PURPOSE, WITH RESPECT TO THE SOFTWARE, THE PROGRAMS, THE SOURCE CODE CONTAINED THEREIN, AND/OR THE TECHNIQUES DESCRIBED IN THIS BOOK. IDGB DOES NOT WARRANT THAT THE FUNCTIONS CONTAINED IN THE SOFTWARE WILL MEET YOUR REQUIREMENTS OR THAT THE OPERATION OF THE SOFTWARE WILL BE ERROR FREE.

(c) This limited warranty gives you specific legal rights, and you may have other rights which vary from jurisdiction to jurisdiction.

6. Remedies.

(a) IDGB's entire liability and your exclusive remedy for defects in materials and workmanship shall be limited to replacement of the Software, which may be returned to IDGB with a copy of your receipt at the following address: Disk Fulfillment Department, Attn: *Official Kai's Power Tools Studio SECRETS*, IDG Books Worldwide, Inc., 7260 Shadeland Station, Ste. 100, Indianapolis, IN 46256, or call 1-800-762-2974. Please allow 3–4 weeks for delivery. This Limited Warranty is void if failure of the Software has resulted from accident, abuse, or misapplication. Any replacement Software will be warranted for the remainder of the original warranty period or thirty (30) days, whichever is longer.

(b) In no event shall IDGB or the author be liable for any damages whatsoever (including without limitation damages for loss of business profits, business interruption, loss of business information, or any other pecuniary loss) arising from the use of or inability to use the Book or the Software, even if IDGB has been advised of the possibility of such damages.

(c) Because some jurisdictions do not allow the exclusion or limitation of liability for consequential or incidental damages, the above limitation or exclusion may not apply to you.

7. <u>U.S. Government Restricted Rights</u>. Use, duplication, or disclosure of the Software by the U.S. Government is subject to restrictions stated in paragraph (c) (1) (ii) of the Rights in Technical Data and Computer Software clause of DFARS 252.227-7013, and in subparagraphs (a) through (d) of the Commercial Computer—Restricted Rights clause at FAR 52.227-19, and in similar clauses in the NASA FAR supplement, when applicable.

8. General. This Agreement constitutes the entire understanding of the parties and revokes and supersedes all prior agreements, oral or written, between them and may not be modified or amended except in a writing signed by both parties hereto which specifically refers to this Agreement. This Agreement shall take precedence over any other documents that may be in conflict herewith. If any one or more provisions contained in this Agreement are held by any court or tribunal to be invalid, illegal, or otherwise unenforceable, each and every other provision shall remain in full force and effect.

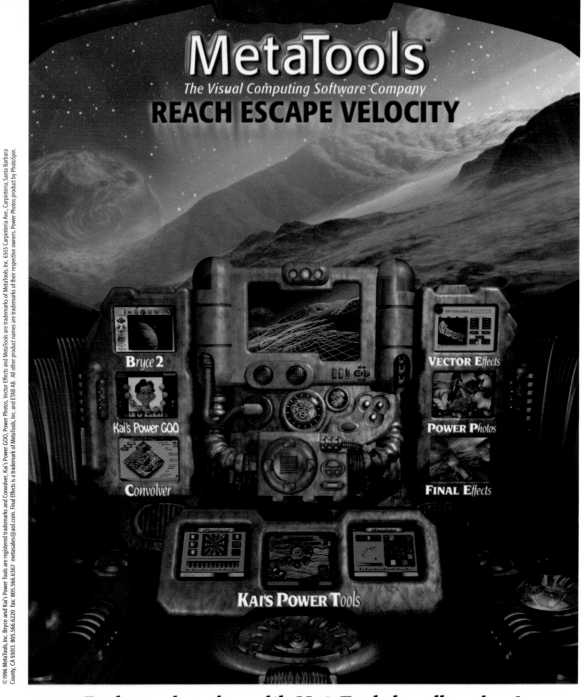